Radical Embodied Cognitive Science

Radical Embodied Cognitive Science

Anthony Chemero

A Bradford Book
The MIT Press
Cambridge, Massachusetts
London, England

First MIT Press paperback edition, 2011

MIT Press books may be purchased at special quantity discounts for business or sales promotional use. For information, please email special_sales@mitpress.mit.edu.

This book was set in Stone Serif and Stone Sans on 3B2 by Asco Typesetters, Hong Kong, and was printed and bound in the United States of America.

Library of Congress Cataloging-in-Publication Data

Chemero, Anthony, 1969–.
Radical embodied cognitive science / Anthony Chemero.
p. cm.—(A Bradford Book)
Includes bibliographical references and index.
ISBN 978-0-262-01322-2 (hardcover : alk. paper) ISBN 978-0-262-51647-1 (pb : alk. paper)
1. Perception—Research. 2. Cognitive science. I. Title.
BF311.B514 2009
153—dc22 2009001697

10 9 8 7 6 5 4

For the crowd at Sweet William's Pub

Contents

Preface: In Praise of Dr. Fodor

Jerry Fodor is my favorite philosopher.

I think that Jerry Fodor is wrong about nearly everything.

Knowing these two facts about me should be helpful for those who wish to understand what this book is all about. My goal is that this book is for nonrepresentational, embodied, ecological psychology what Fodor's *The Language of Thought* (1975) was for rationalist, computational psychology. *The Language of Thought* was a true landmark in (the philosophy of) cognitive science. It set out in great detail just what it is to do computational psychology, what some of the benefits to doing computational psychology are, what some of the results of computational psychology (c. 1975) were, and what the philosophical consequences of the computational approach are. It is admirably clear and rigorous, and also very funny. (See, for example, his discussion of the dispositional properties of Wheaties.) I would argue that *The Language of Thought* is the very best work ever done in the philosophy of cognitive science.

I warn you in advance that this book is not *that* good. I can live with that. I have set lofty goals for this book, fully aware that I would not reach them. My assumption was that if you aim for the stars, you might end up in low orbit, or in a deluxe apartment in the sky. So, although not as good, this book really is intended as a counterpart to Fodor's. Like his book, I describe a way one might pursue the scientific study of cognition and lay out the philosophical consequences of studying cognition this way. Like Fodor's book, the purpose is primarily to say what this way of doing cognitive science is, warts and all. Only secondarily do I try to convince you that what I describe is the *right* way to pursue the science of the mind. I am more than happy to accept the following reaction: "If that is what nonrepresentational, embodied, ecological cognitive science is all about, I'll stick with computationalism. Maybe I'll become a pastry chef instead." In other words, it could be that this book is one big modus tollens. If so, so be it. As Fodor himself puts it, "Hate me, hate my dog" (1990, xii).

The main way that this book is different from Fodor's, apart from the already-apologized-for difference in quality, is the nature of the cognitive science it describes. I suspect that the approach described and defended here, which I call *radical embodied cognitive science*,[1] would make Fodor gag.[2] In defending radical embodied cognitive science, I embrace many of the things that Fodor has railed against (direct perception, American naturalism, connectionist networks, teleological theories of content) and reject many of the things near and dear to him (especially mental representation). Another way that this book differs from Fodor's is in its attitude toward competing approaches in cognitive science. The hilarious and biting first section of *The Language of Thought* is devoted to dismantling behaviorist approaches to cognition in order to make space for his positive story. There is no such section in this book. Indeed, I think that this felt need to "make space" for a new scientific approach by showing that all other approaches are faulty or doomed to fail is a peculiar philosophical malady, and one that desperately needs curing.[3] This is the point of chapter 1. In it, I argue that primarily conceptual arguments against scientific approaches should be taken with a grain of salt, and never as dispositive. This is true in the case of arguments against the computational approach (Dreyfus 1964, 1972; Searle 1980) as well as arguments against radical embodied cognitive science (Clark 1997, 2008; Markman and Dietrich 2000a,b). Having argued against space-making arguments, I do not argue against other theories to argue for radical embodied cognitive science.

In chapter 2, I describe radical embodied cognitive science very broadly, comparing it to plain old embodied cognitive science, and outline a few historical antecedents and factors that make it attractive. Radical embodied cognitive science, very roughly, is the thesis that cognition is to be described in terms of agent-environment dynamics, and not in terms of computation and representation. The point of these chapters is to show that radical embodied cognitive science deserves a place at the cognitive science table, alongside more traditional computational approaches.

In the second part of the book, I explain just what it takes to embrace radical embodied cognitive science. One of the things I try to make clear is that it is actually very difficult to reject internal representations, and that radical embodied cognitive science must be more radical than most of its proponents realize. Representationalists can, and do, claim that things in agents are representations, even when they have few or none of the trappings of classical representations and even when calling them such plays no explanatory role. (See, e.g., Markman and Dietrich 2000a,b; Wheeler 2005.) The way to avoid this problem is to argue for a particular explanatory stance toward cognitive systems and models of them. To defend radical embodied cognitive science, one must take up what I call the *dynamical stance,* a methodological commitment to explaining perception, action, and cognition dynamically and without referring to representations. A strategy similar to this has been employed with considerable success throughout the cognitive sciences, including in studies of perception, motor control, speech, and development. Despite this success, and the promise of considerable future success, there is a particular problem for dynamical cognitive science that is not faced by computational and representational explanation: the problem of discovery.

The problem of discovery is not a new problem: it first sprang up in a debate between Mach and Boltzmann at the beginning of the twentieth century and has been discussed extensively in the philosophy of science. (See, e.g., Hanson 1958.) The problem boils down to the way in which new hypotheses are generated for testing. Since dynamical cognitive science is a commitment to methodology, it is instrumentalist. That is, it has no necessary connection to any particular posit about what its subject matter is like. The dynamical stance, like Dennett's stances on which it is based, is blissfully metaphysics-free. Computationalism and representationalism, though, are not: they are tied to the posit that the mind (or brain) is a computer and full of representations being acted upon by algorithms. This background assumption has been extraordinarily productive in the generation of new hypotheses for testing (as well as productive for papers published and new journals). Without such a set of background assumptions, it might seem that the dynamical stance is without a guide to discovery, without a method of systematically generating new hypotheses. This is, I take it, a serious disadvantage, one that might lead some sympathizers back to representationalism and computationalism. (I am psychoanalyzing Andy Clark here.) In short, radical embodied cognitive science has a methodology in dynamical modeling; it also needs a background theory, a theory of what its objects of study are.

In the third part of the book, I propose that Gibsonian ecological psychology is just the right theory. Gibson's assumptions—that perception is direct, constitutively linked to action, of affordances—are fully compatible with radical embodied cognitive science and with dynamical methodology. Indeed, for the sociologically inclined, much of the dynamical research in the cognitive sciences today can be traced back to two related, Gibson-sympathizing institutions in Connecticut: Haskins Labs in New Haven and the Center for the Ecological Study of Perception and Action at the University of Connecticut. The main problem with the ecological approach as the background theory for radical embodied cognitive science and dynamical modeling is that the key concepts of Gibson's approach are, to be frank, obscure. There is much disagreement, even among ecologically oriented psychologists, over just what affordances are supposed to be, and how they relate to animals, information, and events. The bulk of the third part of the book, therefore, is devoted to setting out a relatively faithful, conceptually sound theory of the main concepts of Gibsonian ecological psychology. Think of this as Gibson for philosophers, or for psychologists who (understandably) are a bit confused about what Gibson was on about.

The first three parts outline a theoretical orientation to cognition (radical embodied cognitive science), a methodology (the dynamical stance), and a background metaphysics and epistemology (shored-up ecological psychology). The union of these three things is what I'm recommending as the way to do cognitive science. Since (as noted above) I don't argue against other views on what is the right way to do cognitive science, you might wonder why you should accept my advice. After all, you'll have to relearn calculus after all that effort learning computability theory. The true test of an approach in any science is how well it answers the questions we want answered with empirical results. Though some empirical results and promises for more are outlined at various places throughout the book, these results are mostly not in. (Though I think that the computational approach has appallingly little to show considering the time and money that have been devoted to applying it.) How, then, to make the proposed reorientation appealing? In the last section of the book I look at a few traditional philosophical problems through the lens of radical embodied cognitive science. The comparative ease with which these problems (reductionism, epistemological skepticism, metaphysical realism, consciousness) are solved or dissolved constitutes, along with the sketched and promised empirical results, a fairly strong recommendation. My hope is that they will convince impressionable, young cognitive scientists that radical embodied cognitive science is worth some of their time and effort.

Acknowledgments

I've been working on this for a long time, and I could not have done it without the help of a great many people. The seeds of this book, and even snippets of text here and there, are from my dissertation. Brian Cantwell Smith, Tim van Gelder, Ruth Millikan, Bob Port, and Mike Dunn all helped immensely way back then. Most of this book, however, is very different from my dissertation. During the long path from there to here, many people read chunks and provided invaluable advice. Michael Silberstein, Colin Klein, Mason Cash, and Ken Aizawa read and commented on nearly the whole thing. Michael Penn, Mike Anderson, Roger Thompson, Fred Owens, Charles Heyser, John Bickle, Andy Clark, Matthias Scheutz, Randy Beer, Eric Dalton, Adam Kovach, Tom Stoffregen, Harry Heft, Bill Mace, Luciano Floridi, Deniz Dagci, Will Cordeiro, Priscila Farias, João Queiroz, Doug Eck, Damian Stephen, and Rob Withagen all provided helpful advice on various chunks. Will Cordeiro, Colin Klein, Dobri Dotov, Chris Silansky, Charlie Fox, and Matt Rosen collected the data presented at various points throughout the book. Dobri Dotov also provided lifesaving help with figures. So did Damian Stephen. Chapter 3 and chapter 8 are based on coauthored work, so some of this book was actually written by Doug Eck and Charles Heyser. Thanks to Doug and Charles for permission to include coauthored work.

The excellent drawing on the cover is *Figure Heads II* by Brant Schuller. Thanks to Brant for making it for me. Thanks to Sarah Coughlin and Aysu Şuben for help with proofreading and with the Index. Thanks too to Tom Stone and Judy Feldmann at the MIT Press. I humbly apologize to anyone I've forgotten to thank. Present this page with your name on it as a coupon, and I will buy you a beer. If your name should be here, but I've forgotten you, I'll buy you two.

The majority of the writing of this book was done during two leaves from Franklin & Marshall College (2003–04 and 2006–07). During one of these leaves, I was hosted by the Center for the Ecological Study of Perception and Action (CESPA) at the University of Connecticut and funded by a grant from the National Science Foundation (NSF 00-04097). During the other leave, I was partially funded by a Central Pennsylvania Consortium Mellon Grant. I am grateful to F&M, UConn, CPC, and NSF for their generosity, and to Franklin & Marshall for providing intellectual stimulation and allowing me to pretend to be a psychologist. My debt to the folks at CESPA, especially Mike Turvey, Claudia Carello, Claire Michaels, Bob Shaw, and Bruce Kay, is enormous. In addition to helping me get funding and providing me an office in their dynamic and stimulating center, they taught me a good deal of what I know about dynamics and ecological psychology, patiently correcting my misunderstandings and tolerating my heterodox views. Furthermore, during my time at CESPA, and many times in the years since, Mike and Claudia fed me, entertained me at their in-house pub, and put me up for the night. I cannot thank them enough.

I also cannot thank Andrea, Ava, and Henry enough. They regularly remind me that, at the end of the day, philosophy is not all that important.

Radical Embodied Cognitive Science

I Stage Setting

We also assumed, at least initially, that a complicated issue involving major conceptual revisions could be solved by a single clever argument.
—Paul Feyerabend, *Killing Time* (1995)

The moral, children, is approximately Baconian. Don't think; look. Try not to argue.
—Jerry Fodor, "Observation Reconsidered" (1984)

1 Hegel, Behe, Chomsky, Fodor

Imagine the scene: An academic conference. Two cognitive scientists, casual but friendly acquaintances, are chatting in a hotel bar.[1]

"So, what are you working on now?"

"I've been doing some stuff with [insert one of: ecological psychology, connectionist networks, dynamical modeling, embodied cognition, situated robotics, etc.]."

"But [insert name(s) here] already showed that that approach is hopeless. The paper was published in . . . "

"Yeah, yeah. I've read that one. I don't buy it at all. [Reinsert name(s) here] doesn't really get it. You see . . . "

If you're reading this, you've probably taken part in a conversation like this. In fact, nearly everyone working in cognitive science is working on an approach that someone else has shown to be hopeless, usually by an argument that is more or less purely philosophical. This is especially true of the not quite mainstream approaches listed above, the approaches that constitute the core of radical embodied cognitive science, the view I will describe and defend in this book. But it is also true for more mainstream computational cognitive science (e.g., Miller, Galanter, and Pribram 1960). We all know about the arguments that purport to show that our research can never succeed; indeed, nearly every book written by a philosopher begins with an argument that the competing approaches are hopeless. Yet, for some reason, we persist. Somehow we're only convinced by the philosophical arguments that everyone else's approaches are hopeless.

The point of this chapter is to make sense of two related phenomena. The first phenomenon is the large number of philosophical arguments against empirical research programs in cognitive science. Why are there so many of these arguments in cognitive science, but not in, say, botany? The second phenomenon is the collective shrug that greets these arguments, the fact that no one is convinced by them. If people were convinced by such arguments, cognitive science would have died a premature death in the mid-1960s in the face of early critiques by Dreyfus (1964, 1972). I will account for these phenomena by suggesting a way of understanding the power (and lack thereof) of these philosophical arguments. My path to doing so is anything but direct: I will touch upon Hegel, Kuhn, Feyerabend, intelligent design, medieval philosophy, and vertebrate digestion, along with Chomsky, Fodor, and Pylyshyn. All of this will be in the service of an argument that it is just fine, even admirable, for those of us who work on nonmainstream cognitive science to keep on doing so, despite philosophical arguments that our efforts are in vain. I will also suggest that it is just fine, even occasionally admirable, to keep producing arguments that our efforts are in vain.

1.1 Hegelian Arguments

I begin by describing four famous philosophical arguments against empirical approaches.

1.1.1 Hegel and Behe

According to uncharitable legend, Hegel's 1801 *Habilitation* contains an argument that the number of planets in the solar system was necessarily seven. Like most legends, this one is not exactly correct. What Hegel actually argued was that there was necessarily no planet between Mars and Jupiter. This argument was made in the face of contemporary evidence that there was a planet—actually the asteroid Ceres—between Mars and Jupiter, and was based on Hegel's "corrections" to one of the number series descried in Plato's *Timaeus*. Because the purported planet between Mars and Jupiter would be the eighth planet discovered, Hegel concluded that there could not be an eighth planet. We can reconstruct Hegel's argument as follows:

1. If there were a planet between Mars and Jupiter, the distances between the planets would not conform to the corrected *Timaeus* number series.
2. The distances between the planets must conform to the corrected *Timaeus* number series.
3. *Therefore*, there must be no planet between Mars and Jupiter.
4. *Therefore*, no eighth planet can be discovered.

Hegel's reason for believing the second premise is somewhat obscure. It was in explicit reaction to the Bode-Titius law, which predicted a planet between Mars and Jupiter. The Bode-Titius law was based on a number series derived from the positions of the known planets. Hegel's objection to it was that it was phenomenological: it was based on observation and curve-fitting. The number series that actually predicted the number and location of planets must, he was certain, be derived from rational thought, not curve-fitting. Overall, Hegel's argument was a conceptual one: logically, he claimed, there could be no planets between the ones that were known to exist already at that point. Of course, the final conclusion is unwarranted: the *Timaeus* number series continues to infinity, leaving open the possibility that more planets would be discovered beyond the then-known seven. Furthermore, when more planets were discovered, their positions conformed to the phenomenological Bode-Titius predictions, and not the rational *Timaeus* series. Nonetheless, the inference from premises (1) and (2) to conclusion (3) is valid.[2]

Although formally dissimilar, Michael Behe's argument for an intelligent designer has the same a priori flavor as Hegel's. Behe defines *irreducible complexity* as "a single system which is composed of several well-matched, interacting parts that contribute to the basic function, wherein the removal of any one of those parts causes the system to effectively cease functioning" (1996, 39). He goes on to claim that "[a]n irreducibly complex system cannot be produced directly (that is, by continuously improving the initial function, which continues to work by the same mechanism) by slight, successive modification of a precursor system, because any precursor to an irreducibly complex system that is missing a part is by definition nonfunctional" (ibid.). Based on this definition and claim, Behe argues as follows.

1. Irreducibly complex systems cannot have evolved by natural selection.
2. Many biochemical systems are irreducibly complex.
3. *Therefore*, many biochemical systems cannot have evolved by natural selection.
4. *Therefore*, many biochemical systems have been designed an intelligent agent.

Among the many biochemical systems that Behe cites as being irreducibly complex are the cilium and the protein transport system. He goes on to claim that "[e]xamples of irreducible complexity can be found on virtually every page of a biochemistry textbook" (ibid.). As in the case of Hegel's argument, the initial conclusion follows if the premises are true, but the final conclusion does not. And, again, as with Hegel's argument, the argument is conceptual: Behe defines a class of systems, claims they must have certain properties, and then (contrary to empirical evidence) claims that certain biological systems are members of the class.

Hegel's argument has become a target for contemporary analytic philosophers who use it as a means to mock the antiempirical methods of transcendental and continental philosophers. (See, e.g., Popper's *The Open Society and Its Enemies* [1945].) Behe's argument is ridiculed by scientists, philosophers of science, and (thankfully) federal judges. By now, most analytic philosophers and most scientists believe that logical or conceptual arguments against empirical propositions and research programs, such as Hegel's or Behe's, have no place in science. Empirical propositions about the number of planets or about the history of cilia, it is typically thought, are not to be ruled out by logic or by definition. Somehow, though, this attitude has not made its way into cognitive science, where conceptual arguments against empirical claims are very common. Indeed, one could argue that the field was founded on such an argument.

1.1.2 Chomsky on *Verbal Behavior*

In the last section of his review of *Verbal Behavior*, after a withering critique of Skinner's theory of language learning, Chomsky makes an argument, part of which is now typically called a *poverty of the stimulus* argument. It begins with a series of observations about language learning: that language is complex, that it is acquired rapidly, and that it is acquired without much explicit instruction. It continues as follows:

> It is not easy to accept that a child is capable of constructing an extremely complex mechanism for generating a set of sentences, some of which he has heard, or that an adult can instantaneously determine whether (and if so, how) an item is generated by this mechanism, which has many of the properties of an abstract deductive theory. Yet this appears to be a fair description of speaker, listener, and learner. If this is correct, we can predict that a direct attempt to account for the behavior of speaker, learner, and listener, not based on a prior understanding of the structure of grammars, will achieve very limited success. The grammar must be regarded as a component in the behavior of the speaker and listener which can only be inferred, as Lashley has put it, from the resulting physical acts. The fact that all normal children acquire essentially comparable grammars of great complexity with remarkable rapidity suggests that human beings are somehow specially designed to do this, with data-handling or "hypothesis-formulating" ability of unknown character and complexity. (Chomsky 1959/2003, 424)

This argument reaches two conclusions—that there is an innate grammar and that studying language without taking this grammar into account is hopeless—that were crucial to the establishment of cognitive science. I am especially interested here in the second of these conclusions and arguments for conclusions like it. This argument, like Hegel's and Behe's, purports to show that apparently empirical propositions are false as a matter of casual observation and logic and, consequently, that certain ways of trying to understand the natural world are ruled out in advance.

Chomsky's argument can be outlined as follows.

1. Children uniformly and rapidly learn language, without specific reinforcement.
2. Children are presented with evidence insufficient to infer the characteristics of the grammar they attain in learning language.
3. Learning language is the attainment of a grammar, an internal deductive mechanism that allows the recognition and production of appropriate sentences.
4. *Therefore*, the grammar must be largely innate.
5. *Therefore*, any theory that does not posit such an innate grammar cannot account for language learning.

Before criticizing this argument, I should point out its reasonableness. Humans acquire a mechanism that is apparently unlearnable given the opportunities for learning, so it must be innate. This is rather plausible, and many people—nearly all linguists—are convinced by it. There is, however, a problem with this argument, and it is with the evidence for the premises. The problem with the evidence for the premises is that *none is provided*, and no empirical studies of language learning are cited. Chomsky relies entirely on casual observations in the case of the semiempirical premises (1 and 2).[3] The theoretical premise (3) is derived by inference to the best explanation of the semiempirical premises.[4] This, then, is the particular character of Chomsky's argument that I would like to focus on: it is an argument that a class of scientific approaches is doomed to fail, based on theoretical posits and little or no empirical evidence. Note that this is just what Popper mocked Hegel for, and what biologists mock Behe for, and on reasonable grounds. Somehow Chomsky's argument has escaped relatively unscathed. In what follows, I will call arguments like this *Hegelian arguments*. Specifically, Hegelian arguments are arguments, based on little or no empirical evidence, to the conclusion that some scientific approach (observational astronomy, evolutionary biology, behaviorist psychology) will fail.

As noted above, Chomsky's is the first in a string of Hegelian arguments in cognitive science. The majority of these arguments are aimed at showing that particular explanatory styles and mechanisms are incapable of explaining human cognition. I will describe one more of these arguments in the next section. There are lots of Hegelian arguments that I won't discuss concerning original intentionality, qualia, symbol grounding, physicalism,[5] and so on.

1.1.3 Fodor and Pylyshyn on Connectionist Networks

Another famous Hegelian argument is the famous systematicity argument found in "Connectionism and the Cognitive" Architecture by Fodor and Pylyshyn[6] (1988; see also Aizawa 2003, Fodor 2008). Their argument against connectionist networks as a model of the cognitive architecture goes as follows.

1. Human thought is systematic. That is, abilities come in clusters.
2. Systematicity requires representations with compositional structure.
3. Connectionist networks do not have representations with compositional structure.
4. *Therefore,* connectionist networks are not good models of human thought.

This argument is one of the most important and influential in the recent history of cognitive science. It drew stark battle lines soon after Rumelhart, McClelland, and the PDP Research Group (1986) drew attention to connectionist networks. It is also an argument that has been convincing to many people. That this argument is Hegelian can be seen from premises (1) and (3), neither of which is defended in Fodor and Pylyshyn's article by citing empirical studies. In fact, Fodor and Pylyshyn's claim that human thought is systematic was an entirely new one in the cognitive sciences. No prior empirical study supported the claim that human thought came in "clusters," where having one ability was necessarily connected to having others. In fact, Fodor and Pylyshyn cite just one empirical study in the whole of their paper: a chapter in Pinker 1984. In that chapter, the evidence presented indicates that children's speech is *not* systematic, which evidence Pinker attempts to discount. So the only experimental study cited actually contains evidence *against* systematicity.[7] And, in fact, Dennett (1991) and Clark (1997), among others, have argued (against premise 1) that although human language is systematic, the rest of human thought is not. Many other defenders of connectionism, such as Smolensky (1990), van Gelder (1990), and Chalmers (1990), have argued (against premise 3) that connectionist networks can have representations with compositional structure.

My reminder of these two highly respected, highly influential Hegelian arguments from cognitive science is intended to show that these arguments are taken very seriously in the discipline. This is an important difference between cognitive science and other sciences, which are more purely empirical. At first blush, it might seem that the explanation for this difference is that the cognition is *different in kind* from the subject matter of other sciences, and requires a different kind of science. Is this true? To see this, we'll look at the scientific study of a more mundane animal activity: digestion.

1.2 On Digestion

Anatomists and physiologists, whether they are studying humans or other living things, are typically more or less atheoretical.[8] They are primarily interested in gathering data, to see empirically how living things work. Theoretical issues may occasionally motivate their experiments and the observations they choose to make, but that is the only role they play. For example, given theoretical claims about parallel evolution, one might choose to see whether the same or different molecular mechanisms are involved in the adaptation to extreme cold in Arctic and Antarctic fish. Note, however, that the theoretical claims only make this seem like an interesting experiment; they do not lead to claims that molecular mechanisms, but not, say, behavioral tendencies, are *the* way to study differences between Arctic and Antarctic fish. (These claims about biologists come primarily from my experiences talking with biologists. For published confirmation, see Keller 2002.) That is, one rarely sees Hegelian arguments by practicing biologists. Indeed, Behe has disqualified himself from this community by trafficking in them. What one sees instead a lot of fact-finding and an impressive systematization of knowledge of the natural world that psychologists and cognitive scientists ought to envy.

We can see this by looking at an example: vertebrate digestion. Beginning with Galen of Pergamon in the second century CE, digestion has been studied in great detail, by experiment and direct observation via disection and vivisection. The current state of knowledge is that among vertebrates, there are many varieties of digestive system, each of which is aimed at extracting nutrients from substances introduced into the body. The properties of digestive systems are in large part determined by diet, yielding three main classes: herbivorous, carnivorous, and omnivorous. I will briefly describe each of these in turn. (This information comes mostly from Stevens and Hume 1995.)

The digestive systems of herbivores are adapted to maximize the extraction from a typically rough food source that is poor in nutrients. Thus herbivores have relatively complex digestive systems that take advantage of both mechanical and chemical means of digestion. Typically, herbivore digestion begins with chewing, a mechanical means of beginning the process of breaking down foodstuffs. Herbivores must rely on microbial fermentation to digest cellulose. That is, their digestive tracts must have specialized fermentation vats in which bacteria can break down the cellulose into simple, digestible sugars. There are two main ways this is done: foregut fermentation and hindgut fermentation. Foregut fermenters are animals whose major site of fermentation is before the stomach and small intestine. These animals are often called ungulates, and have specialized prestomach regions for fermentation. There are two main classes of foregut fermenters. First there are the so-called ruminants, such as cows and sheep, that regurgitate their food. There are also the nonruminant foregut fermenters, such as the hippopotamus and the kangaroo. These fortunate foregut fermenters animals need not regurgitate their food to digest it. Hindgut fermenters, on the other hand, do not have specialized prestomach fermentation vats. Most of their fermentation takes place in a digestive dead end called the caecum, which houses a huge population of bacteria. Rabbits, horses, and elephants are examples of hindgut fermenters.

Unlike herbivores, carnivores typically have very short, unspecialized digestive tracts. Given the richness of their food, they also typically have no major sites of microbial fermentation for breaking down cellulose, though some hindgut microbial fermentation typically does occur. The differences among carnivores occur at the front end of the digestive tract. Carnivores either (1) masticate their food, tearing it to pieces and mixing it with saliva for predigestion (cats, dogs); (2) swallow it whole, allowing intestinal chemicals to do all the work (carnivorous birds, lizards); or (3) use a filtration to allow only relatively small, digestible animals to enter the body for chemical digestion (some whales).

Omnivores have digestive systems that, unsurprisingly, share features with both herbivores and carnivores. Like herbivores, they typically have complex digestive tracts and they rely significantly on microbial fermentation. Like carnivores, their fermentation is always hindgut. The main differences one sees among the omnivores are in their strategies for mechanical digestion, an essential part of dealing with tough foods such as seeds and insects. Some omnivores (humans, pigs) masticate their food by chewing. Others (especially birds) cannot afford a bulky set of teeth and must use swallowed stones in their muscular gizzards to do the mechanical work other omnivores do by chewing.

To sum up this brief discussion of the varieties of digestion, there are many different ways that evolution has solved the problem of turning energy stored in environmental foodstuffs into forms usable by vertebrates. (Here, I have discussed seven main varieties of digestive system.) Given this great variety, and the relative "earthiness" of the digestive process, it is unsurprising that our knowledge of digestive diversity came via patient empirical research over hundreds of years. Indeed, I would suggest that our knowledge of the diverse types of vertebrate digestion could not have come from armchair reasoning and argument. Could anyone have just *deduced* that microbes and swallowed stones are crucially involved in vertebrate digestion? This is in great contrast to the cognitive sciences, in which what I have called Hegelian arguments are marshaled in attempts to constrain empirical research and close down nascent research programs. The difference, it might seem, may be in the subject matter. Digestion is eating and excreting, as "merely animal" an activity as humans go in for. Cognition, on the other hand, is the pinnacle of our humanity. Thus, one might expect philosophers to make Hegelian arguments about cognition, but not about the gut. Think again.

1.3 Hegelian Arguments about Digestion

In the twelfth and thirteenth centuries, there was a vigorous debate among Scholastics concerning what was called the multiplication theory. The theory, first described in Peter Lombard's *Sentences*, concerns the origin of the matter that composes human bodies, and ultimately impacts the nature of digestion. According to the multiplication theory, all the matter in every human is derived by copying from the matter that composed Adam.[9] That is, we are each made up of the very same stuff that God breathed life into in the Garden of Eden. The medievals could believe this counterintuitive claim because they were atomists, and believed that there was a smallest indivisible unit of nature. Thus, they could believe that Adam's atoms could multiply; that is, if an atom "splits," it becomes two atoms that are not smaller than the original because atoms are the smallest units of nature. The idea, roughly, was this. Adam's semen contained a number of his atoms, which he deposited into Eve. During fetal and postnatal development, these atoms divided to become Cain, Abel, and so on, who in turn deposited their atoms into their wives for development, and so on until we have the entirety of thirteenth-century humanity, all composed of atoms that are Xerox-like copies of Adam's atoms. This affects the role of digestion by making it the case that digestion cannot involve the incorporation of food into the body. Incorporation of food would conflict with multiplication because if food were incorporated, the percentage of the stuff of the original man in humans would diminish over the generations. Suppose that by reproductive age, incorporated food made up 20 percent of a man. Then, because he was born ten generations later, Noah would be just 13.4 percent Adam; the next ten generations would make Abraham just 1.4 percent Adam. But we know, according to the multiplication theory, that Noah, Abraham, and everyone else are 100 percent composed of Adam's atoms. Thus food must not be incorporated during digestion. Here, we have a Hegelian argument about digestion.

Unlike the arguments from cognitive science described above, this one seemed counterintuitive even at the time. Even in the twelfth century, it was obvious that excessive eating led to weight gain and that weight loss came with fasting. One could counter this by saying that food provided energy for multiplication, thus accounting for these results; but this also seems counterintuitive. Why, then, did people believe the multiplication theory? Reynolds (2001) describes two main reasons why the medievals might have believed in multiplication. First, multiplication can help explain original sin. According to Catholic doctrine, Adam's original sin taints all of us. Since we ourselves did not commit the original sin, how could that be? Multiplication theory provides a ready explanation. Suppose that Adam's body (not his soul) was tainted by original sin. If our bodies are made of material copied from Adam's, the taint of original sin could also be copied. Thus, you and I are guilty of Adam's original sin, despite our never having been to the Garden of Eden, because our bodies are made of tainted material. Notice that this allows a parallel Hegelian argument about digestion similar to the one above. If food were incorporated, each generation would be less tainted by original sin than the previous one. Furthermore, the children of overweight fathers would be less tainted. This was, of course, the stuff of reductio ad absurdum to medieval scholars.

A second reason to believe in multiplication, and yet another Hegelian argument about digestion, is related to the Resurrection. According to Catholic doctrine, after the second coming of the Son of God, the souls of the righteous will rejoin their bodies and live in Heaven on Earth. But this is a problem if food is incorporated. For what if Shem were eaten by a fish named Japheth, and during digestion was incorporated into Japheth the fish. Then, later, Ham catches Japheth and eats him, including the stuff that was originally part of Shem, incorporating it into his (Ham's) body. When the Resurrection comes, and righteous Shem and righteous Ham return to Earth to rejoin their bodies, who would get that bit of stuff? (This circle could be tightened, leaving Ham out altogether, if Japheth were not a fish but a cannibal. But then he wouldn't get to rejoin his body due to lack of righteousness, and ownership would presumably revert to Shem.) This problem goes away immediately if the multiplication theory is true, and if food is not incorporated during digestion.

The purpose of this digression into the Middle Ages is to show that Hegelian arguments have also had a role in the history of the study of digestion.

So, the prevalence of Hegelian arguments in cognitive science cannot be because of the fact that cognition is a biological function different in kind from digestion. Indeed, one of the guiding principles of this book is that cognition is not a special kind of biological function. Instead, I would suggest that the reason we see Hegelian arguments in both medieval theories of digestion and contemporary cognitive science stems from their immaturity as fields of study. That is, both approaches to their subject matter lack a unifying set of conceptual principles and experimental methodologies, what Kuhn (1962) called a *paradigm*.[10]

1.4 Stages of Scientific Inquiry and Hegelian Arguments

I have just suggested that Hegelian arguments are prevalent in cognitive science because cognitive science is immature. This in itself does not indicate anything about how one ought to react to Hegelian arguments. In this section, I will discuss the role and force of Hegelian arguments in each of Kuhn's (1962) stages in the evolution of a science. This will require saying a little about Kuhn's stages. What I will say about Kuhn concerns his historical account of scientific theory change, and this can stand independently of the stronger conclusions he draws concerning incommensurability, metaphysics, and the possibility of scientific progress.[11]

According to Kuhn's (1962) famous analysis of theory change in science, a field of study at any point in time is in one of three stages: it is immature, it is in the stage of normal science, or it is in a period of revolution. Hegelian arguments can have different effects in each of these stages. In immature science, thinkers have not yet come to agreement on a unifying paradigm to guide research. In this kind of science, there is vast disagreement on principles, methods, and even accepted facts. For convenience, I will refer to these principles, methods, and accepted facts as the *theoretical background*. This lack of agreement on theoretical background allows, even encourages, Hegelian arguments. If there are several competing theoretical backgrounds, we should expect devotees of theoretical background A to use their assumptions to argue against the assumptions of the devotees of theoretical background B. Because immature sciences often lack organized, agreed upon bodies of data, these will typically be Hegelian arguments. This is even more to be expected when there is intense competition over grants, space in journals, and good graduate students. This, I would argue, is the current situation in cognitive science.[12] But note that the lack of agreement on theoretical background blunts the force of Hegelian arguments. Devotees of background B are not likely to be persuaded by arguments based on assumptions from background A that they do not accept. As Fodor puts it,

> There is in general no point to my convincing you that belief *B* is derivable from theory *T* unless *T* is a theory you endorse; otherwise my argument will seem to you merely a reductio of its premises. This is a peculiarly nasty property of inferential belief fixation because it means that *the more we disagree about, the harder it will be to settle any of our disagreements*. (1984, 24)

This contrasts with contemporary study of digestive anatomy and physiology, which are mature and more fully empirical in nature. Digestion, unlike cognition, is a field whose study has come of age. It is in the stage that Kuhn calls *normal science*, when there is broad agreement on the theoretical background, now solidified into what Kuhn calls a *paradigm*. In this stage of science, Hegelian arguments will be rare. If everyone agrees on the paradigm, arguments will be arguments over matters of fact. This is the current stage of anatomical and physiological studies of digestion, as well as many other more established sciences. Note, too, that astronomy in the nineteenth century was normal, so Hegel's own Hegelian argument was, unsurprisingly, rejected by astronomers. Similarly for Behe and evolutionary biology.

Kuhn's third stage, *revolutionary science*, occurs only after years of normal science, when a series of findings is inexplicable given the current paradigm and/or problems that were thought to be easily solvable present unexpected difficulties. When difficulties such as these accumulate, a science is said to be *in crisis* and scientific revolutions or *paradigm shifts* might occur. For this to happen, a new set of assumptions must arise that accounts for persistent anomalies, one that is sufficiently compelling so that the field of study is reoriented around a new paradigm. Paradigm shifts will typically be based on largely nonempirical arguments. For example, Einstein's reconceptualization of simultaneity and importation of non-Euclidean geometry were nonempirical assumptions that structured his arguments for relativity theory. In most cases, though, the arguments that lead to a paradigm shift will not be Hegelian in the sense described above. In particular, they will serve to energize a field around a set of new assumptions by laying out this set of new assumptions and showing what phenomena they promise to account for. The Hegelian arguments described above are negative: they argue from a set of assumptions that some existent theory *cannot* account for phenomena. We should, however, expect Hegelian arguments during times of crisis, as scientists begin to lose confidence in the dominant paradigm, and begin to question some of its assumptions. We should also expect rearguard Hegelian arguments defending the in-crisis paradigm, by attacking potential replacements.[13]

If this analysis is correct, we should expect to see Hegelian arguments in science primarily in times of theoretical flux: when science is immature or in crisis. We should not see them in business-as-usual normal science. Of course, those who make these arguments should expect them to meet great resistance. At times of revolution, these arguments essentially claim that the current paradigm is insufficient. In the cases of present interest (medieval digestive science and current cognitive science), there is no single, dominant paradigm guiding a field and, hence, little agreement on theoretical background. Thus Hegelian arguments in immature sciences have very little chance of convincing those committed to the approach being called into question. In particular, we should not expect those who are working with a particular set of assumptions *S* to be convinced by arguments based in another nonidentical set of assumptions *T*, several of which they do not believe. (See the Fodor quote above.) This, finally, is the reason that we noncomputational cognitive scientists typically reject out of hand the Hegelian arguments proffered by proponents of computational approaches, just as computationalists rejected earlier arguments by Dreyfus and Searle.

Looking back to the Hegelian arguments discussed above, it is easy to see why proponents of competing "preparadigms" would not be convinced. In immature science, there is no universally accepted paradigm, so background assumptions that structure the research of one faction are optional to those of other factions. In the case of Chomsky's argument described above, the positing of a grammar is typically rejected. In the case of Fodor and Pylyshyn, proponents of connectionist networks deny that human thought is, in general, systematic and insist that connectionist representations are structured. Rejecting these premises, of course, means that one can also reject the conclusions that supposedly follow from them. It is for this reason that my radical embodied cognitive scientist colleagues can continue in their research, still assuming that mental representations and computations play a very limited role in cognition.

1.5 Recommendations

The purpose of this chapter has been to make sense of two puzzling features of cognitive science: the frequency of Hegelian arguments, and the fact they fail to serve their intended purpose. The comparison with both medieval and contemporary digestive physiology suggests that both these features result from cognitive science's immaturity. In fields like cognitive science, there will be a plurality of theoretical perspectives. (See note 13.) So computational cognitive scientists (e.g., Fodor and Pylyshyn 1981) argue against the ecological approach (e.g., Gibson 1979) as part of an effort to establish their approach as a unifying paradigm for the discipline, and hence to attract research funding and good graduate students. Ecological psychologists (e.g., Turvey et al. 1981) reject these arguments because they share few of the assumptions that structure the computational cognitive scientist's argument. And both sides continue with their experimental research, ideally having clarified and adjusted their own assumptions based on the critique from the other side.

Ultimately, it is likely that experimentally discovered facts will largely determine the appropriate theoretical approach in cognitive science. We should let the facts on the ground do that. Indeed, my bet is that the empirical facts will ultimately show that we need more than one theoretical approach in cognitive science (Chemero and Silberstein 2008a; Dale 2008). This is in effect a recommendation that we embrace the kind of *theoretical pluralism* that (preanarchist[14]) Feyerabend (1963, 1965) argued for. According to this view, allowing several incompatible theories to simultaneously guide research is good for science—having competitors enhances individual theories by providing potential falsifiers and by forcing theoretical development to deal with the empirical findings of rivals. Feyerabend's point, and mine in this chapter, is that we should allow many theoretical flowers to bloom. To stretch this metaphor, we should not allow Hegelian arguments to lead to inappropriate, preemptive weeding, likely to take the tulips (paradigms-to-be) along with dandelions (false starts). Even dandelions are lovely in their way.

1.6 Pointing Forward

Books by philosophers almost always begin by arguing that everyone else is incorrect. I have just explained why nobody believes these arguments. I will, therefore, not be presenting arguments that all approaches other than radical embodied cognitive science are somehow bad. We will not choose a scientific research program by process of elimination. To argue in favor of radical embodied cognitive science, I will, instead, explain in detail how it connects to other theories, how it explains, what it has explained, what it promises to explain, and how adopting it transforms perennial philosophical problems.

2 Embodied Cognition and Radical Embodied Cognition

I've just suggested that arguing against scientific approaches philosophically is never convincing. So unlike most works in philosophy, I will not be arguing to make space for radical embodied cognitive science, the position I will articulate in this book. But despite the fact that I won't be arguing that other approaches are incorrect, I will say a few things about them, primarily to give some sense of how radical embodied cognitive science fits in. One rather surprising outcome of this will be that situated, embodied cognitive science of the sort that has become increasingly popular in recent years (e.g., Clark 1997, 2008) is both very similar to and very different from radical embodied cognitive science. Although the taxonomy of scientific psychologies I'm about to set out will include many nonembodied approaches, my focus will be on embodiment.

2.1 A Taxonomy of Theories of Mind: The First Pass

In their connectionist-bashing article of 1988, which we discussed in chapter 1, Fodor and Pylyshyn say the following:

> There are two major traditions in modern theorizing about the mind, one that we'll call "representationalist" and one that we'll call "eliminativist." Representationalists hold that postulating representational (or "intentional" or "semantic") states is essential to the theory of cognition; according to representationalists, there are states of the mind which function to encode states of the world. Eliminativists, by contrast, think that psychological theories can dispense with such semantic notions as representation. According to eliminativists, the appropriate vocabulary for psychological theorizing is neurological or, perhaps, behavioral, or perhaps syntactic; in any event, not a vocabulary that characterizes mental states in terms of what they represent. (1988, 7)

Although they say nothing else about eliminativist theories in their article, the point of which after all is to develop a contrast among representation-

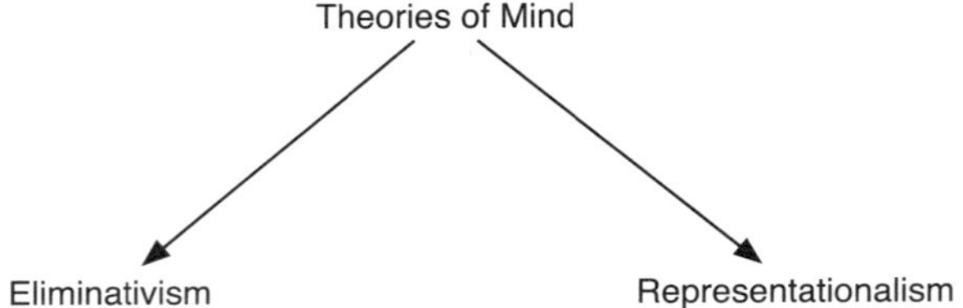

Figure 2.1

alist theories, what Fodor and Pylyshyn have in mind are views of the sort defended by American pragmatists (Peirce, James, Dewey; see Heft 2001; Rockwell 2005) and some of their intellectual offspring (Skinner, Gibson), along with Gilbert Ryle, Richard Rorty (1979), Stephen Stich (circa 1983), and Daniel Dennett (circa 1969). What these eliminativists have in common is that they don't take the mind to be a mirror of nature; they are, that is, *antirepresentationalists*. This, then, is the first cut on theories of mind and cognition: there are those who think the main business of cognition is what I will sometimes call *mental gymnastics*, the construction, manipulation, and use of representations of the world, and there are those who believe that the business of cognition is to do something else. (See figure 2.1.)

It is worth pointing out that this first cut *almost* lines up with the distinction between functionalists and structuralists from the early years of scientific psychology in the United States. The first point to make about this distinction is that the functionalists of early twentieth-century psychology have nothing in common with the functionalists of later twentieth-century philosophy of mind. Indeed, philosophical functionalists are direct descendents of the psychological structuralists. In early twentieth-century parlance, then, structuralism was psychology derived from William Wundt's German psychology program, and ultimately from Kant and Descartes. Structuralists, generally, believed that the only way to do psychology was to start by determining the structure of the items in our mental lives, and only then was it appropriate to try to understand their function. Their claim was that, as in biology, one had to understand anatomy before one could understand physiology. Functionalism, on the other hand, derived from the American psychology of William James, and ultimately from Darwin. Functionalists generally thought that mental acts could only be understood in terms of their functions. One will misunderstand the mind if one tries to look at parts of it, outside the context of the whole of mental life and behavior. In what follows, to minimize the confusion wrought by dueling terminologies, I will call old-fashioned, psychological functionalists *American naturalists*. (In doing so, I follow Fodor 1990.)

The debate between the structuralist and American naturalist camps was a series of Hegelian arguments[1] that began in earnest with the structuralist Titchener's "Simple Reactions" (1895). In it he argues in favor of using timing experiments to determine the nature of mental processes. An example of such an experiment, described by Titchener, by Ludwig Lange involves an attempt to determine the duration of attention. In Lange's experiment, subjects were asked to complete two tasks, which, Lange thought, differed only in that in one but not the other subjects needed to attend to sensations. The results of the experiment allowed Lange to determine the duration of sensory attention. The logic behind this is as follows. According to structuralists like Titchener and Lange, mental acts have the following structure: first, there is a stimulus, caused by physical stimulation of receptors; then there is a linear series of mental acts; then there is a behavioral response. Of course, then as now, which mental acts occur, and in which order, is a matter of speculation on the part of the experimenter. Suppose that there are two simple reactions *X* and *Y*, which differ only in that *X* requires mental acts *M1* through *M4* whereas *Y* requires only *M1*, *M2*, and *M4*. Then one can determine the duration of *M3* by subtracting the time it takes to perform *Y* from the time it takes to perform *X*.[2] To do psychology, Titchener argued, one must focus on the structure of the mental acts in the series, and not on their function.

American naturalist John Dewey responded in his classic paper "The Research Arc Concept in Psychology" (1896), in which he explicitly criticized the Lange experiment. Dewey describes the structuralist view of simple reactions as a "reflex arc." (It is an arc because it begins in the body, ascends to the mind, and returns to the body.) Dewey argues that the structuralist understanding of the reflex arc commits "the empiricist fallacy," the assumption that the parts of something are prior to the whole. Instead, according to Dewey, all actions, from simple reactions to the most complex intelligent behavior, are *organic circuits* that cannot be understood by breaking them into parts. Out of context, a part of an action is devoid of meaning of any kind, a "series of jerks" in Dewey's memorable phrase. Furthermore, the division of a simple reflex into parts can only be done *ex post facto*. Something can only be identified as a stimulus *after* one identifies the response. In other words, in an organic circuit, what the response is *determines* the nature of the stimulus. That is, a visual stimulus never results in mere seeing; rather it leads to seeing-in-order-to-grasp-and-bring-to-the-mouth or seeing-in-order-to-grasp-and-swing. So, the idea that different simple reactions are composed of the same parts, mixed and matched, is fallacious. So too, Dewey claimed, is any psychology that attempts to explain cognition solely in terms of mental gymnastics, that is, any representational theory of mind. It is, therefore, unsurprising that Fodor often picks on Dewey (e.g., in Fodor 1983, 1990).

The point here is that the distinction that Fodor and Pylyshyn draw between eliminativism and representationalism is as old as psychology itself. And we should notice that contemporary cognitive science has been squarely on the side of the representationalists/structuralists.

2.2 Making Some Finer Distinctions

Before commenting on how the representationalist side is divided up, I should say a few words about the representational theory of mind. I assume that the representational theory of the mind (RTM) is familiar to most readers, so I will describe it briefly. Jerry Fodor (1981) sets out RTM as a commitment to the following five hypotheses:

a) Propositional attitude states (e.g. beliefs and desires) are relational.
b) Among the relata are mental representations.
c) Mental representations are symbols: they have both formal and semantic properties.
d) Mental representations have their causal roles in virtue of their formal properties.
e) Propositional attitudes inherit their semantic properties from those of the mental representations that function as their objects. (1981, 26)

So thoughts (propositional attitudes) are relations between people and mental representations that stand for things in the world (their semantic properties). Any theory, then, that takes cognition to involve semantically evaluable internal entities is a variety of representational theory of mind. Historically speaking, RTM has been a very widely held theory of the mind, one that goes back at least to St. Augustine.

All RTMs have the above in common. Where they differ is in how these symbols are used in cognition. One particularly important variety of RTM, the computational theory of mind (CTM), also has a long history, going back to Hobbes. In *Leviathan*, Hobbes says "By ratiocination, I mean computation." More specifically, he claims that rational thought (ratiocination) is the processing of internal symbols that represent external objects (computation); these symbols are processed according to rules, which, when applied correctly, yield rational thought.

When a man reasoneth, he does nothing else but conceive a sum total, from addition of parcels; or conceive a remainder, from subtraction of one sum from an-

> other. . . . These operations are not incident to numbers only, but to all manner of things that can be added together, and taken one out of another. For as arithmeticians teach to add and subtract in numbers . . . the logicians teach the same in consequences of words; adding together two names to make an affirmation, and two affirmations to make a syllogism; and many syllogisms to make a demonstration. (1651, Part 1, chapter 5; quoted in Haugeland 1985)

Actual thinking is the manipulation of the mental representations (done via their causal, formal properties alone). This just is today's computational theory of mind. The only difference is in how mental computation works. For Hobbes, it literally is addition ("adding together two names to make an affirmation, and two affirmations to make a syllogism"). Contemporary computationalists, of course, have the benefit of the twentieth-century picture of computation. So, for them, computation is the rule-governed manipulation of the formal symbols in what Fodor calls a language of thought. These formal symbols share many properties with idealized natural language words. They are discrete, context-independent tokens; they are combinable into larger molecular representations (similar to sentences) whose meaning is a function of the parts that make them up. The classical computational theory of mind, the one in which cognition is rule-governed manipulation of formal symbols that have all of these properties, is often referred to as good old-fashioned artificial intelligence or GOFAI (Haugeland 1985). There are many other versions of RTM, in which symbols do not have all the properties of symbols in a language of thought, or are used differently in cognition, or both. Because of current interests, and in unfair denigration of much good work, I will simply call these different styles of symbol and symbol-manipulation "other RTM" and "other CTM." See figure 2.2.

We can also make some slightly finer distinctions on the eliminativist side. As noted above, the most prominent version of eliminativism in psychology has been American naturalism, in which it is believed that cognition cannot be understood as a mirror of the world, and cannot be understood apart from the activities, indeed the whole life, of the animal. Two very different descendents of American naturalism are behaviorism (which itself comes in many varieties) and Gibsonian ecological psychology (Gibson 1966, 1979). A second form of eliminativism, one mentioned by Fodor and Pylyshyn in the quote at the beginning of this chapter, is actually a close relative of the computationalist theory of mind. Dennett and Stich have at certain points in their careers each argued that cognition is the rule-governed manipulation of sentences in a logical calculus, but because of systematic difficulties of semantic interpretation, these sentences

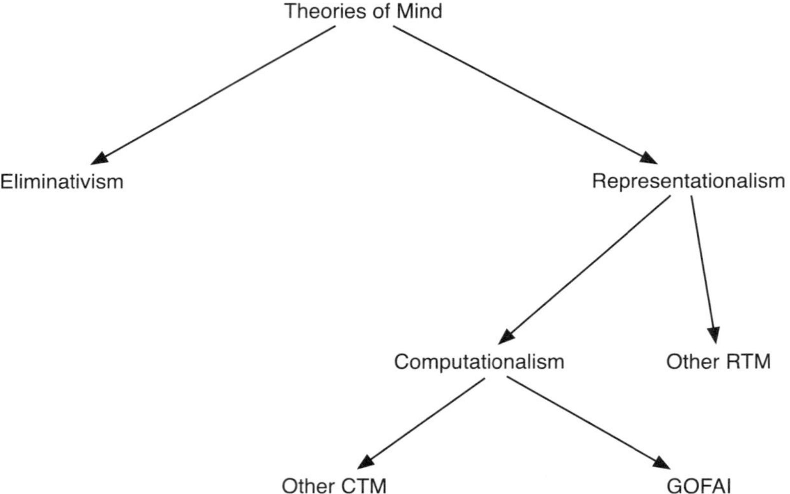

Figure 2.2

are not representations. That is, Dennett (1969) and Stich (1983) both thought that cognition was a form of nonrepresentational mental gymnastics. Stich (1996) has certainly repudiated this position; Dennett probably has as well. (See his introduction to Millikan 1984.) We can, then, split up the eliminativist portion of the tree as seen in figure 2.3, which shows the ambiguous position of early work by Dennett and Stich. This picture is, I admit, a bit convoluted. But it is in this context that we must try to understand the embodied cognition movement that sprang up in cognitive science beginning in earnest in the early 1990s.

2.3 Embodied Cognitive Science

Nowadays lots of cognitive science claims to be embodied or situated[3] or both. Typically, those writing about situated, embodied cognition start with the early work of Rodney Brooks (1991). (See Smith 1991, 1996; Clark 1997, 1999, 2003, 2008; Agre 1997; Clancey 1997; Lakoff and Johnson 1999; Pfeiffer and Scheier 1999; Dourish 2001; Breazeal 2002; Anderson 2003; Wilson 2004; Gallagher 2005; Wheeler 2005; Gibbs 2005; Rowlands 2006; Menary 2007.) To give credit where it is due, I will go back further, to the work of American naturalist offspring James Gibson (1979) and the collaborations between John Barwise and John Perry (1981, 1983).

Gibson's (1979) ecological theory of vision was intended as a direct response to the increasing dominance of computational theories of mind,

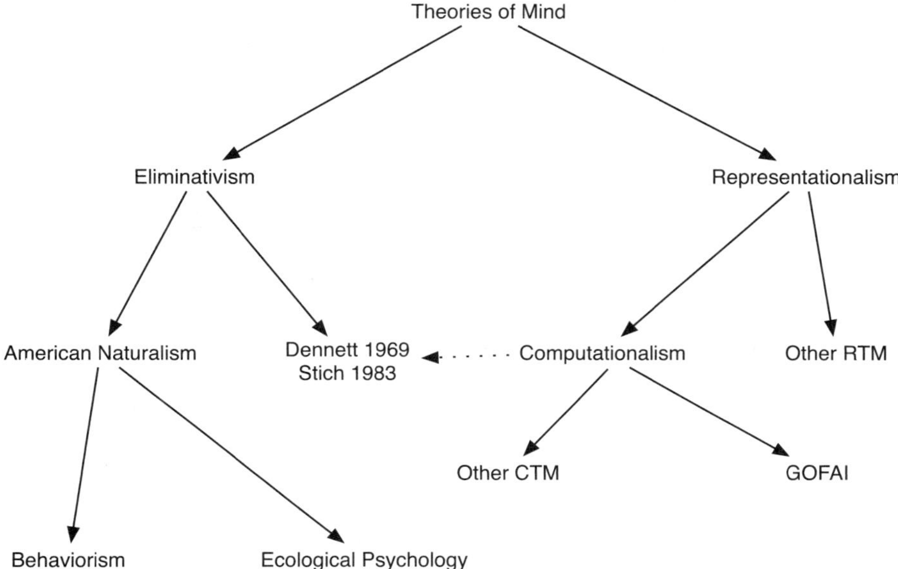

Figure 2.3

according to which perception and thought are rule-governed manipulations of internal representations. Gibson's ecological approach to perception has three major tenets. First, perception is direct, which is to say that it does not involve computation or mental representations. That is, Gibson thought that perception was not a matter of internally adding information to sensations. Second, perception is primarily for the guidance of action, and not for action-neutral information gathering. We perceive the environment in order to do things. The third tenet follows from the first two. Because perception does not involve mental addition of information to stimuli, yet is able to guide behavior adaptively, all the information necessary for guiding adaptive behavior must be available in the environment to be perceived. Thus the third tenet of Gibson's ecological approach is that perception is of *affordances*, that is, directly perceivable, environmental opportunities for behavior. Affordances, as Gibson was well aware, are ontologically peculiar:

> [A]n affordance is neither an objective property nor a subjective property; or it is both if you like. An affordance cuts across the dichotomy of subjective-objective and helps us to understand its inadequacy. It is equally a fact of the environment and a fact of behavior. It is both physical and psychical, yet neither. An affordance points both ways, to the environment and to the observer. (1979, 129)

Despite this ontological peculiarity and the controversy over how to best understand affordances (Turvey 1992; Reed 1996; Stoffregen 2003; Chemero 2003a; Scarantino 2003; Sahin, Cakmak, Dogar, Ugur, and Ucoluk 2007; Chemero and Turvey 2007a; see also chapter 7 below), the idea of affordances—divorced of their relation to direct perception—is the one aspect of Gibson's theory that gained significant attention from the beginning, for example, from designers (see Norman 1988). The rest of Gibson's ideas were not widely accepted by cognitive scientists upon their appearance. They were, however, widely discussed (see Fodor and Pylyshyn 1981; Turvey et al. 1981), and did attract a small, solid core of devotees. More recently, Gibson has become one of the heroes of embodied cognitive science, which has adopted these views (substantially softened) as its own. (Much more will be said about this below. See especially chapters 5, 6, and 7.)

Moving slightly closer to the present, we can trace the origins of the *situated* aspect of embodied cognitive science to situation semantics, the work in the philosophy of mind and language done in the 1980s by John Barwise and John Perry (Barwise and Perry 1981, 1983). Taking themselves to be providing a semantics for Gibsonian psychology,[4] Barwise and Perry argued that we can't understand meaning or cognition without taking into account that thinkers are spatially located (i.e., situated) and so have only incomplete, locally available information at their disposal. Every thinker and speaker is someone, who is somewhere, and who is aware of only certain things. One major upshot of this is that indexicals move from the periphery of accounts of cognition to the center. The idea is that because we are situated in the environment, thoughts about "here," "there," "now," and "me" are ubiquitous. This focus on indexicals, we will see, is a crucial but almost incidental feature of embodied cognitive science. A second important feature of Barwise and Perry's was derived directly from its Gibsonian motivation. Barwise and Perry developed their situation semantics in order to account for meaning without reference to mental representations. In their nonrepresentational account, having meaningful thoughts (perceptions, utterances) has nothing to do with having mental representations, or indeed with anything that might be called epistemic. The meaning of thoughts and sentences is a matter of the relationship between thinkers/speakers and information in their environments.

It is this latter aspect of Barwise and Perry's situation semantics that Rodney Brooks (1991, 1999) picks out when he uses the word "situated" to describe his robots. When Brooks says that his simple, mobile robots are situated, he means that, because they are in the midst of a changing world, they do not need to use representations of the world to plan or guide their behavior. Instead they interact with the world itself. The idea is that there is no need to store information on board, and make predictions about how things will change during an action, when you can just act and check again. Brooks sums up this antirepresentationalism with the slogan "The world is its own best model." This Gibson-like[5] skepticism about mental representations is perhaps the most (in)famous aspect of Brooks's early work, but it is not his antirepresentationalism[6] that makes Brooks the model for embodied cognitive science. Instead it is his insistence that intelligence is necessarily embodied. Brooks argues that it is real interaction with the real world, not mental gymnastics, that is the mark of intelligence. In effect, Brooks sees Barwise and Perry and raises them: for Brooks it is not just a thinker's setting, but also its physical constitution, that is essential for understanding it as intelligent, thinking, and so on. And, of course, having a physical constitution that is essential to intelligent behavior guarantees being situated in a physical (not to mention social) environment. Embodied cognition is necessarily situated.

The current work in embodied cognitive science that arose from these sources (among others, of course) is a broad-based movement, incorporating work in robotics, simulated evolution, developmental psychology, perception, motor control, cognitive artifacts, phenomenology, and, of course, theoretical manifestos. Given this variety of subject matter, there is also variety in theoretical approach. The following tenets, though, are more or less universally held among embodied cognitive scientists.

Interactive explanation and dynamical systems Explaining cognitive systems that include aspects of the body and environment requires an explanatory tool that can span the agent–environment border. Many embodied cognitive scientists use dynamical systems theory. That is, many (though not all) proponents of embodied cognitive science take cognitive systems to be dynamical systems, best explained using the tools of dynamical systems theory. A dynamical system is a set of quantitative variables changing continually, concurrently, and interdependently over time in accordance with dynamical laws that can, in principle, be described by some set of equations. To say that cognition is best described using dynamical systems theory is to say that cognitive scientists ought to try to understand cognition as intelligent behavior and to model intelligent behavior using a particular sort of mathematics, most often sets of differential equations. Dynamical systems theory is especially appropriate for explaining cognition as interaction with the environment because single dynamical systems can have parameters on each side of the skin. That is, we might explain the behavior of the agent in its environment over time as coupled dynamical systems, using something like the following equations, from Beer (1995a):

$$\dot{X}_A = A(X_A; S(X_E))$$

$$\dot{X}_E = E(X_E; M(X_A))$$

where A and E are continuous-time dynamical systems, modeling the organism and its environment, respectively, and $S(x_E)$ and $M(x_A)$ are coupling functions from environmental variables to organismic parameters and from organismic variables to environmental parameters, respectively. It is only for convenience (and from habit) that we think of the organism and environment as separate; in fact, they are best thought of as forming just one nondecomposable system, U. Rather than describing the way external (and internal) factors cause changes in the organism's behavior, such a model would explain the way U, the system as a whole, unfolds over time. It is also worth pointing out that dynamical systems theory is neutral over whether to consider parameter or variable values as representations.

Changing the role of representations Although embodied cognitive science's main modeling tool, dynamical systems theory, is neutral about mental representations, with few exceptions (on which see section 2.4), embodied cognitive scientists reject the strongest claims made by Brooks, Gibson, and Barwise and Perry about mental representations. That is, embodied cognitive scientists typically are not antirepresentationalists. Yet although embodied cognitive scientists do call on representations to explain behavior, they call on them in such a way that the need for mental gymnastics is reduced. The representations they call on are indexical-functional (Agre and Chapman 1987), pushmi-pullyu (Millikan 1995), action-oriented (Clark 1997), or emulator representations (Grush 1997, 2004; Churchland 2002). In what follows, I will refer to these collectively with Clark's term *action-oriented representations*. Action-oriented representations differ from representations in earlier computationalist theories of mind in that they represent things in a nonneutral way, as geared to an animal's actions, as affordances. Action-oriented representations are more primitive than other representations in that they can lead to effective behavior without requiring separate representations of the state of the world and the cognitive system's goals. That is, the perceptual systems of agents need not build an action-neutral representation of the world, which can then be used by the action-producing parts of the agent to guide behavior; instead, the agent produces representations that are geared toward the actions it performs from the beginning. By focusing on action-oriented representations, embodied cognitive scientists attempt to minimize the role of what Andy Clark (2001) has called "objectivist" representations: sentence-like representations of the action-neutral environment in a language of thought.

Intelligent bodies, scaffolded environments, fuzzy borders Given this minimization of importance of mental gymnastics, it is a challenge to explain complex, intelligent behavior. In embodied cognitive science, some of the intelligence is "off-loaded" from the brain to the body and environment. On this view, our bodies are well-designed tools, making them easy for our brains to control. For example, our kneecaps limit the degrees of motion possible with our legs, making balance and locomotion much easier. It is only a small exaggeration to say that learning to walk is easy for humans because our legs already know how. (See Thelen and Smith 1994; Thelen 1995.) This off-loading goes beyond the boundaries of our skin. The natural environment is already rich with affordances and information that can guide behavior. As when beavers build dams, in interacting with and altering the environment, animals enhance these affordances. Kirsh and Maglio (1994; see also Kirsh 1995) show that manipulating the environment is often an aid to problem solving. Their example is of Tetris players rotating zoids on-screen, saving themselves a complicated mental rotation. Hutchins (1995) shows that social structures and well-designed tools allow humans to easily accomplish tasks that would otherwise be too complex. This leads many to believe that cognitive systems are not confined to the brain or body, but include aspects of the environment (Clark 1997; Rowlands 2006; Menary 2007; Hutto 2007). Clark (2003) even argues that external tools (including phones, computers, language, and so on) are so crucial to human life that we are literally cyborgs, partly constituted by technologies.

These three tenets make clear that, despite the influence of American naturalist James Gibson, embodied cognitive science is a form of RTM. In fact, for all its breaks with GOFAI, embodied cognitive science is still a *computational* theory of mind. This much can be seen from the way Kirsh and Maglio describe the zoid-rotations of their Tetris players: they say that zoid-rotation is a matter of off-loading computational complexity onto the environment, so that the rotation is *part of the computation*. Clark (2001) concurs, calling for a *dynamic computationalism* in which we can see that certain of the entities of dynamical models are representations in computational systems that span brain, body, and environment. We can, then, add

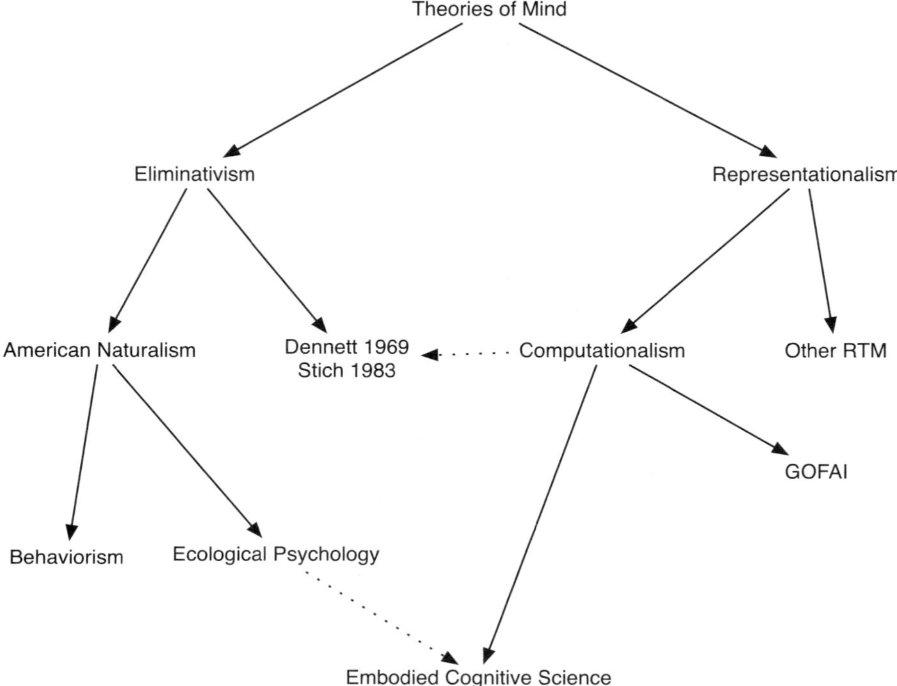

Figure 2.4

to our taxonomy, as pictured in figure 2.4. Embodied cognitive science, like Dennett (1969) and Stich (1983), is in a somewhat ambiguous position. Embodied cognitive science is highly influenced by the American naturalist worldview, especially Gibsonian ecological psychology, but it is also a form of the computational theory of mind.

The final question for this chapter is how radical embodied cognitive science fits in. In particular, how is it related to embodied cognitive science?

2.4 Radical Embodied Cognitive Science

This book is called *Radical Embodied Cognitive Science*. It is high time I say what that is. The term radical embodied cognition is from Andy Clark, who defines it as follows:

Thesis of Radical Embodied Cognition Structured, symbolic, representational, and computational views of cognition are mistaken. Embodied cognition is best studied by means of noncomputational and nonrepresentational ideas and explanatory schemes, involving, e.g., the tools of Dynamical Systems theory. (Clark 1997, 148; 2001, 129)

Clark finds arguments for this position (or set of positions, see below) in Maturana and Varela 1980; Skarda and Freeman 1987; Brooks 1991; Beer and Gallagher 1992; Varela, Thompson, and Rosch 1991; Thelen and Smith 1994; Beer 1995a,b; van Gelder 1995; van Gelder and Port 1995; Kelso 1995; Wheeler 1996; and Keijzer 1998. We might also add Kugler, Kelso, and Turvey 1980; Turvey et al. 1981; Kugler and Turvey 1987; Harvey, Husbands, and Cliff 1994; Husbands, Harvey, and Cliff 1995; Reed 1996; Chemero 2000a, 2008; Lloyd 2000; Keijzer 2001; Thompson and Varela 2001; Beer 2003; Noë and Thompson 2004; Gallagher 2005; Rockwell 2005; Hutto 2005, 2007; Thompson 2007; Chemero and Silberstein 2008a,b; Gallagher and Zahavi 2008; and many others. The point, then, is that this is a genuinely held position, one whose force Clark wishes to deny.

Radical embodied cognition amounts to two positive claims and one negative claim.

Radical embodied cogntion, claim 1 Representational and computational views of embodied cognition are mistaken.

Radical embodied cognition, claim 2 Embodied Cognition is to be explained via a particular set of tools *T*, which includes dynamical systems theory.

Radical embodied cognition, claim 3 The explanatory tools in set *T* do not posit mental representations.

Although I think that claim 1 is correct, I will not argue for it. The point of chapter 1 is that no one believes arguments like that. This leaves claims 2 and 3. These two claims make up radical embodied cognitive science, the science of radical embodied cognition. I hereby define radical embodied cognitive science as the scientific study of perception, cognition, and action as necessarily embodied phenomenon, using explanatory tools that do not posit mental representations. It is cognitive science without mental gymnastics. The goal of this book is to say exactly what it is to do radical embodied cognitive science. For now, though, I would like to say how it fits into the taxonomy of theories of mind described so far in this chapter.

The best way to understand the relation between embodied cognitive science and radical embodied cognitive science is to look back again at the historical forbears of embodied cognitive science. As noted above, embodied cognitive science arose from embracing some of the ideas of Gibson, Barwise and Perry, and Brooks, but backpedaling on the strongest claims

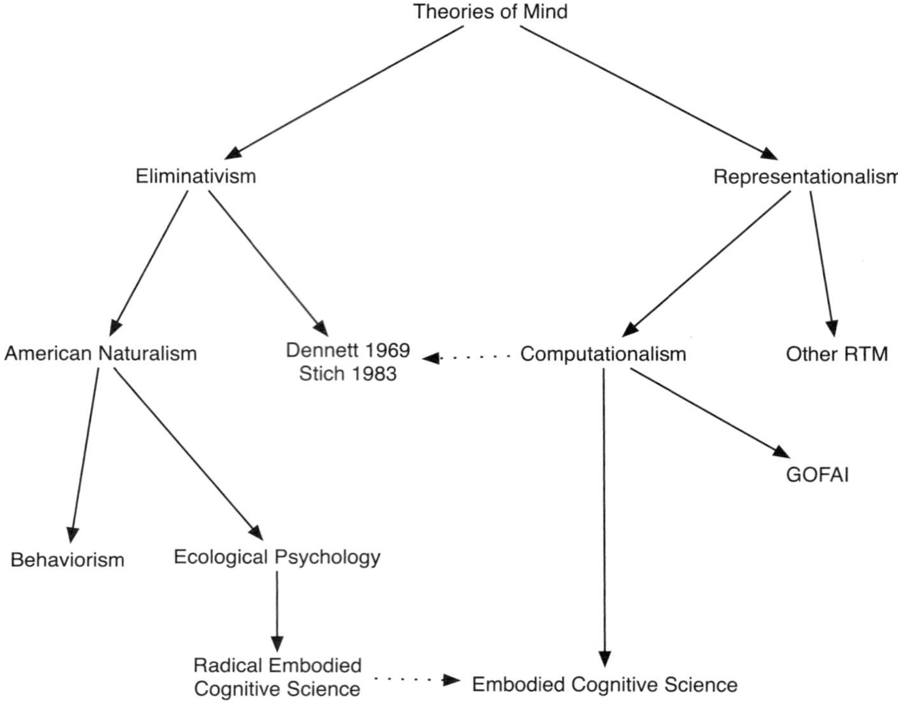

Figure 2.5

these authors made. In particular, embodied cognitive science embraces the necessity of embodiment and the value of dynamical explanation, but combines them with the computational theory of mind. It is the claims that embodied cognitive science rejects that are of interest here. Situated, embodied cognitive scientists typically reject the *antirepresentationalism* of Gibson, Barwise and Perry, and Brooks, while antirepresentationalism (which implies anticomputationalism) is the core of radical embodied cognitive science. Radical embodied cognitive science is a form of eliminativism, one that has its historical roots in American naturalism. (Gibsonian ecological psychology, remember, is a direct descendent of the work of James and Dewey.[7]) I would suggest, then, that radical embodied cognitive science is not a radicalization of embodied cognitive science. Instead, embodied cognitive science should be seen as a watering down of radical embodied cognitive science, and an attempt to combine a theory that is ultimately American naturalist and eliminativist in origin with the computational theory of mind. Thus figure 2.5.

Box 2.1
Extended Mind and Extended Cognition

Inspired in part by embodied cognitive science and radical embodied cognitive science, a vigorous debate has opened over whether cognition systems are extended. On one side are those who argue that wide computationalism and dynamical systems modeling imply that the cognitive system includes aspects of an animal's environment to which the animal is coupled (e.g., Beer 1995a,b; Clark 1997, 2003, 2008; Wilson 2004). On the other side are those who admit that the environment serves as necessary background and input to the cognitive system, but argue that the cognitive system proper has to be understood as encapsulated by the organism's skin or central nervous system (Adams and Aizawa 2008; Rupert 2004). Sometimes this debate slips without justification from being over "extended cognition" to being over "the extended mind." I will speak here only about extended cognition, which strikes me as a debate in (philosophy of) cognitive science, and hence within the scope of this book.

Radical embodied cognitive science is a variety of extended cognitive science. Furthermore, radical embodied cognitive science is not subject to the usual antiextension arguments that can gain traction against (nonradical) embodied cognitive science. In radical embodied cognitive science, the explanation of cognition is dynamical, and (wide) computationalism is explicitly rejected. Agents and environments are modeled as nonlinearly coupled dynamical systems. Because the agent and environment are nonlinearly coupled, they form a unified, nondecomposable system, which is to say that they form a system whose behavior cannot be modeled, even approximately, as a set of separate parts. (See box 2.2, "Dynamical Systems Terminology.") In contrast, the wide computationalist explanation embraced by (nonradical) embodied cognitive science ascribes representations of the environment to the agent. Explaining the agent's activity in terms of its representations invites the anti-extended claim that it is the represented environment, and not the environment itself, that is part of the cognitive system. Adams and Aizawa call this the *coupling-constitution* fallacy: they argue that the fact that a wide computational system is coupled to the environment does not imply that the environment is partly constitutive of the system. I think that there might be something to this when the system in question is a wide computational system and the coupling to the environment is via representations, but not when the system in question is a nonlinearly coupled agent–environment system. When the system is representing the environment, one can carve off the system from the environment, by claiming that it is the environment-as-represented that drives the nonextended cognitive system. On the other hand, when the agent and environment are nonlinearly coupled, they, together, constitute a nondecomposable system, and when that is the case, the

Box 2.1
(continued)

coupling-constitution fallacy is not a fallacy. In other words, the coupling-constitution fallacy is only a fallacy when the coupling is linear. (See Chemero and Silberstein 2008a,b; Silberstein and Chemero, under review for detailed argument for these claims.) Because it rejects computational and representational explanation in favor of nonlinear dynamical modeling, radical embodied cognitive science is not subject to this sort of argument, and might therefore be the only sustainable version of extended cognitive science.

This taxonomy is important for two reasons. First, it needs to be clear that radical embodied cognitive science is part of a venerable scientific tradition, one that begins with the birth of American psychology, and so is in no sense radicalism for its own sake. Second, understanding embodied cognitive science as in part an offspring of radical embodied cognitive science blunts one common criticism. Clark has argued several times (1997, 2001, 2008; Clark and Toribio 1994; Clark and Grush 1999) that the antirepresentationalism of radical embodied cognitive science is misplaced. Really, he thinks, radical embodied cognitive scientists are mistakenly extending their disagreement with GOFAI to a disagreement with all of computationalism. What radical embodied cognitive scientists are really opposed to, he suggests, are objective, sentence-like representations. This suggests, Clark thinks, that radical embodied cognitive scientists are pushing for too severe a break with the good-old fashioned AI of the cognitivist revolution; they should be satisfied with the less severe break that is embodied cognitive science. This line of argument loses a good deal of its force, though, once one realizes that radical embodied cognitive science is not a recent breakaway from computationalism, is not embodied cognitive science plus antirepresentationalism, but is eliminativist root and branch. The onus, I would argue, is instead on embodied cognitive science, which must show that its attempts to incorporate American naturalist ideas into computationalism are truly stable.

This point, that radical embodied cognitive science is not merely antirepresentationalist embodied cognitive science, is, of course, not sufficient to carry the day against radical embodied cognitive science's representationalist critics. It is just a return volley of the burden in argumentative tennis: it is up to embodied cognitive scientists to argue that their hybrid of American naturalism and computationalism is stable. Even with the burden so shifted, it is still true that the difference between embodied cognitive science and radical embodied cognitive science is over the explanatory role of representations. Proponents of embodied cognitive science and other computationalists can still argue against radical embodied cognitive science in either of two ways. First, they can say that it will be impossible to explain truly cognitive phenomena without mental gymnastics. (See, e.g., Clark and Toribio 1994; Adams and Aizawa 2008.) Second, they can say that the models and theories used in radical embodied cognitive science actually do attribute representations to cognitive systems (Clark 1997; Markman and Dietrich 2000a,b; Wheeler 2005). Chapters 3, 4, and 5 are a long response to this second line of argument. The first of line of argument, that real cognition can't be explained without representations, is, obviously, an empirical matter that can't be settled here. In the next section, though, I will briefly outline two examples of radical embodied cognitive science research. Doing so gives a first look at how radical embodied cognitive science explains, what sort of things it has explained already, and a sense of how it can explain genuinely intelligent behavior.[8]

2.5 Example 1: Crossing the Brain–Body–Environment Boundary

Randy Beer's 2003[9] target article in *Adaptive Behavior* gives a good sense of what radical embodied cognitive science is all about: it utilizes dynamical systems theory to describe and explain the behavior of a simulated robot controlled by an evolved, artificial neural network. The work shows the explanatory style of dynamical modeling and makes clear that radical embodied cognitive science is fully compatible with both neural networks research and artificial life methodologies (even though these are often lumped in with computationalism). In the study, Beer uses artificial evolution to produce an artificial agent capable of categorical perception, the classification of environmental entities for the purpose of adaptive behavior. The agent in question is a circular simulated robot, with an array of seven "eyes" laid out horizontally, covering one sixth of the agent's body. These "eyes" are connected to a continuous time, real-valued neural network (CTRNN) of fourteen neurons: seven sensor neurons, each taking input from an "eye"; five interneurons, which take connections from the input neurons and one another; and two motor neurons, which take connections from the interneurons and control the agent's two motors. (See figure 2.6.) The CTRNN was evolved to categorize and respond differentially to circle-shaped and diamond-shaped objects in the environment. On each trial, a circle or diamond dropped from above the agent's arena,

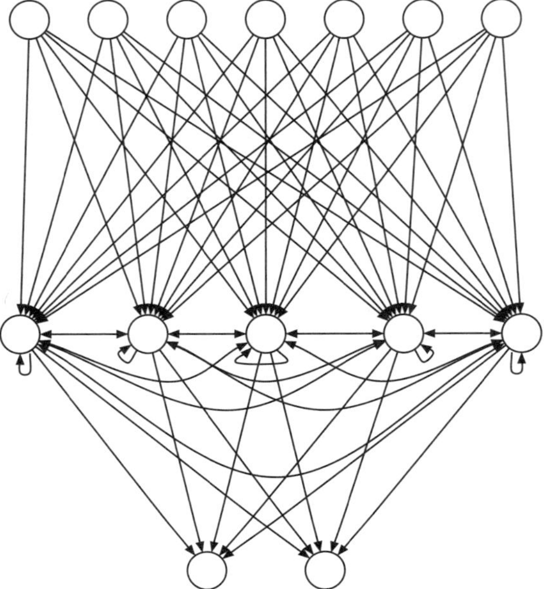

Figure 2.6

and the CTRNN evolved so that the agent would catch circles but avoid diamonds.

Beer's dynamical analysis is of the agent that evolved to complete the task most successfully, where success is defined in terms of avoiding diamonds and catching circles. After eighty generations of evolution, this best agent performed at greater than 99 percent success on twenty-four evaluation trials and at greater than 97 percent success on 10,000 randomly generated trials. The agent achieved this level of success by rotating to "foveate" on the object, then moving toward the object while scanning it by rotating back and forth, and, finally, heading for circles but veering sharply away from diamonds. Before getting to Beer's dynamical analysis, it is important to realize three things about this behavior. First, the behavior on each trial is both a discrimination and an action, but these are not separate. The action is part of the discrimination, and the discrimination determines the final form of the action. The rotational scanning on the way to avoiding or catching the object is essential to the discrimination. Second, because the action is part of the discrimination, the discrimination is not punctate in time, but happens over the whole trial. This is something that will loom large later as a crucial feature of radical embodied cognitive science: perception, cognition, and action take time. Finally, it is important to notice that the model is of an individual agent, not of a collection of agents. This focus on individuals is a common feature of dynamical analyses, which take behavior and, especially, development to be the unfolding of a particular brain in a particular body in a particular environment, and not the playing out of a neural or genetic program. Given this stance toward particulars, individual differences are taken to be data, not noise. (See especially Thelen and Smith 1994; Thelen 1995; Kelso and Engstrøm 2006.) Now, on to Beer's analysis.

Beer sets out a three-part dynamical model of the agent's behavior: one part models the brain–body–environment system; one part models the agent–environment system; and one part models the neural implementation of the agent's behavior in the environment. I will look at these in order, and will, in this case, suppress most of the mathematical details, which are mostly fairly standard neural network math. (Don't worry. There will be plenty of equations later.)

Whole coupled system: Evolved nervous system + body + environment
Beer's first analysis is the most encompassing one, and is therefore the largest system. The model of the CTRNN + agent + environment system is a sixteen-variable dynamical system. There are fourteen variables for the states of each of the neurons; one variable x for the horizontal distance to the object to be avoided or caught; and one variable y for the vertical distance of the object (which, remember, is dropped into the arena from above). Because there are sixteen variables in the system, a graph of the system would have sixteen dimensions. A sixteen-dimensional graph is, of course, not visualizable to those of us with visual systems specialized for three-plus-one dimensions. The vertical distance variable y is not particularly interesting. This variable follows a constant path because the objects fall at a constant rate that does not vary over trials. Most of the action is in the other variables. The seven sensory neurons have states that are a function of the distance to the object (variables x and y) and the identity of the object. The five interneuron variables have states that are determined by the states of the sensory neurons and, because they are laterally connected, by the other interneurons. The states of the variables for the motor neurons are determined by the states of the interneurons. Note that the output of the motor neurons moves the motors, which affect the agent's location, which affects the value of horizontal distance (variable x), which affects the agent's "eyes," which affect the state of the sensory neurons, which affect the state of the interneurons, which affect the state of the

Box 2.2
Dynamical Systems Terminology

Here, I define some terms that I will use in describing dynamical systems and models thereof. I will use them repeatedly throughout the book, so you might want to mark this page. All of these definitions are standard.

1. The *state space* of a system is the space defined by the set of all possible states the system could ever be in.
2. A *trajectory* or *path* is a set of positions in the state space through which the system might pass successively. The behavior of the system is often described by trajectories through the state space.
3. An *attractor* is a point of state space to which the system will tend when in the surrounding region.
4. A *repeller* is a point of state space away from which the system will tend when in the surrounding region.
5. The *topology* of a state space is the layout of attractors and repellors in the state space.
6. A *control parameter* is some parameter of a system whose continuous quantitative change leads to a noncontinuous, qualitative change in the topology of a state space.
7. A differential equation $dx/dt = F(x)$ for variables $x_1 \ldots x_n$ is *linear* if none of $x_1 \ldots x_n$ or functions of $x_1 \ldots x_n$ are among the coefficients of F. Otherwise, the equation is *nonlinear*.
8. Systems that can be modeled with linear differential equations are called *linear systems*. Systems that can only be modeled with nonlinear differential equations are called *nonlinear systems*.
9. Only linear systems are *decomposable*; that is, only linear systems can be modeled as collections of separable components. Nonlinear systems are *nondecomposable*.
10. Nondecomposable, nonlinear systems can only be characterized using global *collective variables* and/or *order parameters*, variables or parameters of the system that summarize the behavior of the system's components.

motor neurons, and so on. The system has just one parameter, the identity of the object, which determines the shape of the state space. The shape of the object, that is, determines the dynamics of the sixteen interlocked variables. Because the object is either a circle or a diamond, and remains so for the duration of a trial, there are two different state spaces for the dynamical system, one for when the object is a circle and one for when it is a diamond.

With this sixteen-variable, one-parameter dynamical model, one can see all the possible ways that the agent could move through the environment and the relation of such movement to the environment and the agent's brain. This model, that is, allows one to *predict* the precise behavior of the agent's brain and the robot in the environment, showing the way the robot will behave in all possible situations, and it provides a detailed picture of the role of the CTRNN, the agent's movement, and the object in categorization and behavior.

Agent–environment system The part of the model just described shows how the system as a whole unfolds over time. The second part of the model, which models the agent–environment system, explains how relative positions of agent and object affect agent movement and how movement affects relative positions of agent and object. The dynamical system that is most relevant to this is determined by the first temporal derivative of horizontal distance to the object, dx/dt, the rate of change of the horizontal distance between the object and the agent. This rate of change is determined by the activity of the agent's motors, and, in turn, the motor neurons. One can use this variable to plot, for every point in the agent's field of view, the speed and direction of the agent's motion through the field, if the object were there. This tells you exactly how the agent's movement and the object's position interact with one another.

Neural implementation of agent dynamics The third part of Beer's model is a model of the CTRNN. Its purpose it to explain how the agent's nervous system produces the agent–object dynamics modeled by the above model of agent–environment dynamics. That is, how, given the mathematics of the neural network, does an object being in a particular location affect the network so that the network makes the motors move in a particular way? This model produces a plot of the activity of the neural network, including especially the motor neurons, for every possible visual situation that the agent might find itself in. One can use this to see the way individual neurons behave over time to study the temporal dynamics of the network, and how those dynamics lead to the movement depicted in the model of the agent–environment system. Notice, however, that this model of the CTRNN is impoverished as a model of the system. Using the model of the CTRNN alone, one can only tell how an instantaneous input will affect a previously inactive network. But because the network is *recurrent*, the effect of any instantaneous input to the network will be largely determined by the network's background activity when the input arrives, and that background activity will be determined by a series of prior inputs. This model of the CTRNN, in other words, is informative only if one knows what flow of prior inputs to the neural network typically precedes (and so determines the typical background activity for) a given input. The impact of the visual stimulus is determined by prior stimuli and the behavioral response to those prior stimuli. The model of the CTRNN is useful, that is, only when combined with the models of the whole coupled system and the agent–environment dynamics. These three dynamical systems compose a single tripartite model.

With this three-part dynamical model, we have a remarkably complete depiction of the agent's behavior in its environment. We know (from part 1) how the system as a whole will evolve over time. We know (from part 2) how an agent's relationship to an object will change over time. And we know (from parts 1 and 3) how the agent's simple nervous system reacts to objects. In each case, we know what we know for every possible situation. Thus, we not only have very complete descriptions of how the agent, CTRNN, and environment actually do behave, we also have enough information to predict their behavior in future and counterfactual situations. The models also show that the agent's "knowledge" does not reside in its evolved nervous system. The ability to categorize the object as a circle or a diamond requires temporally extended movement on the part of the agent, and that movement is driven by the nature and location of the object as well as the nervous system. To do justice to the knowledge, one must describe the agent's brain, body, and environment. Notice that none of these dynamical models refers to representations in the CTRNN in explaining the agent's behavior. The explanation is of what the agent does (and might do), not of how it represents the world. This variety of explanation—of the agent acting in the environment and not of the agent as representer—is a common feature of dynamical modeling, and it exemplifies the connection between radical embodied cognitive science as practiced by Beer and the American naturalism of Dewey and James.

2.6 Example 2: Satisfying Representation Hunger

Randy Beer's dynamical models, just discussed, were presented in a target article in *Adaptive Behavior*. Though there were several interesting replies to it, I want to single out one in particular, not because it is particularly interesting or original, but because it is so common as a response to radical embodied cognitive science. Shimon Edelman's commentary "But Will It Scale Up? Not without Representations" (2003) criticizes both Beer's agent and his dynamical models.

Beer's anti-representation stance seems to be unwarranted . . . in the light of his own example of a system evolved to categorize simple shapes. First, the analytical meth-

> ods he marshals are barely up to the task even in the toy setting of his choice. In this he is in good company: mathematical tools suitable for analyzing complex dynamics in hierarchical, functional terms simply do not exist at the present. Second, and perhaps more importantly, the target of the analysis—the evolved solution to the toy task—hardly seems worth the effort. (2003, 274)

This sort of complaint about radical embodied cognitive science is quite common. Much work in radical embodied cognitive science explores what is often called *minimally cognitive behavior*, such as categorical perception, coordination, locomotion, and the like. Though a far stretch from composing sonnets, this is appropriate given radical embodied cognitive science's commitment to the necessity of perception and action to cognition. The focus on minimally cognitive behavior is also necessary, as Edelman rightly points out, given the current state of analytical and computational tools available. (I would be remiss if I didn't point out, though, that these tools get better every day.) What cognitive science needs, so the objection goes, is an approach that can explain *real* cognition, and for this you need representations.

To my knowledge, the first version of this kind of response to radical embodied cognitive science is by Clark and Toribio (1994). After a sympathetic discussion of nonrepresentational research in robotics and dynamical systems theory, Clark and Toribio argue that the minimally cognitive behavior explained by such work cannot be the whole story. They wonder whether work of this kind (i.e., radical embodied cognitive science) can ever account for what they call *representation-hungry* cognitive tasks. There are certain tasks, Clark and Toribio claim, that simply cannot be accomplished without representations. How, for example, could one think about temporally and spatially distant objects and events without mental representations of them? The response to this quandary that Clark and Toribio recommend is to agree that nonrepresentational analyses may be appropriate for what Brooks (1991) calls "the bulkiest parts of intelligent systems," but that more advanced cognition—thinking about the past, the future, the distant environment—requires internal representation and computation.

A Clark-and-Toribio-style compromise between the representational and the nonrepresentational seems to some to find support in evidence about the brain. Milner and Goodale (1995) famously find evidence that there are two streams for visual activity in the brain. First, there is the dorsal visual stream, which connects to motor areas of the brain and whose function is involved in vision for the guidance of real-time action. Activity in the dorsal stream is outside of conscious awareness. Second, there is the ventral visual stream, which connects to object recognition areas and whose function is (sometimes conscious) identification of objects. Joel Norman (2002) has argued that this division of visual streams necessitates a division of approaches in cognitive science: nonrepresentational approaches are well suited to explaining dorsal stream vision for action, whereas representational and computational approaches are more appropriate for the ventral stream. One could, of course, accept this and resign radical embodied cognitive science to vision for action, using computational approaches for "real" representation-hungry cognition. Wheeler (2005) relies on Heidegger rather than neuroscience to make a similar case. Heidegger famously distinguishes two different kinds of engagement with the world as ready-to-hand and present-at-hand.[10] In agreement with Norman, Wheeler argues that nonrepresentational models might capture our active coping with the world as ready-to-hand, but we need structured representations to explain the way we think about the world when it is encountered as present-at-hand.

Another, less defeatist possibility is to use empirical work to show that radical embodied cognitive science has the resources to explain representation-hungry tasks. Van Rooij, Bongers, and Haselager (2002) pursue this option. (See section 5.1, case 8 for another example of a dynamical explanation of a representation-hungry task.[11]) They gave subjects a series of sticks of varying lengths, in sequences of increasing then decreasing length and vice versa, and asked them to *imagine* whether they could use the sticks to move a distant object. Because the subjects are asked to predict the outcome of an imagined action, one that hasn't yet happened and so is not perceivable, this is a representation-hungry task. It would seem to require a comparison of a judged distance with a judged combined stick-plus-arm length. Indeed, some would argue that judging the distance of the to-be-poked object also requires a mental comparison of the expected size of the object with its apparent size.

Before performing their experiment, van Rooij et al. hypothesized that the task was similar to a speech categorization task explored by Tuller et al. (1994). The details of the speech categorization task are not important for current purposes; what matters is that hypothesizing that the tasks are similar implies that the dynamical model Tuller et al. developed for their data would also account for their subjects' imagined stick pokings. The Tuller et al. model is a potential field, described by the following equation:

$$V(x) = kx - 1/2x^2 + 1/4x^4, \qquad (2.1)$$

where $V(x)$ is the system potential, a measure of the relative stability, at a location x. High potential, relative to neighboring locations, indicates that

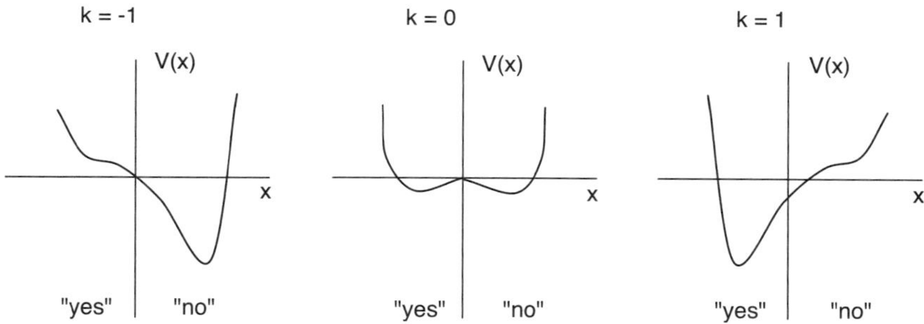

Figure 2.7
Potential landscape defined by equation 2.1. Redrawn from van Rooij et al. (2002), which is redrawn from Tuller et al. (1994).

location x in the potential field is unstable, and the system will tend not to remain at location x. $V(x)$ is this model's collective variable, the variable that determines the overall emergent behavior of the system. In the equation, k is the control parameter that determines the overall shape of the state space; k is a function of the length of a rod on a particular trial, the rod length on previous trials, and the subject's response on previous trials, and is constrained to a range of -1 to 1. The state space determined by equation is shown in figure 2.7. Note that when collective variable $k = 0$ this potential field has two minima, one corresponding to the subject's judgment that *yes* she could poke the distant object with this stick and one to *no* she could not. At such times, the system is said to be *multistable,* and the subject might answer either yes or no. But when $k = -1$ or 1, there is only one minimum, corresponding to only one possible answer to the question.

The hypothesis that the Tuller et al. model can be applied to the imagined pokings leads to four predicted outcomes of the experiment. First, there will be an *assimilative bias*. Because k changes as a function of the previous trial as well as the current stick length, subjects will tend to give the same response on successive trials. That is, the current trial will tend to be assimilated to the previous one. Second, there will be an inverse relation between stick length on the previous trial and the probability of a "yes" answer. That is, if on trial 5 the subject has a particularly long stick, she is more likely to answer "no" on trial 6. Third, multistability will be manifest in two ways. In some cases, there will be *enhanced contrasts*: when stick length increases for a relatively large number of trials and the subject answers "yes," then stick length decreases for several trials, subjects will be

Table 2.1

	Trial n	Trial $n+1$	Trial $n+2$	Trial $n+3$	Trial $n+4$	Trial $n+5$	Trial $n+6$
Enhanced contrast	L = 5 A = "yes"	L = 6 A = "yes"	L = 7 A = "yes"	L = 8 A = "yes"	L = 9 A = "yes"	L = 8 A = "yes"	L = 7 A = "no"
Hysteresis	L = 3 A = "no"	L = 4 A = "yes"	L = 5 A = "yes"	L = 4 A = "yes"	L = 3 A = "yes"		

more likely to answer "no" to a stick of a length that previously was given a "yes." (Mutatis mutandis for shorter, "no.") In other cases, there will be *hysteresis*: when stick length increases for a relatively small number of trials and the subject answers "yes," then stick length decreases for several trials, subjects will be more likely to answer "yes" to a stick of a length that previously was given a "no." See table 2.1. Fourth, as seen in figure 2.7, the multistable region can be of different sizes at different values of k. When the multistable region is large, there will be many cases in which the same stick will be given different answers; when the multistable region is small, there will be fewer such switches.

When van Rooij et al. carried out the experiment, each of the predictions of the Tuller et al. model was borne out. That is, subjects' responses exhibited an assimilative bias, were more likely to be "no" on the trial immediately following a trial with a long stick, showed enhanced contrasts and hysteresis, and showed random switchings at multistable values of k. Thus the subjects' imagined actions can be explained by the interrelationship between the control parameter k, whose value is determined by the current stick length and the stick length and response on the previous trial, and the collective variable $V(x)$. The model accurately accounts for the imagination of the action without calling upon mental representations of the action. Yet this is a representation-hungry task: it involves judgments about something that the animal is not currently interacting with.

Some quick comments on van Rooij et al.'s study are in order here. The first is that it is the beginnings of the answer to those who would claim that radical embodied cognitive science can only account for minimally cognitive behavior and is bound to fail to account representation-hungry tasks. This imagination task manifestly is representation hungry: it required subjects to reason about some action that they had not taken, and which could not be perceived. Note, however, that this is only the beginning of an answer to the criticism lodged by Clark and Toribio, showing by example that there is no in-principle reason that radical embodied cognitive science is not capable of explaining "real cognition." It is still an open question how far beyond minimally cognitive behaviors radical embodied cognitive science can get. We will have to wait and see. The second comment is that this is, in an important sense, an improvement on Beer's post hoc modeling. In Beer's models, the agent was built first and then the dynamical models were developed after the fact. There is nothing particularly wrong with using models to describe phenomena after the fact, but it is more convincing if one can, as van Rooij et al. have, use a model to generate predictions for later experiment. I will discuss this at length in chapter 5. Finally, note that this task is both representation hungry and presumably at least partly dorsal stream. If the task were a perceptual task involved in real action, really poking the distant object, it would presumably require dorsal stream activity. But this is not a perception: it is an imagination of something that has not happened. And because subjects do report on their imagination, the brain activity is not unconscious in the way that is typical of dorsal stream activity. Is this vision for action or vision for perception? It is apparently both, and, to whatever extent it is vision for perception, it problematizes Norman's proposed relegation of radical embodied cognitive science to the non-representation-hungry dorsal stream. It also problematizes Wheeler's Heideggerian distinction between representational and nonrepresentational modes of awareness.

2.7 Summary and Pointer

The point of this chapter has been to see what radical embodied cognitive science is. I have tried to show what it is in two ways. First, I argued that it is part of a tradition of nonrepresentational psychology that includes American naturalism, behaviorism, and ecological psychology. This tradition is separate from the representationalist tradition that runs from Augustine through Descartes to today's computational cognitive scientists. This indicates that radical embodied cognitive science is not just a radicalization of today's situated, embodied movement. Instead, embodied cognitive science is an attempt to combine American naturalism with computationalism. The second way I've tried to show what radical embodied cognitive science is is by example. Beer's dynamically modeled artificial agent and van Rooij, Bongers, and Haselager's dynamical account of imagined action show how radical embodied cognitive science can explain cognition as the unfolding of a brain–body–environment system, and not as mental gymnastics.

It is possible to argue, however, that models such as Beer's and van Rooij, Bongers and Haselager's actually do impute representations to the brains of the agents they account for. (Chemero 2000a points out the possibility; Markman and Dietrich 2000a,b actually make the argument.) Arguments such as these amount to the argument that nonrepresentational psychology (including radical embodied cognitive science) is impossible in principle. The next several chapters (3, 4, and 5) spell out and respond to such arguments. Be warned that the philosophy gets rather thick therein.

II Representation and Dynamics

Members of the Collectivity climb the Ladder, to appearance but curious in a friendly way, and soon the room is full of young Men and Women in avid Disputation. Someone brings up "Sandwiches," and someone else a Bottle, and as night comes down over New-York like a farmer's Mulch, sprouting seeds of Light, some reflected in the River, the Company, Mason working on in its midst, becomes much exercis'd upon the Topick of Representation.

—Thomas Pynchon, *Mason and Dixon* (1997)

3 Theories of Representation

In part II of the book (i.e., chapters 3, 4, and 5), I will describe what it takes to do radical embodied cognitive science, in particular to explain cognition without representations. The way I will do this is to set out a traditional theory of representation (one that has history on its side and has been endorsed in its general form by many philosophers) and argue that it is easy to show that supposedly nonrepresentational, embodied, embedded models of cognition have elements in them that can be called representations according to this traditional theory of representation. This is less surprising than when I first made claims like this (Chemero 1998a). More recently, Markman and Dietrich have been arguing that this ease of application of a traditional theory of representation allows a unification of cognitive science, even purportedly radical embodied cognitive science, under a representationalist and computationalist banner. My point in making the claims will in fact be quite opposite to this. Instead, what this shows is that the traditional theories of representation are not especially useful for arguments over the explanatory value of representations. The radical embodied cognitive scientist must, instead, change the terms of the debate.

This particular chapter has two goals. First, it will talk about what representations are supposed to do and compare different theories of how they manage to do it. This comparison will be done partly in terms of coupled oscillators. That is, I will describe classes of coupled oscillators that meet the requirements of each of the theories of representation I describe. Why coupled oscillators? First, neurons, collections of neurons, and brain areas are all oscillators (among other things). So oscillators are good candidates for representational vehicles. Second, explaining behavior using coupled oscillators has long been a strategy of radical embodied cognitive scientists. So showing that theories of representation can be applied to oscillators will show how far into radical embodied territory one can push representations with a little effort. Third, in addition to providing argument for a particular understanding of representation, this chapter will continue, gradually, to give the reader an introduction to coupled oscillator models, which will play an important role in chapter 5. That gradual introduction is the chapter's second goal.

This chapter itself oscillates: it alternates between describing different understandings of representation and varieties of oscillator that implement them. First, though, some preliminaries.

3.1 Preamble and Oscillators

I'll be comparing four different (classes of) views of what it is to be a representation. I will endorse a theory of representation based on Ruth Millikan's work (also endorsed by Bechtel 1998 and Rowlands 2006[1]). In addition to that, I'll look at the definition put forward by Markman and Dietrich (2000a) and two different views that define representation in terms of decoupling: Brian Cantwell Smith's (1996) theory of registration and Rick Grush's (1997, 2004) emulator theory of representation. Ultimately, I will argue that for different reasons, the decoupling-based definitions of representation aren't appropriate.

3.1.1 Quick Glossary

To facilitate discussion, it will help to pause to introduce the following three possible relationships between a representation and the thing it represents (its target).

A representation *R* and its target *T* are in *constant causal contact* just in case whenever *R* is present in a system, *T* is causing it.
A representation *R* is *decouplable* just in case it can at least sometimes perform its function in a system when it is not in causal contact with its target *T*.
A target *T* is *absent* just in case *T* has no local causal effects when a representation *R* of it is present in a system. (Both my grandmother and the number 3 are absent in this sense.)

Note that representations that are decouplable and representations of absent targets are both cases of representations that do not require constant causal contact with their targets. But notice too that they are different from one another. When I close my eyes for thirty seconds, representations of the objects on my desk (if there are any such representations) are not currently caused by those objects, but those objects are not absent. I will suggest that problems arise in understanding representation because people think decouplability and representing absent targets are the same, when in fact the former is necessary but not sufficient for the latter. I will also use coupled oscillator models to argue that this is not a distinction without a difference.

3.1.2 Coupled Oscillator Basics

The discussion here[2] will be couched in dynamical terms: I will exemplify each definition of representation with a class of coupled oscillators. Coupled oscillators have been suggested as representational mechanisms for a variety of cognitive tasks. McAuley (1996) and Large and Kolen (1994) offer theories of rhythm perception that use oscillators to represent the relative timing of events. (See also Semjen and Ivry 2001.) Jones and Boltz (1989) offer a theory of attention that uses an oscillator to represent the level of temporal structure in a task. Even nontemporal tasks like visual feature binding have been modeled using oscillators as the underlying representational vehicle (Singer and Gray 1995). Furthermore, coupled oscillators are the foundation of the antirepresentationalist dynamical systems movement in cognitive science. Kugler, Kelso, and Turvey (1980) introduced coupled oscillators to explain how, in Gibson's (1979) terms, action could be regular without being regulated. Later, Kelso and Engstrøm (2006) call oscillation "a dynamical archetype of all behavior" (153).

Two broad classes of biologically inspired oscillators are often used in cognitive and brain modeling. The first class of oscillators is inspired by *electrical and neural systems*. Several models of neuron action potential (Fitzhugh 1961; Nagumo, Arimoto, and Yoshigawa 1962; Morris and LeCar 1981) come in the form of *relaxation oscillators*, so named because they slowly accrue voltage and then suddenly fire, relaxing or releasing their energy. These oscillators synchronize readily with themselves and with rhythmic input. However, a problem for these models as useful representational vehicles is that they cannot keep hold of a represented target in the absence of the causal stimulus. To put this in terms of the newly introduced lingo, the target cannot be absent. I argue below that this does not mean that the representation and target must be constantly causally coupled.

The second class of oscillators is inspired by *physical systems* such as mass-spring systems. These models do not synchronize with rhythmic signals as readily as do relaxation oscillators, partly because their mass gives them *momentum*, keeping them from changing their trajectories to match that of a signal. Kelso and Engstrøm (2006) put this by saying that they have *intrinsic dynamics*. Mass-spring systems have been deployed to model many cognitive tasks, though generally those tasks have a motor control component. For example, Thelen and Smith (1994) use mass-spring oscillators to model the development of kicking, stepping, and reaching in infants. Schöner and Kelso (1988b) use oscillators to model the motor control task of finger wagging as studied by Haken, Kelso, and Bunz (1985).[3]

There are also hybrid models that fall into neither category neatly. These systems tend to take desirable properties from relaxation (electrical) systems and combine them with desirable properties from physical (mass-spring) systems. For example, the models of rhythm perception developed by McAuley (1996), Large and Kolen (1994), and Large and Jones (1999) use *adaptive oscillators,* which synchronize quickly with input signals like relaxation oscillators but which have something akin to inertia allowing them to "keep the beat" even in the absence of the signal. These hybrid adaptive oscillators are less stable than relaxation oscillators when coupled together in large groups (Eck, Gasser, and Port 2000) and are neither physically nor neurally plausible.[4]

In the rest of this chapter, I use these varieties of oscillator exemplify different theories of representation.

3.2 A Theory of Mental Representation

Mental representations are theoretical entities, as Fodor's Uncle Wilfrid (Sellars) insists (Fodor 1983; Sellars 1956). That is, just as we might posit dark matter to explain observations in astronomy, we posit mental representations to explain observations of intelligent or adaptive behavior. Mental representations, then, are parts of explanations of behavior, and their existence is vindicated and their proposed properties are confirmed by the success of explanations that call upon them.[5] The role of mental representations in explanations of adaptive behavior is as causally potent, information-carrying vehicles. The representation plays a role in the causal economy of the agent, and, because it carries information about the environment, allows the behavior it causes to be appropriate for the environment. Because representations are posited as theoretical entities and because they do explanatory work in virtue of the information they carry, a theory of representation needs to explain how something inside an agent could be about something outside the agent, as depicted in figure 3.1.

Here, then, is a traditional theory of representation, with a touch of teleology. It is based on Ruth Millikan's teleological theory of representations (Millikan 1984, 1993).

A feature R_0 of a system S is a *Representation for S* if and only if:

(R1) R_0 stands between a representation producer P and a representation consumer C that have been standardized to fit one another.

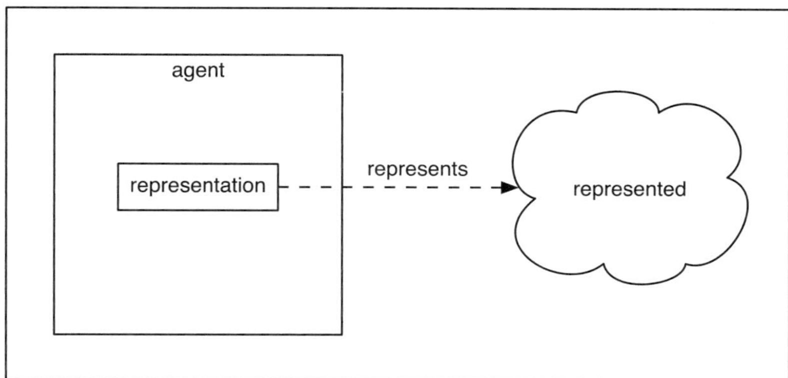

Figure 3.1

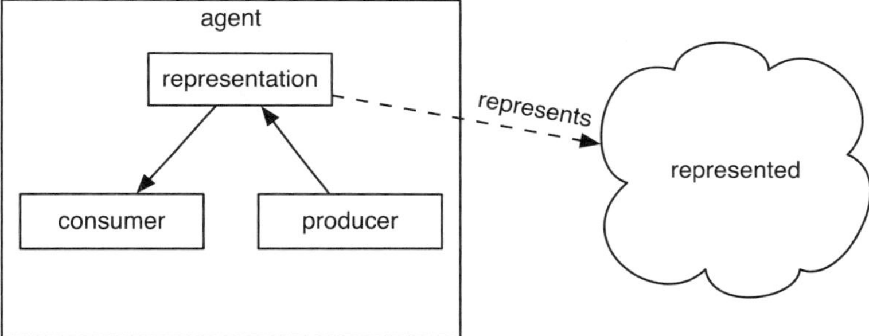

Figure 3.2

(R2) R_0 has as its function to adapt the representation consumer C to some aspect A_0 of the environment, in particular by leading S to behave appropriately with respect to A_0, even when A_0 is not the case.
(R3) There are (in addition to R_0) transformations of R_0, $R_1 \ldots R_n$, that have as their function to adapt the representation consumer C to corresponding transformations of A_0, $A_1 \ldots A_n$.

This definition adds a few wrinkles to the basic notion of representation described above and pictured in figure 3.1. Figure 3.2 shows the changes concerning additional mechanisms required of a system if it is to have representations. Because having functions is a matter of having a particular history, the functional requirements of the definition are not depicted. (Note that in the picture, causal relationships are depicted with solid arrows, and semantic relationships are depicted with dashed arrows.)

As noted above, this definition is a version of Ruth Millikan's teleological theory of content (Millikan 1984). Since so much has already been written about Millikan's views, I will not spend much time describing this definition. I will, however, briefly point out a few of its features. First, as mentioned above, since it requires a representation to have functions, it is *teleological* (R2) and hence explicitly normative. Second, it requires that the representation serve as a representation in the context of producing and consuming devices (R1). Third, it has an explanation of misrepresentation built into it. Since the content of a representation is determined by its function, along with those of the representation producer and consumer, its content will remain constant even in cases in which one or more of the producer, consumer, and representation itself fails to work properly. That is, just as the function of a sperm is to fertilize an egg, despite the fact that the number that do so is vanishingly small, so the function of a token that represents "chicken-here-now" does not change, even in cases in which said token is produced or used improperly. Fourth, it requires that a representation be part of a system of representations (R3). So nothing can represent just one (token) environmental situation. Note that this does not rule out, for example, feature detectors. When a horizontal line detector turns on, that might represent "horizontal-line-here-now," where "here" and "now" have different referents. Fifth, it requires that we follow Millikan (1984) in focusing on the representation consumer in determining the content of a representation—the content is the way the world would need to be for the behavior caused by the representation consumer to be adaptive (R2). Sixth, among the things that meet the criteria of this theory of representation are what Millkan calls *pushmi-pullyu representations* or Andy Clark (1997) calls *action-oriented representations*. As noted in chapter 2, these are the kinds of representations that are typically called upon in representationalist embodied cognitive science.

In what ways is this Millikan-based theory of representation similar to and different from other available theories? In the next few sections, I compare it to several other theories that have been used to analyze embodied, embedded models of cognition. I will argue that the theory just described is as good as or superior to other theories of representation for the purposes of radical embodied cognitive science.

3.3 Markman and Dietrich on "Internal Mediating States"

As mentioned several times already, Markman and Dietrich have argued in a string of papers (2000a,b; Dietrich and Markman 2003) that cognitive scientists should be unified in their acceptance of the necessity of representational explanations of cognition. To do so, Markman and Dietrich outline a theory of representation and point out that such representations can be found in *all* models of cognition. Their main point is that antirepresentationalism is a nonstarter. (The point of this book is that they are wrong about that.) According to Markman and Dietrich, representations in a system are internal mediating states that have the following properties.

(i) There is some entity with internal states which include goal states; we assume that these states undergo changes.
(ii) There is an environment external to the system which also changes states.
(iii) There is a set of informational relations between states in the environment and the states internal to the system. The information must flow both ways, from the environment into the system, and from the system out to the environment. (In the simplest case, this will be a feedback loop, but more complicated loops such as plan-act-detect loops are also possible. Note also that in the typical case, these informational relations will be realized as causal relations, but what is important is the information carried by these causal relations, not the causal relations themselves.)
(iv) The system must have internal processes that act on and are influenced by the internal states and their changes, among other things. These processes allow the system to satisfy system-dependent goals (though, these goals need not be known explicitly by the system). (Markman and Dietrich 2000a, 144)

A minimal system with representations according to this view is depicted in figure 3.3. Note that this is a fairly liberal understanding of representation. Indeed, that is its point: Markman and Dietrich want to bring all the radical embodied cognitive scientists under the representationalist, computationalist umbrella. Their definition is less restrictive even than the teleological definition described above because it does not have the teleological requirement. Mediating states can be representations according to Markman and Dietrich even if they are part of a system by accident. Despite

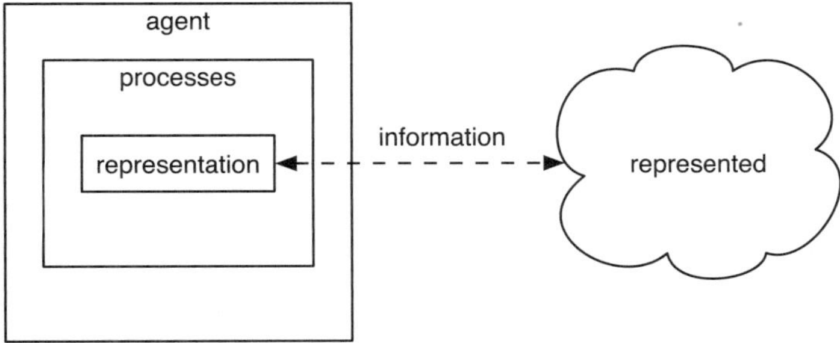

Figure 3.3

this, though, this definition and the teleological one are identical for our purposes. They agree in nearly all cases whether or not some system has representations. In particular, both definitions allow parts of properly functioning systems to count as representations even if they are constantly causally coupled to their targets. The same is true of classical theories of representation put forth by Dretske (1981) and Fodor (1990), as well as Anne Jacobson's "Aristotelian representations" (2003, 2008) and "s-representations," one of the two varieties of representation on offer in William Ramsey's recent book (Ramsey 2007).[6] Given this confluence of opinion, I will henceforth refer to any theory of representation that calls all contentful internal states representations (even if they are not decouplable from their targets) *traditional theories of representation.*

Each of the traditional definitions of representation can be implemented by the same oscillator model: the Fitzhugh-Nagumo simulated neuron (Fitzhugh 1961; Nagumo et al. 1962). This oscillator is a simplification of a model of neuron action-potential developed by Hodgkin and Huxley (1952). As was noted above, Fitzhugh-Nagumo oscillators are a type of *relaxation oscillator*. When presented with an input pattern consisting of voltage pulses, a Fitzhugh-Nagumo oscillator will synchronize its firing with the pulses. If these pulses are rhythmic, the oscillator synchronizes and "beats along" by emitting its own pulses in tandem. A connected group of these oscillators can couple with rhythmic input patterns in ways that mirror the metrical structure of the patterns. That is, a network can distinguish weak beats from strong beats and can even represent *rests* using appropriate inhibitory connections. But when the driving stimulus is removed from a network, the oscillators decouple immediately and return to a quiescent state. In this way the oscillators are unable to couple with a target that is absent. In fact, they simply respond to whatever they are in constant causal contact with. That is, they respond at time *t* only to the input presented to them at time *t*.

Yet despite this inability to maintain an appropriate relation to an absent beat, it is clear that simple relaxation oscillators can play an important role in a system's maintenance of an appropriate relation to its environment. If appropriately connected up within a cognitive system, they can be used by the system to guide its behavior appropriately with respect to an external signal. Indeed, relaxation oscillators can be used to control a robotic arm that taps along with externally supplied beats (see Eck, Gasser, and Port 2000). This kind of intelligent, embodied behavior is exactly the sort that representations are supposed to explain, and it points to the appropriateness of definitions of representation that allow representations that are constantly causally coupled to their targets. That is, these relaxation oscillators are an example that theories of representation ought to include as representations, as the traditional theories do. Not everyone agrees.

3.4 Reliable Presence and Decouplability

John Haugeland's "Representational Genera" (1991) has become the touchstone for discussions of representation in the philosophy of cognitive science, despite the fact that only two of its twenty-seven pages are devoted to discussing representation in general. Haugeland's definition is nicely summarized by Andy Clark (1997) as follows. A system counts as *representation using* just in case:

> It must coordinate its behaviors with environmental features that are not always "reliably present to the system."
>
> It copes with such cases by having something else "stand in" for those features and guide behavior.
>
> The "something else" is part of a more general representational scheme that allows the standing in to occur systematically and allows for a variety of related states. (Clark 1997, 144; see also Haugeland 1991; Wheeler 2005; Clark 2008)

A representation, according to this definition, is something that acts as a stand-in in such a system. This, as it stands, admits of several interpretations. In particular, the phrase "reliably present to the system" is left unanalyzed by Haugeland, who only intended this to be "a few dogmatic and sketchy remarks" (1991, 62). There are, in fact, (at least) two different understandings of this, which lead to two different understandings of representation: a strong version often imputed to Haugeland (Clark and Toribio 1994; Clark 1997) and actually endorsed by Brian Cantwell Smith (1996), and a weaker version that is exemplified in Rick Grush's emulator theory of representation (Grush 1997, 2004; Clark and Grush 1999). Unfortunately, people typically fail to notice the real difference between the strong and weak interpretations of Haugeland's 1991 definition.

3.4.1 Strong Decouplability: Registration

In *Being There,* Andy Clark claims that the Haugeland definition requires what he (Clark) calls *decouplability,* which he defines as "the capacity to use the inner states to guide behavior in the absence of the environmental feature [represented]" (1997, 144). He reads Haugeland's "not always reliably present" as requiring high-level reasoning, the ability to solve representation-hungry problems.

> Adaptive hookup thus phases gradually into genuine internal representation as the hookup's complexity and systematicity increase. At the far end of this continuum we find Haugeland's creatures that can deploy the inner codes in the total absence of their target environmental features. Such creatures are the most obvious representers of their world, and are the ones able to engage in complex imaginings, off-line reflection and counterfactual reasoning. Problems that require such capacities for their solution are representation-hungry, in that they seem to cry out for the use of inner systemic features as stand-ins for external states of affairs. (Clark 1997, 147)

I will call this reading of Haugeland's "not always reliably present" *strong decouplability*. Strong decouplability requires that the representation *R* and target *T* are not in constant causal contact and that target *T* be potentially *absent*. Clark rejects strong decouplability as a necessary condition for something to be a representation. Using a neural group in the posterior parietal cortex of rats as an example, Clark argues that there are systems that are usefully called representational that can never be decoupled from the things about which they carry information. This complex of neurons carries information about the position of the rat's head, but there is no reason to think that "these neurons can play their role in the absence of a constant stream of proprioceptive signals from the rat's body" (ibid., 145). So, in *Being There* at least, Clark agrees with traditional theories of representation: something can be a representation even though it can only function when it is coupled to the thing it represents.

It turns out that Clark's rendering of Haugeland's "not always reliably present" as strong decouplability is rejected by Haugeland himself as too exclusive.[7] I would argue that he (and Clark) are right. This is far too exclusive a definition of representation. Does anyone concerned with the debates over the role of representation in cognitive science actually hold that strong decouplability is a necessary condition on being a representation? Yes: Brian Cantwell Smith (1996) does, taking himself to agree with Haugeland. Smith's theory of what he calls *registration* is an integrated theory of representation and ontology, but we can, for present purposes, take it as theory of representation. Smith contrasts registration with *effective tracking*. We can see effective tracking in the shopworn example of a frog tracking a passing fly. In terms of the physics of the situation, Smith points out, what we have is a continuously moving column of disturbance, beginning at the fly and ending at the frog. This column-shaped disturbance is *just one thing*, and is not separable into frog, fly, and intervening atmosphere, at least not in terms of physics. When a frog tracks a fly in this way, the frog and fly are coupled in a very strong sense: they are not separate. The key for our purposes is that the tracking is a matter of constant causal connection among frog, fly, and intervening air. This, Smith argues, involves nothing worth calling representation. And we can see that in effective tracking, any internal parts of the agent that one might call representations are constantly causally coupled with their targets. Indeed, these parts will be representations according to the traditional definitions of representation.

In registration, on the other hand, the agent must be potentially disconnectable from what it registers, and in a very strong way. First, the agent must be able to continue to track the object despite disruption of constant causal connection. The frog, that is, must be able to continue to track the fly even when the light reflected from it is (temporarily) occluded. For all I know, frogs may not be capable of this, and indeed it is hard to imagine something coming between a frog and a fly at a tongue-reachable distance. But this kind of *noneffective tracking* is the norm in vigilance in the animal kingdom. A nesting bird doesn't lose track of the fox that is temporarily behind a rock. Noneffective tracking, though, is not sufficient for registration. In fact, noneffective tracking could be accomplished just by causal connection and momentum. (The head's momentum keeps it going *that way*, and the bird's eyes meet up with the light that is no longer occluded by the rock.) In registration, there is a further distancing and abstraction. It requires *detachment* in that the subject must "let go" of the object, stop tracking it (even noneffectively). The difference here is like that between knowing your niece will come out from under the other side of the table, and knowing that you won't see her again until next Thanksgiving. This latter requires *abstraction* in that the subject must ignore many of the details of the object to keep track of it. When you're effectively or noneffectively tracking your niece, you are coupled with every detail of her: every freckle, individual hair, and shirt-wrinkle is moving in concert with your head and eyes. When this physical connection is broken, and you register her, you lose or abstract away from much of this detail. It is only here, according to Smith, that one has anything worth calling a representation.

It is in this abstraction that is necessary for registration and representation that we see the vastness of the differences between Smith's understanding and those in which a representation might be constantly causally coupled with its target. In registration, the agent registers not just a target-at-a-moment, but a target as a temporally extended entity, one that can be reidentified later. Smith makes this point by comparing the point-to-point correlation between agent and environmental object that occurs during effective and noneffective tracking. There, the effective connection is between an agent-at-a-moment and an object-at-a-moment. In registration, though, the agent registers an enduring object, with a history and a future.

This, of course, is part of the point of the abstraction and deletion of detail: it would be impossible to represent *all* the details of an object, and anyway not all of those details would be present the next time that object showed up. Thus, registration requires considerable machinery. It requires a stable, disconnectable internal state, one that can maintain its status as being about a particular target, even when that target is distant in space and time, and can then be reapplied to the target later. Part of Smith's theory of registration, then, is a theory of representations that have what was called above strong decouplability.[8]

We can exemplify the difference between strong decouplability, as seen in Smith's theory, and traditional theories of representations by looking again at coupled oscillator models. As shown above, a relatively simple relaxation oscillator was able to meet the requirements of the traditional conceptions of representation. Much more complex *adaptive oscillators* are required to have representations that are strongly decouplable, to be able to represent absent features of the environment. Adaptive oscillators are hybrid oscillators that can beat along in real time to rhythmic stimuli, a task akin to tapping one's foot along with music. In fact, adaptive oscillators have been shown to be able to beat along with noisy rhythmic signals, such as one finds with real human drummers and in the rhythms of human speech (McCauley 1996). They succeed at this task by taking desirable properties from both mass-spring oscillators and relaxation oscillators.

The three most important aspects of the hybridization that make the adaptive oscillator successful are *phase adaptation, confidence rating,* and *frequency adaptation.*

Phase adaptation The adaptive oscillator can instantaneously adapt its phase to match the energy of an input signal. When a pulse comes in that is "loud enough" (greater than some threshold) the oscillator immediately resets its phase to zero. In this way, an adaptive oscillator is like a relaxation oscillator in that it can instantly respond to stimuli, but unlike a pendulum or other mass-spring oscillator where such instantaneous phase resetting is prohibited by momentum.

Frequency adaptation Performed music and spoken language (two types of signal the adaptive oscillator was designed to track) accelerate and decelerate constantly. This poses a problem for a simple phase-adapting oscillator: if the frequency of the input is not matched exactly to the oscillator's resonant frequency, the oscillator will constantly phase reset. This problem is solved by making the oscillator able to tune its resonant frequency to match that of the input, by speeding up or slowing down the oscillator based on where it is in its phase cycle when a phase reset occurs. In other words, the adaptive oscillator acts like a mass-spring oscillator with strong preferred frequency and very much unlike a relaxation oscillator, which has no preferred frequency. This shows the hybrid nature of the adaptive oscillator: phase adaptation is achieved via a relaxation-oscillator type mechanism, frequency adaptation via a tunable mass-spring mechanism. The oscillator has a tuning function that speeds up the oscillator if it is consistently phase resetting *after* a beat and slows it down if it is consistently phase resetting *before* a beat.

Confidence rating Phase coupling and frequency coupling allow the adaptive oscillator to couple to beats at many different frequencies, but they alone do not make it able to represent an absent beat. Beat tracking oscillators are always sensitive to sufficiently loud input. This can present problem for the adaptive oscillator when tracking noisy real-life signals, since beat tracking requires that most sounds be ignored to avoid constant phase resetting. The intuition is that once the oscillator has "found the beat" it should be relatively difficult to make it phase reset. (Compare: you tap along with the beat, even though the melody and background noise are often louder.) This problem is solved by adding a phase-dependent window centered at phase zero. As the oscillator gets more and more confident that it has locked onto the downbeat, it tightens this window (much like putting on blinders so as not to be distracted by events in the periphery) and filters the input. Loudness is no longer enough to cause a phase reset. Now the loud signal must happen at the center of the oscillator's attentional window.

This type of adaptive oscillator can be used as a representation, for example to drive a robotic arm that must tap along with a rhythmic signal. Over time, the phase and frequency of the oscillator are tuned so that the it matches the beat of the rhythmic signal. Furthermore, the oscillator's window is adjusted and narrowed by interactions with the signal so that the beat, when present, always occurs during the window. The oscillator can then be used to drive the robot arm to tap along with the beat. Because the adaptive oscillator has mass-spring properties, its momentum can allow it to continue to tap along after the rhythmic signal has subsided. This means that the adaptive oscillator is able to represent phenomena from which it is strongly decoupled. That is, it can represent beats that are absent. Note too that the windowing is a matter of abstraction. After the window has narrowed, the oscillator expects a beat to occur at a very particular time, and is unresponsive to beats that occur outside the window. Within the window, a physically identical signal is not required, only one that is sufficiently loud and sufficiently close to being correctly timed. That is, just as you recognize your nephew despite his having fewer freckles and a different shirt on, a system with an adaptive oscillator will recognize a physically nonidentical signal that falls into the oscillator's window as being the same beat.

In this way, the adaptive oscillator is capable of what Smith calls registration. In particular, it is able to guide behavior appropriate to an absent signal, and it does so in virtue of ignoring incoming information and relying on its own internal state. Creating adaptive oscillators that can do this is surely an impressive achievement in cognitive science, and one that can be used to significantly advance our understanding of advanced rhythmic behavior. But this sort of ability seems far too complex to be the base case of mental representations. Indeed, it is an ability that many humans do not have: the history of jazz shows that many humans have difficulty registering an absent beat. The Bill Evans Trio's recordings (e.g., 1961's *Sunday at the Village Vanguard*) were revolutionary in that, after establishing the beat in each song, no member of the trio was assigned the role of time-keeper. That is, the beat was only implicit, and each member of the trio respected it in his playing without actually playing it. That this music was taken to be revolutionary, and baffling to many listeners of the early 1960s, underscores the difficulty of maintaining a representation of an absent beat. The point is one that Clark (1997) realized: strong decouplability is simply too strong to serve as a base case of mental representations.

3.4.2 The Weak Reading: Emulators

Realizing that strong decouplability is too strong, one might be driven to look for a theory of representation whose base case is somewhere between Smith's registration and the more liberal traditional representations, a theory that is neurally plausible and not too restrictive (unlike registration), but respects intuitions that representational targets might not be reliably present (unlike traditional theories). Rick Grush's emulation theory of representation (Grush 1997, 2004) aims to be such a theory. Emulators are an attempt to capture the intuition that to count as a representation, something must be able to be decoupled from what it represents. Indeed, Grush advertises his theory as saving us from the confusion engendered by traditional theories of representation that treat mere presentations as representations. *Presentations* are internal contentful states that are constantly causally connected with their targets. To be a representation, Grush claims, a state must be decouplable. Grush offers emulators as the most basic systems with decouplable representations.

An emulator is a mechanism within a system that takes information about the current state of the system and gives a prediction of the next state of the system as output. It is a "forward model" of system behavior. Consider (Grush's example) skilled reaching. Moving an arm and hand toward some object depends on the brain receiving and responding to a stream of visual and proprioceptive feedback concerning the position and trajectory of the arm and hand. But occasionally, owing to the inherent speed limitations of the nervous system, the feedback is required more quickly than it is available. It is in situations like this that emulation is crucial. An emulator in this case could take as input the current position of the arm and hand, along with the direction of their movement, and provide a sort of mock feedback as output, predicting the position and trajectory of the arm before the actual feedback arrives. This mock feedback is then used to control the reach.[9] See figure 3.4 for a depiction of Grush's emulation theory of representation.

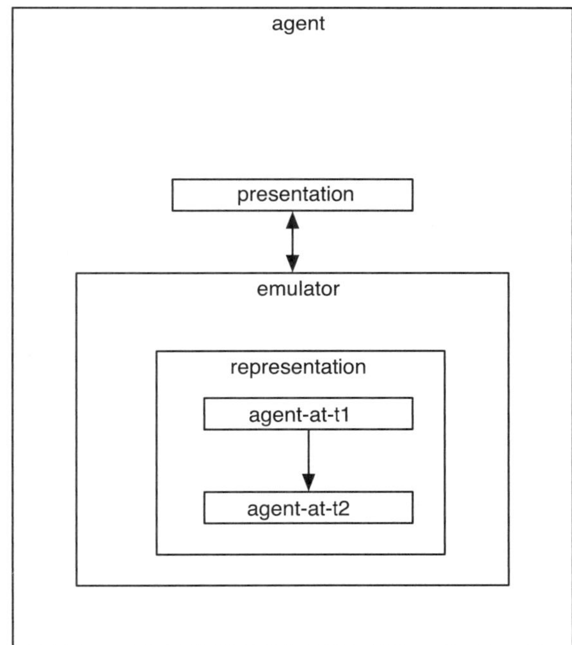

Figure 3.4

Emulation, Grush claims, is important because it is the minimal case of real internal representation, representation that is decouplable. Clark, after initially rejecting decouplability as a necessary condition on being a representation, came to agree.[10] In a coauthored paper, Clark and Grush say:

> In sum, it is our suggestion that a creature uses full-blooded internal representations if and only if it is possible to identify within the system specific states and/or processes whose functional role is to act as *de-couplable surrogates* for specifiable (usually extra-neural) states of affairs. Motor emulation circuitry, we think, provides a clear, minimal and evolutionarily plausible case in which these conditions may be met. (Clark and Grush 1999, 8)

But it is also quite that clear emulators really are not cases of strong decoupling, not requiring that the target be potentially *absent*. There is one sense in which we might say that an emulator controlling skilled reaching is decoupled: in the short time between when it takes its input (the state of the arm, the direction of its motion) and when it gives its output (mock feedback to guide action), the emulator is not receiving input directly from what it is representing; that is, unlike the locus of the actual proprioceptive feedback (which is a mere *presentation* in Grush's lingo), the emulator's hookup with the target is not constant. This, however, is *not* decoupling the strong sense: the capacity to use the inner states to guide behavior *in the absence of* the environmental feature represented. Despite the fact that the emulator is not hooked up to incoming proprioceptive signals for a few milliseconds, the arm and the action it is undertaking are in no way *absent*. Indeed, emulators fall far short of strong decouplability as seen in Smith's theory of registration. Simple emulators, like the ballistic-reach emulator described above, are in fact cases of noneffective tracking. We can see this both by looking at the emulators that are supposed to exist in the CNS and at a coupled oscillator that can implement emulator-based control.

In Grush's original paper on the emulation theory (Grush 1997), he provides nontrivial empirical evidence that there are emulators in the human CNS. He points to models of neural systems that incorporate emulators. This evidence is amplified in later work by Grush (2004), by Clark and Grush (1999), by Patricia Churchland (2002), and by Barbara Webb (2004). Churchland in particular adduces considerable evidence for the presence, perhaps the ubiquity, of what she calls "Grush emulators" in the central nervous system. So it could very well be that emulators are ubiquitous in the nervous system, and that they are in play whenever we see any degree of behavioral control by expectations of sensory feedback. It is vital to realize, though, that the target of emulator representations, at least all those described in the work described above, is the state of the animal's *body*. Indeed, the states of the body are the targets of all of the cases of emulation that Grush describes. But, of course, the animal's body will never be absent in the usual course of things. Thus, although the state of an emulator guiding a ballistic reach may briefly decouple from the stream of incoming proprioceptive information, the emulator's state will almost immediately be updated by fresh proprioceptive information. This is just what Smith calls noneffective tracking, and quite unlike the strong decoupling (real distance, abstraction) that characterizes registration.

We can make the same point in terms of coupled oscillators. Imagine having a conversation with a friend while walking. Your gait in such settings is just the kind of activity that seems to call for both emulation and oscillators. The oscillators are important because walking is a coordinated, rhythmic activity, and oscillators have been shown again and again to be effective in modeling such behavior (Kugler and Turvey 1987; Schöner and Kelso 1988a,b; Haken, Kelso, and Bunz 1985; Kelso 1995; Kay, Saltzman, and Kelso 1991; see also chapter 5). To see that walking also calls for emulators, imagine what happens when, deep in conversation, you step in a small hole. Or, better, imagine walking up the stairs in the dark and being unable to see that you have already reached the landing. The nature of the stumble in both cases makes it clear that you continued to control your locomotion as if you got the proprioceptive feedback earlier than you actually did—that your gait was being controlled by *expected* contact with the ground. It would be easy to implement an appropriate emulator using a Fitzhugh-Nagumo oscillator, the oscillators that were sufficient to serve as traditional, constantly causally connected representations. To make an emulating device from a network of Fitzhugh-Nagumo oscillators one need only implement *time delays* so that the network can use the "stale" information from the proprioceptive stream appropriately. Since locomotion is periodic, such a delay could be found simply by measuring the rate of change in the proprioceptive stream and using it to estimate how fast the legs are moving. Once the delay is found, the emulator is able to predict *current* proprioceptive information using information from exactly one leg cycle before. It is, that is, a forward model of the state of the foot and leg.

A few quick notes on this emulating oscillator are in order. First, the addition of time delays on the "axons" of the artificial neurons is simple to implement and neurally plausible. Second, although Grush's examples typically involve ballistic reaches, this oscillator is an emulator and so a representation by the standards of Grush's theory. Third and most important for current purposes, this emulator is implemented by the very same type of oscillator that is used in the traditional, constantly causally coupled models. Emulators, that is, are simply not very different from the traditional representations that Grush insists on calling "mere presentations." Emulators are much more similar to effective tracking and traditional theories of representation than they are to strong decoupling and Smith's theory of registration.

This, of course, is not a real criticism of Grush's emulator theory as a contribution to cognitive science. Emulators are just more like traditional representations, and more like mere presentations, than Grush's (and Clark's and Churchland's) rhetoric would lead one to believe. Emulators still might be an important (and perhaps widely neurally implemented) subclass of traditional representations. They also provide a very good story about how Brian Smith's distinction between effective and noneffective coupling might be implemented. Indeed, I pointed out above that noneffective coupling could directed by the same mechanisms that direct effective coupling, plus inertia, working to keep eyes or head moving in a particular direction. It should be clear that an oscillator with time delay does just this. The delayed oscillator providing mock feedback causes the leg and foot to keep moving, even without proprioceptive feedback. So, to repeat, the emulator theory of representation is a good and, arguably, very important contribution. Grush is to be commended for bringing the idea to mainstream cognitive scientists. One point made above, though, should make us worry about using emulators as the basic case of mental representations. The problem is that all of the examples of potential neural emulators that Grush, Grush and Clark, and Churchland cite are cases in which the emulators represent parts of an animal's body and not parts of the external environment. To replay part of the quote from Clark and Grush (1999, 8), "In sum, it is our suggestion that a creature uses full-blooded internal representations if and only if it is possible to identify within the system specific states and/or processes whose functional role is to act as *de-couplable surrogates* for specifiable (usually extra-neural states of affairs)" (similar sentiments are found throughout Grush's work on emulation). "Extraneural" does not indicate outside the body. This Cartesian extremism, endorsed explicitly in Grush 2003, in which the central nervous system is taken to be the locus of the mind whereas everything else (the rest of the body and the physical environment) is the world, is worrisome for two reasons. First, it is unusual, and wholly contrary to the philosophical and cognitive scientific traditions, to have a theory of representation whose base cases are representations of parts of the animal. (Notice that there was no need to depict the environment outside the agent in figure 3.4). Second and more important, even if for some reason one is willing to buck tradition in this way, taking the mind to be encapsulated within the central nervous system is contrary to the embodied, embedded movement in cognitive science, whose main purpose is to throw off the Cartesianism of early cognitive science and to allow that cognition is necessarily embodied. For these two reasons, the emulation theory is inappropriate as a theory of the most basic representations.

3.5 Summary

This chapter provided a survey of some theories of representation and a passing introduction to dynamical modeling via coupled oscillators. The main points of this chapter can be summarized in terms of Brian Smith's distinctions among effective tracking, noneffective tracking, and registration. In effective tracking, an agent might be constantly causally coupled to the thing it is tracking. Traditional theories of representation (Millikan 1984, 1993; Fodor 1990; Dretske 1981; Bechtel 1998; Markman and Dietrich 2000a,b; Jacobson 2003, 2008; Rowlands 2006; Ramsey 2007) define representation so that parts of agents that are involved in effective tracking, those that can do their job only when they are in constant causal connection with the environmental object, might be representations. In noneffective tacking, an agent maintains its connection to the environmental object it tracks, despite brief breaks in the causal connection. Emulators, proposed as a base case of representation by Grush (1997), can be used by agents to bridge the short gaps in causal connection that characterize noneffective tracking. Despite the accompanying press, emulator representations are really not very from different traditional representations. This can be seen by the fact that it takes only a trivial alteration of coupled oscillators that implement traditional representations (Fitzhugh-Nagumo oscillators) to turn them into emulators that can maintain connections to their target despite breaks in the causal stream. Furthermore, emulators are problematic in that, in the basic cases, they represent parts of agents, not the external environment. This leads to an unbridgeable gap between an animal's brain, on one hand, and body and world, on the other. So, although there may be emulators in many animals, the emulation theory is not appropriate as a theory of the most basic representations. Finally, to register an object, an agent must be able to reidentify it after a significant absence. This requires that the agent have a representation of the object that is both abstract and redeployable. The coupled oscillator model that implements this sort of representation, adaptive oscillators, is much different from the Fitzhugh-Nagumo oscillators that can implement tracking.

We are left, then, with a choice between a traditional theory of representation that is arguably overly liberal and a newer theory based on strong decoupling that is arguably too restrictive. I take it that using the newer, more restrictive definition to try to argue in favor of nonrepresentational cognitive science would be problematic. "Using my new definition of representations, none of these systems has representations" is a near neighbor of the Hegelian arguments deplored in chapter 1. That is, it allows radical embodied cognitive scientists or their opponents to win arguments by redefining terms.[11] For purposes here, then, the traditional views are more appropriate, and I will stick with the Millikan-style approach outlined in section 3.2. In the next chapters, therefore, I will look at the consequences of using this traditional theory of representation to examine purportedly nonrepresentational models in cognitive science.

4 The Dynamical Stance

In chapter 2, I suggested that the radical part of radical embodied cognitive science is antirepresentationalism. This chapter will primarily be about arguments for antirepresentationalism.[1] In particular, we'll look at how last chapter's traditional theory of representation affects the debate in cognitive science over antirepresentationalism. It turns out that a definition like this one grinds the debate to a halt, making representations mandatory and antirepresentationalism false, almost by definition. As goes antirepresentationalism, so goes radical embodied cognitive science. To deal with this and still have a chance of maintaining antirepresentationalism, I introduce what I call "the dynamical stance."

4.1 Two Claims

When one proclaims oneself to be an antirepresentationalist, as proponents of radical embodied cognitive science do, there are two things one might be saying. First, one might be making a claim about the nature of cognitive systems, namely that nothing in them is a representation. For the rest of this chapter, I will call this the *metaphysical claim*. Second, one might be claiming that our best explanations of cognitive systems will not involve representations. I will call this the *epistemological claim*. These are pretty clearly separate claims. It is easy to imagine, for example, that the metaphysical claim is true and that humans really are just complex dynamical systems, but they are so complex that the best way for us (with our limited intellects) to explain them is by metaphorically or instrumentally ascribing them mental representations. This is roughly Dennett's intentional stance (Dennett 1987), under one interpretation. Nonetheless, the metaphysical and epistemological claims are related at least in that the truth of the epistemological claim might be evidence for the truth of the metaphysical claim. Furthermore, the truth of the metaphysical claim seems to imply the truth of a close relative of the epistemological claim: if cognitive systems really have no representations, then there should be *some* explanation or model of them that does not refer to internal, mental representations, whether or not we can find or understand that explanation.

An antirepresentationalist, then, might defend either (or both) of two distinct claims. The main difference between the claims is that only the epistemological claim is more or less a *scientific* hypothesis. That is, the epistemological claim concerns how we ought to do cognitive science, whatever the mind is really like. The metaphysical claim, on the other hand, is to a much greater extent a *philosophical* hypothesis; it concerns what some region of the world (cognitive agents) is really like, however that region is best explained scientifically. In the next two sections, I will discuss the prospects for these two hypotheses, focusing on two dynamical systems models that have been cited by antirepresentationalists. The point will ultimately be that the metaphysical claim is indefensible, given the way the word "representation" is used in the cognitive sciences. So antirepresentationalists, and radical embodied cognitive scientists, had better try to defend the epistemological claim.

4.2 The Watt Governor and the Dynamical Stance

In a landmark paper that introduced dynamical modeling to the philosophical community, Tim van Gelder (1995) describes the operation of the Watt governor of steam engines, which he intends as a benchmark dynamical system, and argues that it supports antirepresentationalism. In this paper, he is ambivalent between the metaphysical claim and the epistemological claim. His arguments are based on a contrast between two cases: the actual Watt governor and a fictional computational steam governor. Here I will compare three cases: (1) van Gelder's dynamically modeled Watt governor; (2) van Gelder's account of a fictional computational governor; and (3) a representational, though noncomputational, account of the governor as described in (1). Doing so will show that the Watt governor can be seen as using traditional representations, so it should not be seen as supporting the metaphysical claim. This leaves open whether it can be cited as evidence for the epistemological claim.

Start with the actual Watt governor, and its dynamical systems model. The Watt governor controls the speed of a steam engine as follows.

It consisted of a vertical spindle geared into the main flywheel so that it rotated at a speed directly dependent on that of the flywheel itself. Attached to the spindle by hinges were two arms, and on the end of each arm was a metal ball. As the spindle turned, centrifugal force drove the balls outward and hence upwards. By a clever arrangement, this arm motion was linked directly to the throttle valve. The result was that as the speed of the main wheel increased, the arms raised, closing the valve and restricting the flow of steam; as the speed decreased, the arms fell, opening the valve and allowing more steam to flow. The engine adopted a constant speed, maintained with extraordinary swiftness and smoothness in the presence of large fluctuations in pressure and load. (van Gelder 1995, 349)

In van Gelder's proposed dynamical explanation of the governor, its operation is described mathematically. Just as Newton did in his descriptions of the physical world, the behavior of the system of interest is observed, and mathematical equations that describe that behavior are found. In the case of the Watt governor, the instantaneous acceleration of the arm angle when the steam engine is disconnected from the throttle valve is described by the following equation:

$$\frac{d^2\theta}{dt^2} = n\omega^2 \cos\theta \sin\theta - \frac{g}{l}\sin\theta - r\frac{d\theta}{dt} \tag{4.1}$$

where θ is the angle of the arms, n is a gearing constant, ω is the speed of the engine, g is the gravitational constant, l is the length of the arm, and r is a friction constant (see van Gelder 1995; this paragraph and the next follow van Gelder's discussion of the Watt governor closely). This equation describes the instantaneous acceleration of the arm angle, given the instantaneous arm angle. That is, at any moment and for any arm angle, it describes how the movement of the arm is changing. Only θ, the arm angle, is a variable in this equation; n, ω, g, l, and r are parameters, which remain constant and fix the dynamics of the system. This equation is general in that it gives the acceleration for any arm angle. Solutions to this equation specify a state space, and trajectories through this space can be used to predict future instantaneous accelerations and arm angles, given the current values of these variables.

The governor's behavior when connected to the throttle valve can be described by the following, more complicated equation:

$$\frac{d^n\omega}{dt^n} = F(\omega, \ldots, \tau, \ldots,) \tag{4.2}$$

where τ is the setting of the throttle valve. This equation, also perfectly general, describes the instantaneous change of the speed of the engine ω as a function of the throttle setting, which is itself a function of the arm angle θ. Just as ω is a parameter in the former equation, θ is a parameter in this equation, so these two dynamical systems are nonlinearly *coupled*. Any change in the arm angle θ changes the total dynamics of the system that describes the speed of the engine ω, in which it is a parameter; and any change in the engine speed ω changes the total dynamics of the system that describes the change of the arm angle θ, in which it is a parameter. Indeed, just as with the Beer robot described in chapter 2, the engine and governor form a single, nondecomposable system.

In this, as in all dynamical explanations, once we have found equations such as these for the Watt governor, it is agreed that we have explained the Watt governor's behavior: we have a perfectly general, counterfactual-supporting description of its behavior, as is provided in Newtonian physics. Note also that, again as in physical explanation, there is no reference to representation, computation, or teleology in the explained system. If cognitive systems are dynamical systems like the Watt governor, cognition can be explained just as any other complicated physical system is explained.

Van Gelder contrasts the actual Watt governor with a *computational governor*, a fictional machine that is meant to embody a computationalist approach to the problem of smoothly controlling the speed of a steam engine. To design such a governor, one would find a description of the task to be performed, then implement that task description in a finite number of simple steps. The computational solution van Gelder imagines to the problem, which would in fact be easily implemented on a digital computer, consists in running the following program:

(1) Begin:
(i) Measure the speed of the flywheel;
(ii) Compare the actual speed against the desired speed.
(2) If there is no discrepancy, return to step 1; otherwise:
(i) Measure the current steam pressure;
(ii) Calculate the desired alteration in steam pressure;
(iii) Calculate the necessary throttle-valve adjustment;
(iv) Make the necessary throttle-valve adjustment.
(3) Return to step 1. (van Gelder 1995, 423)

Of course, this governor is much different from the one that Watt actually built. Suppose one were to use this computational description to empirically investigate Watt's actual governor. One would observe the governor carefully, searching for the devices that implement the computations it is assumed to perform, perhaps precisely measuring the time it takes the governor to change the engine's speed to the desired value in an attempt to determine how many steps its computation uses. But here, the computational description is misleading. One could look forever and not find the way that these computations are implemented because the Watt governor does not implement the computational task as described.

The computational and dynamical governors that van Gelder describes, however, do not exhaust the space of possibilities: we can also imagine a representational but noncomputational description of the Watt governor. The Watt governor is designed so that the speed of a flywheel controlling the flow of steam into the engine is in turn controlled by the angle of the rotating arms. In the functioning of the Watt governor, the spindle spins, causing changes in the arm angle, in turn causing the valve to open and close. Given the traditional theory of representations described in chapter 3, it is possible to view the governor's arm angles as representations. To see this, consider that the angle of the arm is used by the valve to control the engine speed: the higher the arm, the slower the valve makes the engine run; the lower the arm, the faster the valve makes the engine run. It is the function of particular arm angles to change the state of the valve (the representation consumer[2]), and so adapt it to the need to speed up or slow down. The governor was *designed* so that the arm angle would play this role; that is, arm angle tokens are parts of the functioning of the governor *because* they lead to appropriate control of the engine speed (satisfying criterion R2 of the definition). So the function of arm angles is to control the speed of the engine, and since each arm angle indicates both a speed and the appropriate response to that speed, is both map and controller, it is an action-oriented representation, standing for the current need to increase or decrease the speed. Since different arm angles are appropriate for different engine speeds, this is a system of representations (satisfying R3). Furthermore, the arm angle can "be fooled," causing behavior for a nonactual engine speed: imagine what would happen if we used a flat surface to hold the arm at an artificially high angle. If we held the arm up in this way, the speed of the engine would decrease and finally halt altogether because the representation used to control the engine speed is of a situation (and its corresponding action) that does not obtain. Thus the arm angles of the Watt governor are action-oriented representations, according to our traditional definition of representation from chapter 3.

Since van Gelder offers the Watt governor as a prototypical dynamical system and a new paradigm for the modeling of cognition, the fact that it can be seen as representational is significant, and it suggests that other dynamical systems models of cognition can also be viewed as having representations.

Notice that the noncomputational, representational explanation of the Watt governor begins with and adds significantly to the dynamical story, but it does not displace it. The representational explanation can be seen as providing a teleological explanation of the Watt governor, as telling us *why* the Watt governor works the way it does. The explanation begins by assuming that the governor was designed to perform a certain task, and then assigns content to its states based on the way it performs that task. Since we know that the task is to control the speed of the steam engine, we look for parts of the system that are designed to adapt the governor to aspects of the environment relevant to controlling the engine's speed. We find that we can assign the roles of representation producer and consumer to the spindle and throttle valve, respectively. And the arm angles are action-oriented representations of situations relevant to controlling the engine's speed.

Because the Watt governor has representations according to our definition, it does not provide support for the metaphysical claim. To be sure, there is nothing *computational* (by the standard account) in these models: there are no rule-governed transformations of these representations. The representations in the Watt governor are produced and used, without being subject to rule-governed manipulations, and without necessarily taking part in anything like an inference.[3] So as a model of cognition, the Watt governor is much different from business-as-usual computational cognitive science. Indeed, it is an oft-cited example of embodied cognitive science. But it still contains entities that meet the standards of the traditional definition of representation, and so would be counted as representations by most cognitive scientists. This suggests that radical embodied cognitive scientists should leave the metaphysical claim behind, and focus on the epistemological claim.

Systems like the Watt governor might support the epistemological claim. Indeed, to many people, the representational explanation of the Watt governor seems superfluous. The same will be true for many other models favored by dynamical systems theorists, for example Beer's robotic insects (Beer 1995a,b, 2003), the evolutionary robots built at the University of Sussex (e.g., Harvey, Husbands, and Cliff 1994; see below), and research on coordination dynamics (see chapter 5). For these models, as for the Watt governor, the teleological, representational story doesn't seem any more informative than saying that the robots evolved or were designed for their tasks. Thus one can take up what we might call, with apologies to Dennett, *the dynamical stance* toward these models, explaining their behavior with the tools of dynamical systems theory and avoiding representational vocabulary, while remaining agnostic on the status of the metaphysical claim. In doing so, one admits that the representational story could be told but claims that that's not particularly relevant, because the dynamical systems theory explanation tells us everything important about the system. In fact, this is a natural reaction to the argument that the Watt governor is a representational system. Why should we bother with representational explanations when we have precise, perfectly general, counterfactual-supporting mathematical ones? Perhaps part of the reason for this feeling is that the representations in the former set are action oriented, so it is fairly difficult for us to say exactly what they represent. Another reason, which will be discussed below, is that one must have the dynamical story first, before one can concoct a representational story. If one has the complete dynamical story, what is left to be explained? The point of the dynamical stance is that representational stories about cognitive systems, especially those that already have dynamical explanations, are not likely to be satisfying.[4]

This sense of dissatisfaction with the representational explanation may be just what is necessary for the dynamically inspired cognitive scientist to affirm the epistemological claim, and in so doing to defend radical embodied cognitive science. The radical embodied cognitive scientist can argue for the epistemological claim, via the dynamical stance, as long as (1) there is a large class of dynamical models for which representational glosses add little to the mathematical explanation, and (2) the best explanations of cognitive phenomena fall within this class. The second of these is an empirical matter: we will simply have to wait and see how much of cognition can be explained using dynamical systems models without representational glosses. (I will describe several explanations like this in chapters 5, 6, and 7.) In the next section, I make a case for the first claim.

4.3 Evolutionary Robots and the Epistemological Claim

Work in robotics at the University of Sussex ("Sussex robots" hereafter; see Harvey, Husbands, and Cliff 1994; Husbands, Harvey, and Cliff 1995; Harvey et al. 1997; Di Paolo 2003; Wheeler 2005) presents a case of dynamical cognitive science that, we will see, supports the epistemological claim. In this work, control systems for robots are artificially evolved from a randomly generated initial population. Members of this initial group are selected to be "parents" (subject to mutations, etc.) based on their ability to complete particular tasks, for example, finding and moving toward a (potentially moving) target. The researchers purposefully take a hands-off approach to the architecture of the control systems; the only criterion used to determine which systems get to become parents is success at the particular task being selected for. (In fact, it is often success in their worst trial.) Thus, the theorists have no bias for any particular cognitive architecture. Instead they are concerned with achieving skilled performance of the task. By focusing on evolution of skillful behavior, the robot-builders avoid building models of the task domain themselves and coding them into the robot.

Wheeler (1996)[5] claims that one would be hard pressed to produce a representational story for the control system of the successful Sussex robots. It seems, he claims, that the robots get by not just without a set of representations constructed by their builders, but without any representations at all. But the fact that the Watt governor (advertised as a prototypical dynamical system) has representations suggests that *any* dynamical model of cognition will be a representational model. That is, it seems that any such model will posit entities that are representations according to the traditional definition of representation we are using. To see that this is also true of the Sussex robots, we must take a closer look at the model than Wheeler does when he claims that it has no representations.

According to the definition of representation in chapter 3, to argue that Sussex robots do in fact traffic in internal representations, one must find a set of states of the system that are produced by one part of the system, for use by some other part of the system in adapting the system to some aspect of the environment; then one must argue that these parts were designed to interact with one another in this way. This is easily done for Sussex robots, despite the large number of recurrent connections, which leads Wheeler to describe the control system as resembling a bowl of spaghetti (Wheeler 1996, 220).

Consider a robot with a control system as depicted in table 4.1. This robot, described by Harvey, Husbands, and Cliff (1994), was the most successful of those that were evolved for target following. After the artificial evolution process, which standardizes the parts of the system to work together to produce the desired behavior, the system works as follows. Nodes 0 and 1 take input from separate visual fields (V1 and V2, respectively). When there is strong input in V1, whatever V2 is like, node 0 causes a pattern of activation that speeds up the left and right motors, causing motion straight ahead. When there is strong input to V2 and weak input to V1, node 1 causes a pattern of activation that leads to increased excitement in node 14, which excites itself and slows the left motor. This causes the robot to rotate in a circle, until a strong input is found in V1. When there is strong input to neither visual field, the noisy node 5, which has no connections from either input node (0 and 1), creates feedback loops that cause the robot to spin in place, until one of the visual fields has input. Thus activation of node 0, from V1, causes a pattern of activation that leads the motors—via nodes 13, 14, and 15—to behave appropriately with respect to the target being straight ahead of the robot. Activation of node 1, from V2, causes a pattern of activation that leads the motors—again, via nodes 13, 14, and 15—to behave appropriately with respect to the target

Table 4.1

Connections in a Sussex Robot. This table shows the connections in the most successful target tracking robot discussed in Harvey, Husbands, and Cliff 1994. A mark in a square indicates that there is a connection from node with that row number to the node with that column number. A "+" indicates an excitatory connection; a "–" indicates an inhibitory connection. Nodes 0 and 1 take input from visual fields V1 and V2, respectively; node 13 increases voltage to the left motor; node 14 decreases voltage to the left motor; node 15 increases voltage to the right motor. Node 5 is an extra noisy unit that takes no input from either visual field.

node	0	1	4	5	6	8	9	10	12	13	14	15
0			–					+		+		
1		–	+								+	
4			–			+						
5*	+				+			+				
6	+						+					+
8						–			+			
9							–		+	+		
10		–			+							
12				–								–
13												
14								+	+		+	
15		–										

being in sight, but not straight ahead. And, perhaps most interestingly, self-activation of node 5 (when there is strong visual input from neither field) causes the robot to behave appropriately with respect to the target being out of visual range. These patterns of activation of the robot's control system are representations according to the teleological definition of representation: the input nodes play the role of representation producers; nodes 13, 14, and 15 are representation consumers; patterns of activation across intermediate nodes are representations.

But compare this description to the purely dynamical one that the Sussex roboticists prefer, the one that comes from adopting the dynamical stance toward the system. In their preferred analysis, the robot and the environment are coupled dynamical systems. To explain their operation, Sussex roboticists give mathematical descriptions of the structure of each separately, and then, based on those, they give a unified account of the robot–environment coupled dynamical system. (In what follows, I will provide only a sketch of their argument, leaving out the mathematical details. See Husbands, Harvey, and Cliff 1995.) The control system of the robot is given a mathematical account—in fact, I exploited this account in giving my representational account of the robot. Consider the noisy node 5, which excites itself in the absence of visual input to the system: this node, which they call a *generator unit*, provides input to a feedback loop comprising nodes 1 (a visual input unit), 6, 9, 10, 12, and 14 (a motor output unit), which has connections to the other two output nodes, 13 and 15, as well. To see how such a complicated loop works, they begin by providing a mathematical analysis of the behavior of a simple, single self-exciting node. This analysis is extended to multiple-unit feedback loops, where the behavior is equivalent, but with time delays depending on the number of additional units. Since two of the nodes that give output to the motors (14 and 15) have connections back to the nodes that take input from the visual fields, the analysis in terms of feedback loops can be extended to cover the behavior of the whole network. With such an account, the behavior of the network, given any input to the visual fields, can be predicted.

The next step in the analysis is a dynamical description of the robot's task environment. This description is done in a space of egocentric polar coordinates $r\phi$, where r is the distance from the robot to the center of the task environment and ϕ is the clockwise angle from the front of the robot to the center of the task environment. It is possible to determine what the robot's visual input will be for every possible coordinate in the $r\phi$ space, providing a full description of the robot's visual environment. Finally, as in the Beer 2003 model described in chapter 2, they combine these two dynamical accounts into a combined system that captures the properties of the agent–environment coupling. Once one knows the visual input at every point in the task environment and the behavior given every type of visual input, one can construct a phase portrait that predicts the robot's behavior no matter where it is in its environment. For the robot whose control system we have been discussing, this phase portrait has just one attractor, corresponding to the location of the target. Furthermore, every point in the phase portrait is in the basin of attraction for the target's attractor. So one can predict that the robot will succeed at its task every time; and, when the robot's performance was tested, it did succeed every time.

There are reasons to prefer the dynamical account to the representational one described above. First, the representational story depends on the dynamical story about the control system, but not vice versa. It was that mathematical description of the control system in terms of feedback loops that allowed me to predict what behavior would be produced when particular patterns of activation were produced in the system. To find out what those patterns of activation represented, I determined what environmental situations those activations would adapt the agent to, in particular, by determining what environmental situations the ensuing behavior would be appropriate to. So the representational description is dependent upon the dynamical one. Perhaps more important, though, the representational description of the system does not add much to our understanding of the system. Once we have the full dynamical story, we can predict the behavior of the robot in its environment completely, and we can do so without making reference to the representational content of any states of its control system. The same is true of the Watt governor. In both cases, the dynamical stance pays off: fully predictive mathematical descriptions of the systems are provided. And despite the fact that one can cook up a representational story, once one has the dynamical explanation, the representational gloss does not predict anything about the system's behavior that could not be predicted by the dynamical explanation alone.

The lack of a need for representational explanation to accompany dynamical models can be made more clear via a historical parallel. As van Gelder (1998) points out, dynamical cognitive science can be seen as an attempt to fulfill Hume's goal of a scientific psychology similar to Newton's mechanics—a psychology in which cognition would be explained by mathematical laws. One of the most striking and important features of Newtonian physics is that the sort of covering law explanations[6] that were provided by Newton's mechanics obviated any need for teleology in physical explanation. In providing a fully general set of mathematical laws for physics, Newton sidestepped speculation about Aristotelian final (=teleological) causes, taking his laws of motion as axioms not in need of further explanation. Similarly, once one has mathematical covering laws for psychology, laws that predict the behavior of agents in their environments with great accuracy, there may be no need for teleological explanations in psychology. And since representational explanations are a species of teleological explanations, a mature dynamical cognitive science might make them obsolete.

So dynamical models of cognition like Sussex robots do indeed provide support for the epistemological claim, and, thereby, for radical embodied cognitive science. They show that it is possible that significant portions of cognition might be explained without mental gymnastics. But it must be noted that these robots, like the Beer robots discussed in chapter 2, are capable of only very simple behaviors. This is not to say that dynamical cognitive science is incapable of explaining cognitive abilities more straightforwardly. The van Rooij, Bongers, and Haselager (2002) study from chapter 2 showed that nonrepresentational dynamical accounts can be given for representation-hungry abilities. There has also been significant work using dynamical systems theory to account for language use, decision making, and social coordination. See, for example, Schmidt, Carello, and Turvey 1990; Busemeyer and Townsend 1995; Roe, Busemeyer, and Townsend 2001; Busemeyer, Townsend, and Stout 2002; Port 2003; Richardson, Marsh, and Schmidt 2005; Oullier et al. 2005; van Orden, Holden, and Turvey 2005; Dale and Spivey 2006; Spivey and Dale 2006; Marsh et al. 2006; Turvey and Moreno 2006; Richardson, Dale, and Kirkham 2007; Richardson et al. 2007; Stephen et al. 2007; McKinstry, Dale and Spivey 2008. For dynamical cognitive science to vindicate the epistemological claim, for the dynamical stance to pay off, its proponents must continue to provide models—and covering law explanations—of representation-hungry behavior, and these models must not be usefully viewed as representational. Only time will tell to what extent this will be possible.

4.4 A (Potential) Problem for Dynamical Accounts

Although it seems to be an empirical matter whether dynamical cognitive science will provide compelling, nonrepresentational explanations of great stretches of cognition, there is a potentially serious methodological problem for dynamical accounts, one that might arise for any research program that provides only covering law explanations. And if there is a serious methodological problem for dynamical cognitive science, there is reason to think that dynamical cognitive science will not provide sufficient explanations to vindicate the epistemological claim. This, of course, would be a problem for radical embodied cognitive science. In what follows, I will explain this potential methodological problem and explore a possible resolution to it. This will require a brief digression into the history of physics.

The debate between computationalists and dynamicists in cognitive science runs closely parallel to that between atomists (e.g., Boltzmann) and phenomenalists (e.g., Mach) in theoretical physics at the beginning of the twentieth century. Because of this, the argument made by Boltzmann against Mach's physics can also be made by computationalists against dynamical cognitive science. This argument, which I will call the "guide to discovery" argument, was devastating to the phenomenalist picture of physics, and it is potentially devastating to the dynamical hypothesis in cognitive science.

Boltzmann made the guide to discovery argument in response to Mach's philosophy of science (see Mach 1886). Mach was a *phenomenalist*; that is, he believed that everything that there is is available to the senses. This constrains the sort of theories that might be admissible in the sciences; they too must posit no nonsensible entities or properties. Thus Mach argues for a strictly phenomenological physics, the purpose of which is to provide covering law explanations for physical phenomena. He was therefore opposed to any theory that posited nonsensible entities of any kind, as atomists in physics did. This led to an ongoing, sometimes heated debate between phenomenological and atomist physicists.

In his "The Recent Development of Method in Theoretical Physics" (1900), Boltzmann makes the "guide to discovery" argument in favor of atomistic physics. Boltzmann begins the argument as follows:

> The question simply is whether there are not additional results which atomism only could have achieved, and of such results the atomistic theory has had many remarkable specimens to show, even long after the period of its greatest glory. (1900, 253)

As an answer to "the question" Boltzmann describes some recent triumphs of atomistic physics, such as Van der Waals's greatly improved formula to predict the behavior of the aggregate states of simple chemical substances, improvements to Avogadro's law, Gibb's theory of dissociation, and hydrodynamics. All these successes, Boltzmann claims, could not have been achieved without atomistic assumptions. He concludes the argument:

> If phenomenology deems it expedient, as it certainly must, constantly to institute new experiments for the purpose of discovering necessary corrections for its equations, atomism accomplishes much more in this respect, in that it enables us to point definitely to the experiments which are in most likelihood to lead to its correction. (Ibid., 254)

Atomism, then, is the best methodology for physics because it provides a *guide to discovering* new equations that describe the phenomena more accurately; by assuming that there are atoms, one is led to testable predictions of new phenomena.

The point of this argument is best seen by coopting Peter Clark's (1976) account of the ultimate failure of phenomenological physics. Clark characterizes phenomenological physics as *fact dependent*. In other words, phenomenological physics proceeded by making empirical generalizations about substances and then altering the parameters of descriptive equations to fit anomalies in the experimental results. Thus the only way to improve phenomenological physics was by ad hoc additions to the theory, in light of new empirical facts. That is, phenomenological physics, because it refuses to postulate underlying, unobservable structure, provides no guide to discovery. And, as Clark puts it, "[t]his quite marked limitation of the heuristic of thermodynamics meant that there was no way of systematically improving the theory" (Clark 1976, 44).

Boltzmann's criticism of nonatomistic theories in physics boils down to the observation that they are fact dependent, and so unlikely to offer reasonable testable predictions that might improve our ability to explain new phenomena. That is, unlike atomistic theories, phenomenological theories offer no guide to discovery, and can only proceed in an ad hoc manner. Atomistic physics, on the other hand, is not fact dependent; its practitioners, therefore, can make substantial predictions and then test them. Put simply, phenomenological physicists must constantly alter their theories to fit *existing* empirical results after experimentation, whereas atomists can use their microtheory to *predict* empirical results before experimentation. This is a significant methodological advantage for the atomists.

We can substitute computational and dynamical cognitive science into this debate. Computationalism, like atomism, posits an underlying mechanism—computations performed upon representations. This mechanism can be used to predict new, as-yet-unobserved phenomena, and then perform tests in order to improve our understanding of cognition. There are literally thousands of results in cognitive science that, like the improvement to Avogadro's number that depended on the assumption of atomism, would not have been achieved without the positing of internal mental representations. One obvious example is the results on mental rotation (see Shepard and Cooper 1982). In a well-known experiment, Shepard and Metzler posited picture-like mental representations and predicted that there would be temporal effects associated with the operations performed upon them. In particular, they predicted that to determine whether two similar three-dimensional shapes were the same shape at different orientations, subjects would mentally rotate one of them and the time it would take them to decide would be proportional to the degree of rotation. The experiments showed exactly the temporal effect that was predicted.

On the other hand, it might seem that dynamical cognitive science—at least the dynamical cognitive science of radical embodied cognitive scientists who do not posit mental representations—is like phenomenological physics in that it posits no underlying mechanism for cognition. It is essentially a phenomenological psychology: it is successful when it provides equations that capture observed behavior. It would seem, therefore, that it is fact dependent. Radical embodied (i.e., antirepresentationalist, dynamicist) cognitive scientists must first make empirical observations and then alter their theory to fit them. This, then, is the "guide to discovery" criticism of the dynamical hypothesis: dynamical systems theory, because it posits no underlying mechanism for cognition, is a fact-dependent theory. It provides no guide to discovery, and therefore it is inferior scientific method. Indeed, given the Humean nature of dynamical cognitive science (van Gelder 1998) and Mach's intellectual debts to Hume, it is not surprising that dynamical cognitive science has the same problems as Mach's phenomenological physics.

Notice that the guide to discovery argument can only be an argument for *instrumental theories*, such as methodological atomism or representationalism. If we conclude that atomism is better equipped to yield progress than fact-dependent theories, then we conclude only that we should do atomistic physics, as opposed to phenomenological physics. On the face of it, this is different from arguing for what we might call *realist* atomism. A realist atomism would claim not just that we should do atomistic physics, but also that the world really is composed of atoms, unobservable though they may be. The guide to discovery argument cannot lead to such a conclusion. It can only support a conclusion such as this: whatever the underlying nature of reality, atomism is more likely than fact-dependent theories to increase our ability to describe the world. Similarly, it is not possible to argue from the claim that dynamical cognitive science is fact dependent to the conclusion that cognition *really* is representational or computational. The argument is instead for the *practical necessity* of positing mental gymnastics. But since we are considering the epistemological claim, the claim that the best explanations of cognition will not invoke representations, any argument for the practical necessity of positing representations in our explanations of cognition is sufficient. That is, it might be that although cognitive systems really are dynamical systems, our understanding of them requires that we treat them as having representations. The point is that representational stories might provide crucial leverage for understanding behavior. If this were to be true, the dynamical stance would not pay off, and radical embodied cognitive science would be in trouble.

The question, then, is whether dynamical cognitive science can avoid being purely fact dependent, despite the fact that it posits no underlying mechanism. Here is one reason to think that it cannot. Think about the way that one might do dynamical cognitive science: first, one observes some cognitive activity; then one tries to find the relevant parameters and variables that define the dynamical system that the activity instantiates; finally, one finds equations that specify the trajectories through the state space defined by the dynamical system. All of this proceeds ad hoc, by adding another dynamical explanation for another observed phenomenon, just as in the case of phenomenological physics. Taking the dynamical stance toward cognitive systems might not provide enough predictive leverage to be scientifically fruitful.

4.5 Solving the Problem

How serious is this methodological problem, the lack of a guide to discovery? How bad is it for dynamical cognitive science to proceed by ad hoc additions to its overall account? The next chapter will be the beginning of a response to the first, more pressing, of these questions. The second question, about the problem of ad hoc additions, is more easily disposed of. In and of themselves, ad hoc additions to theory are really not problematic. It is well known that in physics ad hoc additions to models are a fact of life. Hacking (1983), for example, discusses Faraday's 1845 discovery that magnets can affect light, now known as the Faraday effect. Although Faraday believed that light and magnetism were interconnected, he had no unified theory of light and magnetism. (Maxwell would outline this theory in 1861.) Faraday also had no mathematical model of his new effect. In 1846, Airy provided a mathematical model of the Faraday effect, based on earlier mathematizations of the wave theory of light. Hacking writes: "Airy added some *ad hoc* further terms, either first or third derivatives. This is a standard move in physics. In order to make the equations fit the phenomena, you pull from the shelf some fairly standard extra terms for the equations, without knowing why one rather than the other will do the trick" (1983, 211).

Thus, ad-hoc-ery is not in and of itself a problem: it is standard practice in mathematical modeling throughout the sciences. The worry for the dynamical stance really is its fact dependence, its lack of a guide to discovery. Compare the dynamical stance with what Airy actually did. Airy's model of the Faraday effect has ad hoc elements, but it is based on a theory of light as waves in elastic ether. Thus Airy's ad hoc model was based on a nonphenomenological theory of the nature of light, one that led from his model of the Faraday effect to the Maxwell equations. Ad-hoc-ery is OK, even inevitable, as long as it is coupled with a guide to discovery. Indeed, as Feyerabend (1975) points out, Gallileo's argument for Copernican astronomy is also ad hoc, yet, because Copernicanism provided a guide to discovery, was the basis for successful science. "*But their task is now well-defined,* for Galileo's assumptions, his *ad hoc* hypotheses included, are sufficiently clear and simple to prescribe the direction of future research" (Feyerabend 1975, 77). So, to solve this problem radical embodied cognitive science needs a guide to discovery. In chapter 5, I will suggest two possible guides to discovery for radical embodied cognitive science. First, I will show that dynamical models themselves can be guides to discovery. Second, I will argue that radical embodied cognitive scientists can use Gibsonian ecological psychology as a guide to discovery just as physicists of the early twentieth century used atomism, that is, as a noninstrumentalist background theory of the nature of the subject matter.

5 Guides to Discovery

To remind us where we have been so far: radical embodied cognitive science includes a commitment to antirepresentationalism. Antirepresentationalism is best defended by adopting the dynamical stance. The dynamical stance seems beset with the same methodological problem that phenomenological physics had: it is fact dependent. But is the dynamical stance *necessarily* fact dependent? I will discuss two ways in which a nonrepresentational, dynamical cognitive science might offer a guide to discovery, a way to predict new phenomena and generate new experiments. The first of these is one I recommended in Chemero 2000a. One might posit a generally applicable type of dynamical model that accounts for a wide range of cognitive phenomena. This would allow scientists to predict that other, similar behaviors would fall under the same covering laws, and then test that prediction. Such a generalizable dynamical model could provide a guide to discovery, putting dynamical cognitive science on equal methodological footing with computational and representational cognitive science.

As it happens, one such nonrepresentational, generalizable dynamical model of cognition has proven widely applicable, and its range is constantly being extended to more aspects of cognition: the well-known Haken-Kelso-Bunz (1985; HKB hereafter) model and its extension to a more generalized coordination dynamics (Kelso 1995; Kelso and Engstrøm 2006). Also, in Chemero 2000a, I mentioned but did not pursue another option for a non-fact-dependent, dynamical cognitive science: Gibsonian ecological psychology. I now think this is a more fruitful option, partly because it can engulf the generalized HKB model (along with a series of other successful mathematical models). Ecological psychology is more than just a unifying dynamical *model*; it is a unifying background *theory*. Ecological psychology, that is, provides a guide to discovery in the same way that atomism did for physics. In the later part of this chapter, and for the two chapters that follow, I will present ecological psychology as radical embodied cognitive science's guide to discovery. I should point out here that this discussion is relevant to all proponents of embodied cognitive science, radical or not. Ecological psychology's core concepts—perception for action, direct perception, affordances, environmental information—form the core of the embodied cognition movement. So you should pay attention, even if you're not a radical.

5.1 Guide to Discovery 1: Generalizing HKB

One way to provide a guide to discovery for radical embodied cognitive science is by finding a generally applicable dynamical model, and using it as the basis for research. That is, with a model that seems to apply to a wide variety of cognitive phenomena, one can generate predictions to be tested with experiments by hypothesizing that as-yet-unexamined phenomena can also be described by the model. That is, if the model describes embodied behaviors A through L, we can proceed by trying to apply it to behaviors M through R. The model's ability or inability to capture new phenomena will lead to refinements of the model for greater accuracy and for greater generality, as well as to realizations of limits of applicability and, perhaps, ultimate replacement by a different model.[1]

The HKB model is an example of a dynamical model in cognitive science that has served as a guide to discovery in exactly this way. In this section, I will describe the HKB model and a series of extensions and modifications that have been made to it over the years. The point will be to show that it has served, and can continue to serve as a unifying model and guide to discovery for radical embodied cognitive science.

The roots of the HKB model and, arguably, the resurgence of the dynamical approach in cognitive science are found in a suggestion by Kugler, Kelso, and Turvey (1980) to the effect that limbs in coordinated actions could be understood as nonlinearly coupled oscillators whose coupling requires energy to maintain and, so, tends to dissipate after a time. It was in the context of this suggestion that Kelso (1984) performed his experiments on finger wagging. The exceptionally robust results of Kelso's experiments were then modeled by Haken, Kelso, and Bunz (1985). Subjects asked to wag their index fingers left to right can produce only two stable patterns of bimanual coordination. In one, called *in-phase* or *relative phase 0*, the fingers approach one another at the midline of the body; in the other, called *out-of-phase* or *relative phase .5*, the fingers move simultaneously to the left, then to the right, like the windshield wipers on most cars. As subjects were asked to wag their fingers out of phase at gradually increasing rates, they eventually were unable to do so, and slipped into in-phase wagging. Haken, Kelso, and Bunz applied a vector field to the relative phase of the fingers. At slower rates, this field has two attractors, one at relative phase .5, and a second, deeper one at relative phase 0. This means that any finger wagging will tend to be stable only when one of these values for relative phase is maintained. But as the rate increases (and passes what HKB call the *critical point*), the more shallow attractor at .5 disappears, so the only remaining attractor is the deeper one at relative phase 0. So finger wagging at higher rates will tend to be stable only when it is in phase. This is, it turns out, not just true of wagging fingers: any coordinated movement of symmetric limbs (arm waving, leg swinging, etc.) works the same way.

The actual mathematical model of this behavior, the actual HKB model, is a *potential* function,[2] where potential $V(\phi)$ is a measure of the stability of the system, with its two oscillating parts (wagging fingers) at relative phase ϕ. The simplest potential function that will capture all of the data on finger-wagging is

$$V(\phi) = -A \cos \phi - B \cos 2\phi. \tag{5.1}$$

This formula can be visualized as shown in figure 5.1. To understand the graph, it must be imagined as on the surface of a tube. That is, relative phase 0 and relative phase 1 are actually the same points on the graph. In the graph, the potential V has two minima: a deep one at relative phase $0 = 1$, and a shallower one at relative phase .5. This accounts for the stability of the system when fingers are wagged at these relative phases, and the lack of stability at any other relative phases. Put differently, the graph

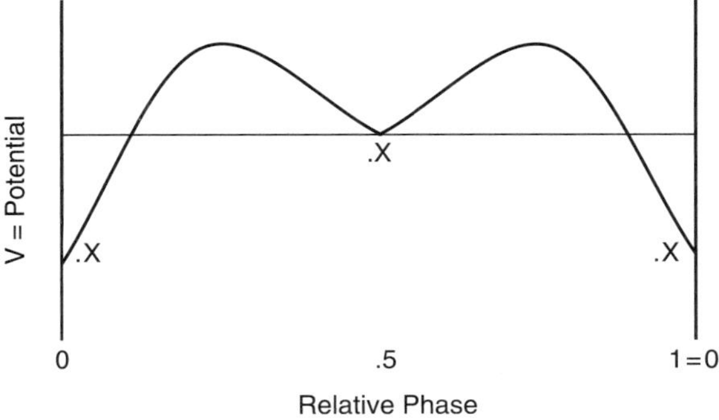

Figure 5.1
Potential as a function of relative phase in the HKB model.

shows the degree of difficulty of maintaining coordination at all possible values of relative phase. The deep well at 0 = 1 and the shallower one at .5 indicate that these are the relative phases to which the system tends. Increasing the rate of finger wagging changes the shape of the graph. As rate increases, the minimum at .5 disappears, leaving only one well, at relative phase 0 = 1.

Equation 5.1 can be combined with the first temporal derivative of ϕ,

$$d\phi/dt = -dV/d\phi, \tag{5.2}$$

to yield this motion equation for relative phase

$$d\phi/dt = -A \sin \phi - 2B \sin 2\phi. \tag{5.3}$$

Equation 5.3 describes the way relative phase ϕ will change, given its current value. The ratio B/A is a *control parameter,* assumed to vary inversely with frequency of oscillation, which determines the nature of the change in behavior of the system. That is, B/A determines the shape of the phase space, the layout of attractors and repellers. (This is depicted in more detail in figure 2.7 of Kelso 1995.)

The HKB model is an example of a general strategy for explaining behavior. First, observe patterns of macroscopic behavior; then seek collective variables (like relative phase) and parameters (like rate) that govern the behavior; finally, search for the simplest mathematical function that accounts for the behavior. Because complicated dynamical systems (like the one involving the muscles, portions of the central nervous system, ears, and metronome in the finger-wagging task) have a tendency to behave like much simpler systems, one will often be able to model these systems in terms of extremely simple functions, with only a few easily observable parameters. Importantly, the HKB model makes a series of specific predictions. First, it predicts that as rates increase, experimental subjects will be unable to maintain out-of-phase performance. Second, even at slow rates, only relative phase of 0 and .5 will be stable. Third, the behavior should exhibit *critical fluctuations*: as the rate approaches the critical value, attempts to maintain out-of-phase performance will result in erratic fluctuations of relative phase. Fourth, the behavior should exhibit critical slowing down: at rates near the critical value, disruptions from out-of-phase performance should take longer to correct than at slower rates.

Because HKB makes these four predictions, it has been possible to design experiments to see whether it can model a wide variety of behavioral, cognitive, and perceptual phenomena. These experiments have led to refining the basic model, and then further predictions. As Schöner and Kelso

(1988a) put it, "we show here how it is possible to (i) establish quantitative and reproducible relations among observables in the form of laws, and (ii) make novel predictions that can be checked experimentally" (1514). In short, HKB has become a guide to discovery for nonrepresentational, dynamical cognitive science, that is, for radical embodied cognitive science. In the rest of this section, I will illustrate this by tracing a bit of the history of the HKB model. (Some of the "cases" I discuss here are discussed in more detail in Kelso 1995; I first heard about some of the others in a lecture by Michael Turvey in 2004.)

Case 1: Changing the basic model for better fit with the data The first modification to the HKB model, made soon after the publication of the original paper, was by Schöner, Haken, and Kelso (1986). This modification changed the equation from a deterministic model to a stochastic one. In particular, Schöner et al. added a noise term to equation 5.3 to deal with microscopically generated fluctuations of the oscillating limbs, providing a better fit with data. The new equation was thus:

$$\frac{d\phi}{dt} = \underbrace{-A \sin \phi - 2B \sin 2\phi}_{HKB} + \underbrace{\sqrt{Q}\xi_t}_{noise}, \tag{5.4}$$

where ξ_t is a stochastic noise term of strength $\sqrt{Q}$. This equation is simply HKB plus a noise term. It is an adjustment to the model, caused by a desire to improve fit with data.

Case 2: Using the model to change our conception of a related phenomenon Within a few years, the model had been extended to cover new phenomena several times. One noteworthy extension was to learning (Schöner and Kelso 1988b), in which learning is understood as a phase transition. That is, the control parameter B/A, which determines the shape of the attractor layout, changes as subjects improve their abilities to coordinate their activities. For example, with practice, it becomes easier for subjects to maintain out-of-phase finger wagging at faster rates. This is modeled by varying the control parameter B/A with the number of trials. Here, HKB has not just been used to model learning; it has also been used to reconceptualize learning as deforming the attractor layout. This reconceptualization led to the discovery of new phenomena several years down the road: Amazeen, Sternad, and Turvey (1996), basing experiments on learning as deformation of the attractor layout, showed that learning a difficult coordination task affects more basic coordination. That is, teaching subjects to wag their fingers in, say, 5:4 (five wags of the left index finger for every four wags of the right one) causes a dramatic change to basic abilities. Before learning, subjects wagged their fingers as the HKB model predicts: they were able to maintain in-phase coordination at fast and slow speeds, but out-of-phase coordination only at slow speeds. After they learned the complex rhythm this had flip-flopped, so that out-of-phase coordination was easier to maintain at high speeds. In terms of the model, before learning, there was a deep attractor at relative phase 0 and a shallow one at relative phase .5. But after learning, which is conceptualized as *phase-space deformation*, these attractors had switched so that the one at relative phase .5 was deeper than the one at relative phase 0. This is a case of the basic model leading to a new conceptualization of a familiar phenomenon (learning), which leads in turn to further experiments and new phenomena to be modeled.

Case 3: Extending the model to cover perception–action coupling A second noteworthy change to the basic model was made so that it could be extended to more complicated forms of coordination, in particular to the coordination of action with perceived features of the environment. The original HKB model can only account for 1:1 coordination. That is, the oscillators in question have to have the same intrinsic frequency, the same frequency at which they "prefer" to oscillate. For example, the HKB model works quite well for wagging fingers or kicking legs, but less well for coordination of one leg and one arm or one finger with a metronome. To account for more complicated forms of coordination and for coordination of unlike parts, Kelso, DelColle, and Schöner (1990) added another term to the already amended HKB model:

$$\frac{d\phi}{dt} = \underbrace{\Delta\omega}_{\substack{\textit{frequency}\\ \textit{difference}}} \underbrace{-A \sin \phi - 2B \sin 2\phi}_{\textit{HKB}} + \underbrace{\sqrt{Q}\xi_t}_{\textit{noise}}, \tag{5.5}$$

where $\Delta\omega$ is the intrinsic frequency difference between the components of the system when they are uncoupled. With this addition, the coordination of one finger with another, for which the original HKB model was developed, could be seen as a special case in which $\Delta\omega = 0$. So with this change to the basic model, Kelso et al. (1990) were able to account for a case of basic perception–action coupling, in which subjects were asked to wag a single finger along with a metronome with a variable frequency. Subjects, that is, had to change the frequency of their moving finger based on their perception of changes to the metronome.

Case 4: Extension to socially coupled oscillators The Kelso et al. (1990) extension of the model was important because it showed that the model could account for oscillators coupled in a different way than in the original finger-wagging experiment. When an individual subject wags her or his fingers, the oscillating fingers are coupled by a nervous system. But when a subject wags a finger along with an environmental source, the coupling is via light and sound in the environment, via environmental information.[3] Because HKB-modelable coupling can occur via the environment, it makes sense to wonder whether coupling can be social. Schmidt, Carello, and Turvey (1990) showed that it can. In Schmidt et al.'s experiments, seated subjects were asked to coordinate their leg swings with one another. Three of the four HKB predictions occurred. First, subjects were only able to maintain coordination at relative phase 0 (in phase) and relative phase .5 (out of phase). Second, at faster leg-swinging rates subjects spontaneously switched from out-of-phase to in-phase swinging. Third, at rates approaching that at which out-of-phase coordination becomes impossible, critical fluctuations appear. Only the fourth criterion, critical slowing down, was not observed; but only because it was not tested by Schmidt et al. So the basic HKB model (even without the term added by Kelso et al. 1990) was able to account for social coupling. More recently, there has been a great profusion of work on social coupling. See Richardson, Marsh, and Schmidt 2005; Oullier et al. 2005; Marsh et al. 2006; Richardson, et al. 2007; Lopresti-Goodman et al. 2008.

Case 5: Extending the model to cover asymmetries As noted above, the basic HKB model and its extensions are designed to cover coordination of *symmetrical* body parts. Of course, even the hands of a single individual aren't really symmetrical in their functionality. Nearly everyone is either left- or right-handed. Does handedness produce an asymmetry significant enough to affect finger wagging? Treffner and Turvey (1995) showed that it does, especially as the rate of finger wagging increases during out-of-phase wagging. Because the wagged fingers are functionally asymmetric, the symmetry between them takes work to maintain. As subjects approach the critical rate at which out-of-phase wagging becomes impossible, handedness contributes significantly to breaking the enforced symmetry between the hands. Treffner and Turvey showed that the HKB model could be extended to account for this, by adding two symmetry-breaking terms to the model. The model, as amended by Turvey and Treffner, is:

$$\frac{d\phi}{dt} = \underbrace{\Delta\omega}_{\substack{\text{frequency}\\ \text{difference}}} \underbrace{-A \sin \phi - 2B \sin 2\phi}_{HKB} - \underbrace{C \sin \theta - 2D \sin 2\phi}_{\text{symmetry breaking}} + \underbrace{\sqrt{Q}\xi_t}_{\text{noise}}, \tag{5.6}$$

In this equation, the value of D accounts for handedness, with $D > 0$ for right-handed subjects and $D < 0$ for left-handed subjects. Later work, inspired by Treffner and Turvey's extension of HKB, led to the investigation of another potential source of asymmetry: attention. Riley et al. (1997) found that attention has significant effects on the ability to maintain out-of-phase finger wagging. They accounted for this via manipulations of D in equation 5.6. In particular, D was expanded to

$$D = D_{handedness} + D_{attention}, \tag{5.7}$$

where $D_{attention} < 0$ indicates attention to the left hand and $D_{attention} > 0$ indicates attention to the right hand. Here, changes to the model to account for one source of asymmetry led to experiments showing that another small change to the model could account for another source of asymmetry.

Case 6: Getting away from limbs 1: Speech production Port (2003) has suggested that one might be able to develop a *general theory of meter*, based on the HKB model. First, Port performed experiments showing that certain simple speech tasks conform to the predictions of the HKB model. These results show, Port claims, that the HKB model captures something general that might underlie speech actions as well as limb motions. Furthermore, it suggests that a more general variant of the HKB model might explain large swaths of human behavior, not just wagging limbs. Port's general model of meter derives from the fact that the speech task matches the predictions of the HKB model, but shows additional attractors. The speech task has attractors at relative phases of 0 and .5, as in HKB's finger wagging task, and weaker attractors at .33 and .67. These two new attractors can be accounted for by adding a term to the basic HKB equation:

$$\frac{d\phi}{dt} = \underbrace{-A \sin \phi - 2B \sin 2\phi}_{HKB} - \underbrace{C \sin 3\phi}_{extra\ term}, \tag{5.8}$$

If C is large, attractors appear at relative phase .33 and .67, along with those at 0 and .5. The HKB model is a special case of this more general model, where $C = 0$. Such a model, Port says, might be fully general: we might be able to apply it to every repetitive motor pattern (such as walking, running, swinging a hammer, chanting), as well as to the perception and production of music and speech.

Case 7: Getting away from limbs 2: Cortical coordination dynamics Based on their work with the HKB model, Bressler, Kelso, and their colleagues

(Bressler and Kelso 2001; Bressler 2002) have begun to extend coordination dynamics (as exemplified in equation 5.5) to patterns of activity in the cortex. Studying coordinated activity among cortical brain areas of rhesus macaques involved in cognitive tasks, they have seen coordinated electrical activity oscillations between cortical areas, coordinated oscillations that are characteristic of coupled oscillators with different preferred frequencies. That is, observing the patterns of neural activity among monkeys engaged in cognitive tasks, they have found coupled oscillation that can be modeled by equation 5.5. In particular, they found that cortical areas remain uncoordinated in their activity for long periods, then have a rapid increase of in-phase field potential oscillations. These bursts of in-phase activity coincide with changes of task or cognitive state. Furthermore, they have found distinctive patterns of coordination among cortical areas that accompany identifiable cognitive states. This particular application of the extended HKB model is especially important for proponents of radical embodied cognitive science, who are often accused (falsely) of ignoring or (less falsely) underestimating the import of the brain. Radical embodied cognitive science now has a nonrepresentational dynamical model that applies to brains, individuals, and groups of individuals.

Case 8: Accounting for "real" cognition: Solving gear problems In nonlinearly coupled dynamical systems, one typically sees a spike in system entropy just prior to a phase transition, such as when coordination moves from out-of-phase to in-phase. As noted above, this spike in entropy is called *critical fluctuation*: as a system approaches a critical point, the coupling among its parts becomes highly variable. For example, the HKB model predicted, and then observed, critical fluctuations in coordinated finger movement. Finger movements become more entropic just prior to switching from out-of-phase coordination to in-phase coordination, a key factor in demonstrating that the system controlling the coordination is nonlinearly coupled. But, as many proponents of computational cognitive science point out, finger wagging is not a paradigmatically cognitive activity. Recent research, however, has demonstrated that more paradigmatically cognitive, and undeniably representation hungry, phenomena also exhibit critical fluctuations. One example of this is research by Stephen, Dixon, and Isenhower (2007, in press; Stephen and Dixon in press) on solving gear problems. In a gear problem, a subject is shown a picture of a sequence of connected gears like in figure 5.2. The subject is told the direction of motion of one of the gears (the driving gear) and asked to determine the direction of another gear in the array (the target gear). In the example

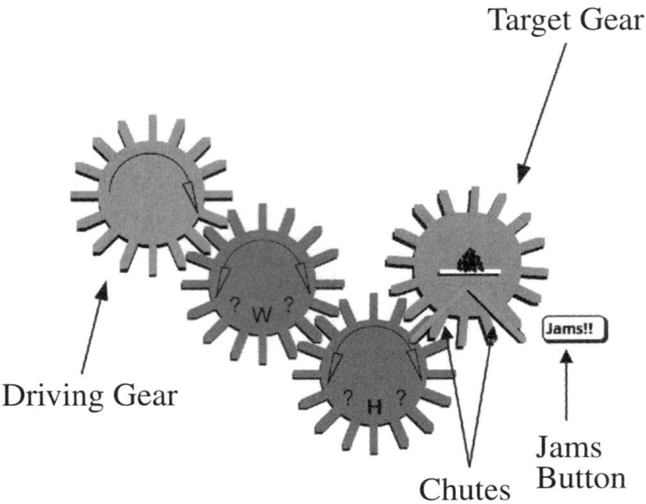

Figure 5.2
Sample of a gear problem used in studies by Stephen et al. Thanks to Damian Stephen for the figure.

pictured in figure 5.2, subjects are shown that the driving gear in the sequence is turning clockwise, and are asked to determine the direction of the target gear, with an intervening sequence of two connected gears. The subjects in these studies were adults and preschool children, who wore finger motion trackers as they solved a series of gear problems presented to them on a computer monitor.[4] Nearly all of the subjects began by employing the strategy of tracing the gears on the monitor with their fingers, and eventually switched to the strategy of alternating gears after some number of trials. (Because directly connected gears move in opposite directions, the first, third, fifth and so on gears in a train will turn in the same direction.) The moment of insight when the subject realizes that she can use the faster and more reliable alternating strategy is easily detected in the eye and finger tracking data. Most important for current purposes, this "a-ha!" moment is preceded by a spike in system entropy. That is, the finger movements exhibit critical fluctuations, indicating that the extended system solving the problem is a nonlinearly coupled dynamical system undergoing a phase transition of exactly the kind predicted by the HKB model. The problem solver's insight, the moment of the change in problem solving strategy, is a phase transition that predictably follows the critical fluctuations.

This work is a nonrepresentational dynamical explanation of a manifestly cognitive, representation-hungry activity. This can be seen by noting that there is a tradition in studying gear problems (and in cognitive psychological studies of problem solving, more generally) of referring to learning a new strategy for solving a problem as learning a new "representation" of the problem domain. Thus even Stephen et al. sometimes refer to the phase transitions as "learning a new representation" of the gear problems. They also point out that the new strategy has all of the features that lead cognitive psychologists to invoke representations: the new strategy is transferrable to new domains; it comes with a suite of predictable new behaviors; and it organizes activity at multiple levels. But Stephen et al. explain this new strategy in purely dynamical terms. That is, their experiments and models explain what cognitive psychologists typically refer to as a change in representation, but they do so without using representations as part of the explanation. Stephen and Dixon (in press) make this point emphatically, and argue that representational approaches are likely to be unable to account for insight. This example shows that radical embodied cognitive scientists can explain genuinely cognitive phenomena using an HKB-like model.

These eight cases demonstrate just what can be achieved with a model like HKB. It has been used to demonstrate that one can get quite far by modeling aspects of human behavior as a nonlinearly coupled dynamical system, that is, as oscillators whose coupling requires energy to be maintained. We have seen that this model can be used to produce explanations of activity at multiple scales relevant to psychology—coupled activity of brain areas, intrapersonal coordinated behavior, coupling of brain–body–environment systems, and interpersonal (i.e., social) coupling—and accounts for them using a unifying explanatory strategy. Thus these cases show that the lack of a posited underlying mechanism need not be a problem for radical embodied cognitive science. Radical embodied cognitive scientists can instead rely on a unifying model for a guide to discovery. A rich and extensible unifying model like HKB can provide, indeed has provided, suggestions for new experiments, which in turn lead to adjustments to the model, further new phenomena to study, and on and on. In the case of HKB, the model even points the way to its own successor. Kelso and Engstrøm say:

> After over 20 years of detailed study, it is probably time to put the more idealized HKB model of coordination to bed. It has served its purpose well. By explicitly showing that crucial observations about the stability and change of human behavior

> could be understood in terms of self-organizing dynamical systems, the HKB model stimulated a great deal of empirical research. (2006, 168)

Their explicit aim is to replace the HKB model with a more general science of coordination dynamics.

Given the success of the HKB model and the promise of its successor, there is reason to think the dynamical stance per se is a sufficient guide to discovery in cognitive science, as long as it is coupled with a fruitful and extensible unifying model. This shows that Boltzmann's arguments needn't worry us. We can be phenomenalists like Mach, or instrumentalists like Newton, who refused to hypothesize about the underlying cause of gravity. Though such instrumentalism is possible, many will find it unattractive. And indeed, as I noted above, the HKB model arose from the suggestions that coordination was the result of dissipative coordination of coupled oscillators, whose tenuous and temporary stability required energy to be maintained (Kugler, Kelso, and Turvey 1980). Although this, it is admitted, is rather vague, it is still a claim about what coordinative structures *are*. The payoff of this approach has been, of course, purely instrumental. In a series of works that followed (a few of which have just been recounted), the vague suggestion concerning what coordinated structures *are* bore fruit in more concrete suggestions concerning how such structures were to be *modeled*. So the significant advances to our understanding that have been brought about by the HKB model are not purely instrumental in origin, even if they are in practice. This will not be enough to satisfy those who are dissatisfied with instrumentalism, those who wish to be realists of some kind. (See chapter 9.) For them, the dynamical stance with HKB as a unifying model will not be attractive. Another reason to worry is that the HKB model is a model of coordinated activity, and a good deal of cognition seems not to be coordinated activity. For these reasons, the radical embodied cognitive scientist may want something more in the way of a guide to discovery. In the rest of this chapter, and then in more detail in the following chapters, I will recommend Gibson's ecological psychology as the guide to discovery for radical embodied cognitive science. Ecological psychology will serve as a guide to discovery differently from the way HKB did; ecological psychology will be a unifying background *theory*, rather than a unified model. But having ecological psychology as a unifying background theory will not conflict with dynamical modeling, including HKB. Dynamical modeling will retain its role in explaining cognition as part of a bigger picture of the nature of cognition.

5.2 Transitional Material

The dynamical stance, with HKB as a unifying model, has just been shown to be a workable guide to discovery for radical embodied cognitive science. Indeed, HKB-based science has been extraordinarily successful in accounting for phenomena and for spurring new studies of coordinated, rhythmic behavior. Yet I have also just suggested that HKB-as-guide-to-discovery is not fully satisfactory, and for two reasons. First, it does not give an account of what cognition *is*, but rather tells us how to model it and only under some rather unusual circumstances: finger wagging just is not something most people do most of the time. I should point out that this is not particularly damning. Most experiments work by putting subjects in unusual circumstances and getting them to perform unusual tasks, and models only account for these highly simplified circumstances. Still, what is wanted is a theory of what cognition is, a true competitor to the theory that cognition is computation. As we saw in chapter 4, the dynamical stance must be instrumentalist to avoid representationalism, and *qua* instrumentalist it cannot tell us what cognition is. One can, of course, adopt an empiricist or positivist attitude (e.g., van Fraassen 1980, 2002) that just accepts this as the role of science. This is surely a defensible philosophical move, but not one that most are willing to make. A second worry cannot be placated by the adoption of a defensible, though counterintuitive, philosophy of science. We must wonder just how much of cognition is a matter of coordination. Before stating the obvious, I want to make clear that a lot more of cognition can be accounted for as coordinated behavior than one might realize intuitively. Look, for example, at the "cases" described in the previous section, especially the extensions to speech, cognition, and the workings of the brain. Then consider how much of our action involves coordination of our body parts, or of doing something in a pattern that is partly determined by an external source. It is quite easy to draw a lot of intelligent behavior under the coordination umbrella.

Now for the obvious: there is also a lot of cognition that will be getting wet. (Because it's not under the metaphorical coordination umbrella.) Not everything that cognitive science wants to explain is coordinated activity. The upshot of these two worries is a push toward an explanatory structure that is (1) broader and (2) tells us what cognition is—a push, that is, toward a *theory* of cognition. The theory recommended here is ecological psychology, which I introduced briefly in chapter 2. In the rest of this chapter, I will discuss ecological psychology itself only briefly. Mostly I will focus on how it can serve as a guide to discovery for radical embodied cognitive science.

5.3 Guide to Discovery 2: Ecological Psychology

In chapter 2, I introduced Gibson's ecological psychology as a commitment to three principles. Here they are again, slightly less briefly.

Principle 1: Perception is direct To claim that perception is direct is to claim that perception is not the result of mental gymnastics, of inferences performed on sensory representations. The direct perception view is anti-representationalism about perception, so it is just the right kind of theory of perception for radical embodied cognitive science. When an animal perceives something directly, the animal is in nonmediated contact with that thing. This implies, of course, that the perceiving isn't inside the animal, but rather is part of a system that includes both the animal and the perceived object. The idea of direct perception is intimately intertwined with a particular theory of environmental information. I will discuss both in detail in chapter 6.

Principle 2: Perception is for action The purpose of perception is for the generation and control of action. It is usually added to this that a good deal of action is also for perception or cognition. The intimate, two-way connection between perception and action has an immediate ring of evolutionary plausibility, and has been the rallying cry of the whole of the embodied cognition movement, radical or otherwise.

Principle 3: Perception is of affordances This third principle actually follows from the first two. If perception is direct (i.e., noninferential) and for the guidance of action, there must be information sufficient for guiding action available in the environment. Gibson introduces affordances to fill this role. Affordances are often misunderstood, and their precise nature is the subject of significant controversy both within the ecological psychology and in the wider cognitive science communities (Turvey 1992; Reed 1996; Heft 1989, 2001; Chemero 2003a, 2008; Stoffregen 2003; Scarantino 2003; Chemero and Turvey 2007a,b). For now, it is sufficient to say that affordances are environmental opportunities for action. Because affordances are supposed to be objective features of the environment and dependent in some sense on animals, it is difficult to say exactly what kind of things affordances are. (Gibson himself said some unusual things.) For the moment, I ask that you take affordances to be directly perceivable opportunities for action and trust that one can tell a coherent story about the ontological nature of affordances. (Chapter 7 will tell such a story.)

The next two chapters will make all of this clear. For now, I would like simply to suggest that a theory based on these three principles can serve as a guide to discovery for radical embodied cognitive science, providing a background theory about what cognition is that can be part of a successful scientific endeavor. To do so, ecological psychology has to provide a nonrepresentational background theory that allows the generation of hypotheses for testing. One way it might do so is by licensing *models* of cognition in which representational explanation gets no foothold. The easiest argument that ecological psychology might serve as a guide to discovery for radical embodied cognitive science by licensing nonrepresentational dynamical models comes from the fact that it already has done so. For example, the HKB model is fully compatible with, indeed is inspired by, ecological psychology. The point, then, is that the HKB model is a crucial explanatory tool for ecological psychology, and ecological psychology includes much more that is helpful to radical embodied cognitive science to boot. To start in explaining this, I will need to say a few things about how I understand the relationship between theories and models. None of the claims I make about this relationship are original and they are not intended to be controversial, though perhaps they are among philosophers of science. As a way to sidestep some controversies, I will point out that the views on models described below are much less influenced by careful consideration of the arguments and counterarguments of philosophers of science (though I have considered many of these of course) than by my own (admittedly limited) experience as a modeler and from conversations and collaborations with expert dynamical modelers in the cognitive sciences. So, although I suspect that the relationship between theories and models described in the next few paragraphs is generally correct, those who strongly disagree are invited to imagine that the claims are limited to the use of dynamical models in the cognitive and neural sciences. That said...

In general, theories are far too complex to be tested against empirical phenomena (Hartmann 1999). Consider as an example recent evolutionary psychologys (for overviews, see Barkow, Cosmides, and Tooby 1992; Buller 2005; Richardson 2007). According to evolutionary psychology, the mind is composed of a very large number of largely independent, evolutionarily hardwired, computational modules, each of which has its own job in the cognitive economy. Or consider the hypothesis, less outlandish in my view, that we've been discussing so far: the mind is a dynamical system incorporating aspects of brain, body, and environment. Neither of these theories can be directly tested against actual phenomena. First, in both cases, the theories are simply too complex to be *computationally* tractable. The number of modules in the former case and the number of variables and parameters in the latter are simply too great. Furthermore, in the case of the dynamical hypothesis, the differential equations are *analytically* intractable; there is simply no way to solve them. The same is true in all the natural sciences: theories typically contain or imply equations that are not solvable. (Cartwright 1983, 1999 makes this case about physics; Winsberg 2001 does so for fluid dynamics.)

This is where models come in. Models are tractable, both computationally and analytically, relatives of theory, whose role is to put theory in mediated contact with data. The first, easiest step is to turn analytically intractable differential equations into solvable difference equations. After this, it gets more complex, for in almost no case is a model strictly derived from theory, and every theory is compatible with many models, even many conflicting models of the same group of phenomena. Modeling is, to use a cliché, an art form. Models necessarily bring in simplifications and assumptions that are not strictly part of the theory, and often include ad hoc elements, approximations, and guesses, among other kinds of theory-external sorcery. This motley of modeling techniques is aimed at satisfying two ends simultaneously. First and foremost, models account for the data that have been collected without being necessitated by the data—there are always many models that will account for data. Secondarily, models must respect the theory, so that in some unformalizable way they seem appropriate to the theory despite the aforementioned modeler's artistry.[5]

Given this pair of relationships, theory–model and model–data, we can see that the way for theory to come into contact with the world is via models. Thus one important criterion for goodness of theory is its fruitfulness as a source of models that can then be applied to data. Boltzmann's guide to discovery argument criticized phenomenological physics because it had no means of predicting as-yet-unobserved phenomena to test and extend it as a theory. We can see now that the real problem that Boltzmann pointed to is that phenomenological physics is not a theory at all, it is a set of models created on the fly to be applied to incoming data.[6] In the first part of this chapter, I argued that basing a science on a model is not necessarily inappropriate, so long as that model is widely applicable and easily extensible. Yet we can also, as in atomistic physics, base our science on a theory, which in turn can generate models to be applied to data. The appropriateness of a theory as a guide to discovery, then, is partly a function of how well it does at generating models for application to laboratory findings (as well as for hypothesis generation, etc.). We can apply this to the appropriateness of ecological psychology as a guide to discovery for radical embodied cognitive science.

Ecological psychology, in addition to providing a rich background theory of the nature of cognition, perception, and action, has generated several models that have been just as flexible and extensible as HKB. Gibson's work on ecological psychology describes an exceptionally complex world, and complex relations between perceivers and that world. There is no mathematics anywhere in Gibson's theory. Yet ecological psychology has been exceptional as a producer of successful mathematical models. As noted above, HKB grew from a paper by Kugler, Kelso, and Turvey (1980). At the time of the writing of that paper, all three were working at both Haskin's Laboratory at Yale and Center for the Ecological Study of Perception and Action at the University of Connecticut (the latter, the hub of the ecological psychology world). Their goal was to account for action in a way that respected Gibsonian ecological psychology, so that the control of action was not the result of a centralized executive making plans based on representations of the environment. Gibson's solution to this problem, like his solution to most problems, was in terms of the environment surrounding the animal: he argued that the information in the surrounding environment was sufficient to control behavior (without, that is, mentally added information, computation, or inference, and without a mentally represented plan). Kugler, Kelso, and Turvey asked how that information could actually generate the action. More particularly, they asked how action could be organized without being the result of mental gymnastics. The answer they came up with was that action is *self-organized*. This answer led to the finger-wagging experiments and to the models that explained them.

There is no sense, of course, in which the three tenets of Gibsonian ecological psychology logically imply the HKB model. A bit of mathematics (the beginning of the Fourier sequence) was pulled off the shelf by modelers who knew tricks of the trade; then a phenomenon (finger wagging) was produced in the lab; then over several years the math was tweaked to fit the details of the produced phenomenon. The only thing specifically Gibsonian about the model is that it describes the created phenomena in a way that is acceptable to ecological psychologists: without mental representations, with a direct link between perception and action, and so on.

Thus one way that ecological psychology acts as a guide to discovery for radical embodied cognitive science is in virtue of inspiring nonrepresentational, mathematical models like HKB. HKB is not the only such model that was inspired by ecological psychology. I will discuss two others: the optical variable τ as a model of the information available that specifies time-to-contact and the inertial tensor as a model of haptic information for affordances. I will discuss these two models in some detail in the next two chapters. The variable τ will be discussed in chapter 6 on information; the inertial tensor will be discussed in chapter 7 on affordances.

5.4 Wrap Up

In this chapter we've seen two related ways for radical embodied cognitive science to have a guide to discovery. There are no doubt others. First, one might pursue the instrumentalist dynamical stance, using highly extensible dynamical models such as HKB. We've seen that HKB has served as a guide to discovery, prompting a series of further studies and changes to its basic form to account for new data, and even inspiring its own successor. Alternatively, one might pursue the dynamical stance in concert with a background theory, such as Gibsonian ecological psychology. Ecological psychology is appropriate here because it provides the inspiration for several dynamical models, and provides a story of what cognition is really like, one that does not license representational interpretations. In the next few chapters, I will pursue this second course, dynamical modeling plus ecological psychology as an antirepresentational background theory. This, I think, is the best way to pursue radical embodied cognitive science. To this end, the next several chapters will be devoted to making sense of Gibson's ecological approach. Specifically, I will outline conceptual stories about direct perception and information (chapter 6) and about affordances (chapter 7).

III Ecological Psychology

The rules that govern behavior are not like laws enforced by an authority or decisions made by a commander: behavior is regular without being regulated. The question is how this can be.

—James J. Gibson, *The Ecological Approach to Visual Perception* (1979)

6 Information and Direct Perception

The purpose of this chapter and the next is to describe Gibsonian ecological psychology and to show that it can serve as an appropriate theoretical backdrop for radical embodied cognitive science. It hardly makes sense to do so other than in the context of the theoretical work of Michael Turvey, Robert Shaw, and William Mace. Since the 1970s, Turvey, Shaw, and Mace have worked on the formulation of a philosophically sound and empirically tractable version of James Gibson's ecological psychology. It is surely no exaggeration to say that without their theoretical work ecological psychology would have died on the vine because of high-profile attacks from establishment cognitive scientists (e.g., Fodor and Pylyshyn 1981). But thanks to Turvey, Shaw, and Mace's work as theorists and, perhaps more important, as teachers, ecological psychology is currently flourishing. A generation of students, having been trained by Turvey, Shaw, and Mace at Trinity College and/or the University of Connecticut, are now distinguished experimental psychologists who train their own students in Turvey-Shaw-Mace ecological psychology. Despite the undeniable and lasting importance of Turvey, Shaw, and Mace's theoretical contributions for psychology and the other cognitive sciences, their work has not received much attention from philosophers. It will get some of that attention in the next two chapters. I will point to shortcomings in the Turvey-Shaw-Mace approach to ecological psychology, and will offer what I take to be improved versions of each of the four main components of it. In this chapter, I will describe theories of information[1] and of direct perception that differ from the Turvey-Shaw-Mace account; in the next chapter I will tackle affordances and abilities.

Given the debt that those of us interested in ecological psychology owe to Turvey, Shaw, and Mace, this, no doubt, seems ungrateful.[2] Perhaps it is. But I would argue that because of the success of the Turvey-Shaw-Mace approach to ecological psychology, the field has become a true contender in psychology, cognitive science, and artificial intelligence. Given the stability of ecological psychology and its standing as a research program, it can withstand some questioning of the assumptions on which its current practice is founded. This is especially the case if the questioning is aimed at firming up foundations rather than tearing down the house.

6.1 Gibson on Direct Perception and Information

Gibson's posthumous magnum opus, *The Ecological Approach to Visual Perception* (1979), is perhaps alone among books about perception in devoting nearly 50 percent of its pages to discussion of the nature of the environment that animals perceive. This half of the book is a description of Gibson's theory of the information available for vision, which goes hand in hand with his theory of visual perception. There are two main points to Gibson's theory of perception. First, Gibson disagreed with the tradition that took the purpose of visual perception to be the internal reconstruction of the three-dimensional environment from two-dimensional inputs. Instead, the function of perception is the guidance of adaptive action. Second, Gibson (1966, 1979) rejected classical views of perception in which perception results from the addition or processing of information in the mind to physically caused sensation; that is, he rejected perception as mental gymnastics. This information-processing way of understanding perception, Gibson thought, places an unbridgeable gap between the mind (where the information is added, and the perception happens) and the world (where the merely physical light causally interacts with the retina). Instead, Gibson argued, perception is a direct—noninferential, noncomputational—process, in which information is gathered or picked up in active exploration the environment.

Combined, these two theses give rise to Gibson's most well-known contribution, his theory of affordances (Gibson 1979; see chapter 7 for a detailed story about affordances). If perception is direct, no information is added in the mind; if perception also guides behavior, the environment must contain sufficient information for the animal to guide its behavior. That is, the environment must contain information that specifies opportunities for behavior. In other words, the environment must contain information that specifies affordances. These views place significant constraints on the theory of information that Gibson can offer. First, because it is used in noninferential perception, information must be both ubiquitous in the environment and largely unambiguous; second, because perception also guides behavior, the information in the environment must specify opportunities for behavior, which is to say it must specify affordances. Although the theory of information outlined in Gibson 1979 does meet these criteria quite nicely, it is spelled out in too plainspoken a manner to be convincing to most philosophically inclined readers.[3] I will try to do better here.

The first thing to know about what Gibson meant when he used the word "information" is that he was not talking about information as described by Shannon and Weaver. ("The information for perception, unhappily, cannot be defined and measured as Claude Shannon's information can be," Gibson 1979, 243.) The best first pass at an understanding of what Gibson *did* mean by "information" is his distinction between stimulation and stimulus information. To see the difference, consider standing in a uniformly bright, densely fog-filled room. In such a room, your retinal cells are stimulated. The light in the room enters your eye and excites the rods and cones. But there is no information carried by the light that stimulates your retina. This is the case because the uniform white light that converges on the eye from the various parts of the room and is focused by the eye's lens does not specify the structure of the room. So stimulation, the excitement of sensory cells, is not in itself information and is not, therefore, sufficient for perception. The differences between the normal environment and the fog-filled room are instructive. In the fog-filled room, the light that converges on any point that could be occupied by an observer's head and eyes has been scattered by the fog. Thus, when it reaches the observer it has not come directly from any surface in the room, and hence cannot inform the subject about the surfaces in the room. In the more typical, nonfoggy situation, the light that reaches any point in the room has been reflected off the room's surfaces. The chemical makeup, texture, and overall shape of the surfaces off which the light reflects determine the characteristics of the light. Since surfaces are interfaces of substances with the air in the room, the nature of the surfaces is, in turn, determined by the substances that make them up. This set of facts is what allows the light that converges at any point to carry information about the substances in the environment. It also allows animals whose heads occupy the point to learn about their environment by sampling the light.[4]

This story allows us to understand what it is for light (or other energy) to carry information, but it says nothing about what sort of thing information is. When Gibson and his followers claim that information is ubiquitous, are they saying that in addition to the substances, objects, and energies in the room, there is extra stuff, the information? Yes and no. Yes: information is a real, unproblematic aspect of the environment. But information is not a kind of measurable, quantifiable stuff that exists alongside the objects or substances in the environment. Instead, information is a relational feature of the environment. In particular, the light converging on some point of observation is in a particular relationship to the surfaces in the room, that of having bounced off those surfaces and passed through a relatively transparent medium before arriving at the point. The information in the light *just is* this relation between the light and the environment.[5]

A few quick points about this. First, note that information relation between the light and the surfaces does not hold in the case of a fog-filled room. So the light in this case bears no information about layout of the environment. Second, it is worth noting that this way of understanding information allows it to be ubiquitous in the environment. Light reflected from surfaces in the environment converges at every point in the environment. Third, the information in the environment is more or less complete: the light converging at every point has reflected off *all* of the nonobstructed surfaces. Fourth, and most important for Gibson's project, is that the light can contain information that specifies affordances. To see this, a little needs to be said about affordances. (Much more will be said in chapter 7.)

Affordances are opportunities for behavior. Because different animals have different abilities, affordances are relative to the behavioral abilities of the animals that perceive them. In some cases, these abilities are significantly related to an animal's height. To take just two examples, Warren (1984) has established a relationship between leg length and stair climbing affordances, and Jiang and Mark (1994) have established a relationship between eye height and the perception of gap-crossing affordances.[6] Given the relationship between height and some affordances, information about height is also (partial) information about affordances. Remember that at every point in the environment reflected light converges from the surfaces in the environment. Among these surfaces is the ground, so one relatively obvious source of information concerning height is the light reflected from the ground beneath the point of observation. Sedgewick (1973) points out a less obvious source of information: the horizon cuts across objects at a height that is equal to the height of the point of observation. That is, whenever light is reflected to some point in the environment from the horizon and also from some object between that point and the horizon, the light will contain information about the height of the point of observation relative to the height of the object. Of course, information about the height of a point of observation is also information about the height of an animal. So, at least for the types of affordances that have some relationship to an animal's height (reaching, stair climbing, gap crossing), there is information in the light about the affordances. More generally, this means that information in light is not just about the things the light bounces off. It is also information about the perceiver and the relation between the perceiver and the environment. Gibson put this point by saying that proprioception and exteroception imply one another.

We will look at affordances in detail in the next chapter. For now, the following are the key points of this brief description of Gibson's theory of the information available in the environment for perception.

1. Information for perception is not Shannon-Weaver information.
2. Ontologically speaking, information is a relation between energy in the environment (light, vibrations, etc.) and the substances and surfaces in the environment.
3. Along with the substances and surfaces of the environment, the energy in the environment also contains information about animals that perceive it and about what is afforded to these animals.
4. Because of (3), information can be used by animals to guide behavior directly. That is, information about affordances can guide behavior without mental gymnastics.

6.2 The Turvey-Shaw-Mace Approach

Gibson's ecological theory of vision (Gibson 1979) was intended as a response to the increasing dominance of computational theories of mind. Unsurprisingly, Gibson's ideas were not widely accepted by cognitive scientists upon their appearance. Indeed, as noted above, they were subjected to withering criticism from an establishment in psychology that was committed to understanding perception and cognition as mental gymnastics. The ecological approach was not helped by Gibson's writing style, which, though highly readable, was often imprecise.

Enter Michael Turvey, Robert Shaw, and William Mace. Along with a few colleagues, Turvey, Shaw, and Mace wrote a series of papers outlining a detailed philosophical account of the ontology and epistemology of Gibson's ecological approach (Shaw and McIntyre 1974; Mace 1977; Turvey 1977; Turvey and Shaw 1979; Shaw, Turvey, and Mace 1982; Turvey, Shaw, Reed, and Mace 1981[7]). The most complete and rigorous of these papers is Turvey et al.'s 1981 reply to criticism from Fodor and Pylyshyn, so I will focus my discussion of the Turvey-Shaw-Mace view on this work.[8] The goal of Turvey et al. 1981, stated in the first sentence, is to provide a more precise explication of Gibson's work, specifically his claim that "there are ecological laws relating organisms to the affordances of the environment" (237). There are four key notions here, which come in pairs: the first pair is affordance and effectivity; the second is ecological law and information. I will look at them in order, suppressing as much formalism as possible. On the Turvey-Shaw-Mace view, an object *X* affords an activity *Y* for an organism *Z* just in case there are dispositional properties of object *X* that are complemented by dispositional properties of organism *Z*, and the manifestation of those dispositional properties is the occurrence of activity *Y*. Conversely, an organism *Z* can effect the activity *Y* with respect to object *X* just in case there are dispositional properties of *Z* that are complemented by dispositional properties of object *X*, and the manifestation of those dispositional properties is the occurrence of activity *Y*. The idea here is that affordances, or opportunities for behavior, are dispositions of things in the environment to support particular behaviors, and effectivities are dispositions of animals to undertake those behaviors in the right circumstances. Thus, a copy of *Infinite Jest* has the affordance "climbability" for mice in virtue of certain properties of the book (height, width, stability, etc.) and of the mouse (muscle strength, flexibility, leg length, etc.); the mouse has the effectivity "being-able-to-climb" in virtue of the same properties of the mouse and the book. The dispositional affordance and effectivity complement one another in that the climbing-of-book-by-mouse occurs only when the climbability and the being-able-to-climb interact. This, according to the Turvey-Shaw-Mace view, is what affordances and effectivities are.

To understand how organisms perceive and take advantage of affordances, and, in particular, how they do so directly, Turvey et al. define information and natural law. As with affordances and effectivities, the definitions of information and ecological law interact. Ecological laws, according to the Turvey-Shaw-Mace view, are quite different than they are according to what they term the *establishment/extensional analysis*. Most of the differences don't matter to us here, so I will focus on just one key point of ecological laws: their being bound to contexts. According to Turvey et al., ecological laws are defined only within settings and do not apply universally. Thus, the ecological laws relating to things in the niche of mice do not necessarily hold in outer space, or even in the niches of mackerel or fruit flies. So, instead of taking laws to be universal relationships between properties as the "establishment/extensional analysis" does, Turvey et al. say that properties-in-environments *specify*, or uniquely correspond to, other properties-in-environments. The most important ecological laws on the Turvey-Shaw-Mace view are those relating ambient energy to properties in the environment, for example, those relating patterns in the the light of the optic array to affordances. Thus, in virtue of ecological laws, particular patterns of the ambient optic array specify the presence of affordances in particular environments. It is this specification that allows the arrays to *carry information* about the affordances: because there is a lawful connection between patterns in ambient energy and the properties specified by those patterns, organisms can learn, or be informed about, the properties by sensing the patterns. Crucially, among the properties about which information is carried in the array are affordances.

Here's what we have so far: Ecological laws make it such that ambient arrays specify properties (including affordances), and this specification is what makes the arrays carriers of information. The presence of this kind of information underwrites direct perception. If the information required to guide behavior is available in the environment, then organisms can guide their behavior just by picking that information up. Ecological laws guarantee that if a particular pattern is present in the optic array in a mouse's niche, affordances for climbing by mice are also present. Hence perception of those properties can be direct. This view of direct perception is clearly represented by Shaw's principle of symmetry (Shaw and McIntyre 1974; Turvey 1990a). We can represent the symmetry principle as follows. Let E = "The environment is the way it is," I = "The information is the way it is," and P = "Perception is the way it is." Also, let ">" stand for the logical relation of adjunction, a nontransitive conjunction that we can read as "specifies." Then, the symmetry principle is

$$[(E > I) \& (I > P)] \& [(P > I) \& (I > E)].$$

In English, this says: "That the environment is the way it is specifies that information is the way it is and that information is the way it is specifies that perception is the way it is, and that perception is the way it is specifies that the information is the way it is and that information is the way it is specifies that the environment is the way it is." We can simplify this to say that the environment specifies the information, which specifies perception, and perception specifies the information, which specifies the environment. This principle is symmetrical in that the environment, information, and perception determine one another. This, on the Turvey-Shaw-Mace view, is what it is for perception to be direct. By law, the environment determines the information, which determines the perception. This makes the perception a lawful guarantee of the presence of the information and also of the environment. So direct perception is perception that, by ecological law, is guaranteed accurate.

6.3 Issues with the Turvey-Shaw-Mace Approach

The Turvey-Shaw-Mace approach is a sensible and faithful account of an epistemology and ontology to accompany Gibsonian ecological psychology. I think, though, that there are problems with the account. Over the last several years, I have developed an alternative ontological and epistemological background for ecological psychology, one that attempts to be equally faithful to Gibson's vision. I will restrict my comments here to differences concerning direct perception and information. I will have some critical comments about the Turvey-Shaw-Mace view of affordances in chapter 7. The main problem with the Turvey-Shaw-Mace account of information is that, by insisting that information depends on natural law, they have made it such that there is too little information available for direct perception. In particular, on the Turvey-Shaw-Mace view, there is no information about individuals, in social settings, or in natural language. I will discuss these in order.

On individuals Because Turvey, Shaw, and Mace take direct perception to be infallible, they insist that it be underwritten by information, which is, in turn, underwritten by natural law. They are careful to maintain that the laws in question are *ecological* laws, laws that hold only in particular niches. Thus laws need not be universal in order to allow information to be carried in the environment. But, of course, ecological laws must still be general in that they apply to a variety of individuals. For example, there would be an ecological law that connects a particular optical structure, a visible texture, to the bark of a particular kind of tree: in the environment of gray squirrels, say, optical structure *O* is present only when light has reflected off a silver maple. Note that making the ecological law niche specific makes it so that the presence of optical pattern *O* in other environments, where lighting conditions or tree species differ, doesn't affect *O*'s information carrying in the squirrel's environment. So far so good, but in each gray squirrel's environment there are a few trees that have special affordances in that, unlike most trees in the environment, they contain nests. There are no ecological laws relating these trees, as individuals, to properties of the optic array, so there is no information about these trees, as individuals, available to the squirrels. This, of course, does not apply only to trees. If information depends on laws, ecological or otherwise, there is also no information about individual people available for perception. So although a human infant might have information available about humans, she has none about her mother. So, on the Turvey-Shaw-Mace view, either babies do not perceive their mothers (because the information for direct perception is unavailable) or they do not perceive them directly. I take it that either alternative is unacceptable to radical embodied cognitive scientists.

On social and linguistic information Another facet of the Turvey-Shaw-Mace requirement of lawlike regularities for information to be present is that no information can be carried in virtue of conventions. Conventions hold, when they do, by public agreement or acquiescence and thus are easily violated. Because of an error at the factory or a practical joke, a milk carton may not contain milk and a beer can may not contain beer. This is true in any context in which milk cartons and beer cans appear. Similarly, through ignorance or dishonesty, spoken and written sentences can be false and words can be used to refer to nonstandard objects. In fact, these things happen all the time even in the environments where the conventions in question are supposed to be most strongly enforced, for example, at the grocery store or presidential press conferences. None of this is to imply that there is no information to be picked up at grocery stores or when the president speaks. Ecological laws determine the way that collections of aluminum cans in a cardboard box will structure fluorescent light and the way exhalations through vocal cords that pass by moving mouth, lips, tongue, and teeth will structure the comparatively still air. So there is information that there are cans on the shelf and that the president has said that he and the prime minister use the same toothpaste. But, because these things are merely conventionally determined and conventions may be violated, there is no information concerning the presence of beer or the president's toothpaste of choice. And since direct perception depends on the presence of such information, we must, according to the Turvey-Shaw-Mace view, perceive that there is Boddingtons in the cans and that the president and prime minister use the same toothpaste either indirectly, or not at all.

Radical embodied cognitive scientists require theories of information and direct perception that allow children to directly perceive their mothers and for beer cans to inform us about the presence of beer. This requires different accounts of what it is for perception to be direct and of the nature of information. Before presenting my alternative views of information and direct perception, I should point out that there is an active controversy in the ecological psychology community over what I'm calling the Turvey-Shaw-Mace view of information. In recent years, mounting empirical evidence gathered by ecological psychologists indicates that humans regularly use nonspecifying variables to perceive, in successful perception and in perceptual learning (Jacobs, Michaels, and Runeson 2000; Jacobs, Runeson, and Michaels 2001; Fajen 2005; Withagen and Michaels 2005; Jacobs and Michaels 2007; Withagen and Chemero 2009). But according to the Turvey-Shaw-Mace view, a variable that does not specify (i.e., is not lawfully connected to) a particular environmental feature cannot carry information about that feature. There is mounting evidence, that is, that the Turvey-Shaw-Mace view of information is inadequate. So, even if you are unconvinced by the philosophical arguments I have offered against the Turvey-Shaw-Mace view, there are other compelling reasons to worry about it. Among those who have felt compelled to worry are Jacobs and Michaels (2007), who offer a theory of learning that attempts to rescue most of the Turvey-Shaw-Mace view. I am less confident that it is savable.

6.4 An Alternative Approach to Direct Perception

On the Turvey-Shaw-Mace approach, direct perception is defined as perception that is grounded in ecological law, so is always accurate. Indeed, Turvey et al. (1981, 245) define *perception itself* as direct and law-governed. As argued above, this rules out information about, and so direct perception of, individuals and things partly determined by convention. To make it possible for these things to be perceived directly, we need a different understanding of direct perception. In this section, I describe perception as direct when and only when it is noninferential, where being noninferential does not guarantee accuracy. Direct perception is perception that does not involve mental representations. This understanding of direct perception, I would argue, is what Gibson had in mind. For example, he writes: "When I assert that perception of the environment is direct, I mean that it is not mediated by retinal pictures, neural pictures, or mental pictures" (Gibson, 1979, 147).

We can get started in seeing what this kind of direct perception is by recalling Brian Cantwell Smith's notions of *effective* and *noneffective tracking*, already described in chapter 3. An outfielder effectively tracks a fly ball when the light reflecting off the ball makes contact with her eyes, and she moves her eyes and head so as to maintain that contact. In terms of the physics of the situation, the ball, the outfielder, and the intervening medium are just one connected thing. In effective tracking, that is, the outfielder, the ball and the light reflected from the ball to the outfielder form a single coupled system. No explanatory purchase is gained by invoking representations here: in effective tracking, any internal parts of the agent that one might call mental representations are causally coupled with their targets. This effective tracking is direct perception. We can also have direct perception during *noneffective tracking*. Often an animal must continue to track an object despite disruption of causal connection. The outfielder, that is, must be able to continue to track the fly ball even when the light reflected from it is (temporarily) unavailable, as when her head turns directly past the low, late-afternoon sun. This noneffective tracking, though, also does not require mental representation. There are three reasons for this. First, noneffective tracking could be accomplished just by causal connection and momentum. The head's momentum keeps it going that way, and the light coming directly from the sun no longer overwhelms that reflecting off the ball. Second, as Gibson points out, perception is an activity, and as such happens over time. So directly perceiving something may involve periods of time when it is being tracked effectively and periods when it is tracked noneffectively. Third, and this is getting ahead of myself because I haven't said what information is yet, there is still information in the light about something that is temporarily occluded. Thus we can have direct, that is nonrepresentational, perception even when tracking is noneffective.[9]

There are two relevant consequences of taking tracking as the model of direct perception. First, we can see that perception is, by definition, direct. Perception is always a matter of tracking something that is present in the environment. Because animals are coupled to the perceived when they track it, there is never need to call upon representations during tracking. Effective and noneffective tracking are nonrepresentational, hence direct. Explaining how we write novels or plan vacations might require invoking something like a representation in the sense of strong decoupling described in chapter 3. But perception never does.

The second consequence of taking tracking as the model of direct perception is that perception can be direct and mistaken. First, and perhaps obviously, when tracking is noneffective, it is possible for the animal to lose track of its object. The fox might stop behind the rock, yet the bird's head and eyes might keep moving along the path that the fox was following. This kind of minor error is typically easily corrected, of course. Another possibility is when an animal is coupled with an inappropriate object. For example, the same optical pattern can be caused by a full moon and a lightbulb on a cloudy night. And there will be the same sort of continuous column of disturbance connecting a moth to each. So the moth will be effectively tracking whichever of the two it happens to be connected with. When the moth is effectively tracking the lightbulb, it is making a mistake. But this does not mean that it is tracking the bulb via a mental representation of the moon. For if it did, then it would also be tracking the moon via a mental representation of the moon when it was doing things correctly, and perception would never be direct. Instead, the moth is directly perceiving the moon or misperceiving the lightbulb via a nonspecifying optical variable (Withagen 2004; see also Withagen and Chemero 2009). A variable is nonspecifying when its presence is not one–one correlated with some object in the environment. Like the moth when it is coupled with the moon, many animals rely on nonspecifying variables. Yet according to the Turvey-Shaw-Mace view, nonspecifying variables do not carry information about the environment, and so cannot be used for perception, direct or otherwise. So to make sense of the moth's effective coupling with the moon as a case of direct perception, we need a different theory of information, according to which nonspecifying variables can carry information. The same is true if we want to understand my perception of beer-presence in beer cans and meanings in words.

6.5 An Alternative Approach to Information

There is a theory of information that has considerable currency in cognitive science that is consistent with Gibsonian information: Barwise and Perry's (1981, 1983) *situation semantics*, discussed briefly in chapter 2, and the extensions of it by Israel and Perry (1990), Devlin (1991), and Barwise and Seligman (1997). Situation semantics is a good candidate here because Barwise and Perry's realism about information was directly influenced by Gibson. Barwise and Perry (1981, 1983) developed situation semantics in order to, as they said, bring ontology back to semantics. That is, they were interested in a semantics based on how the world is, and not on minds, knowledge, or mental representations. Information according to this view is a part of the natural world, there to be exploited by animals, though it exists whether or not any animals actually do exploit it. According to situation semantics, information exists in *situations*, which are roughly local, incomplete possible worlds. Suppose we have situation token *s*1, which of type *S*1, and situation token *s*2, which is of type *S*2. Then situation token *s*1 carries information about situation token *s*2 just in case there is some *constraint* linking the type *S*2 to the type *S*1. Constraints are connections between situation types. See figure 6.1. To use the classic situation semantics example (Barwise and Perry 1983; Israel and Perry 1990; Barwise and Seligman 1994), consider the set of all situations of type *X*, in which there is an x-ray with a pattern of type *P*. Because patterns of type *P* on x-rays are caused by veterinarians taking x-rays of dogs with broken legs, there will be a constraint connecting situations of type *X* with situations of type *D*,

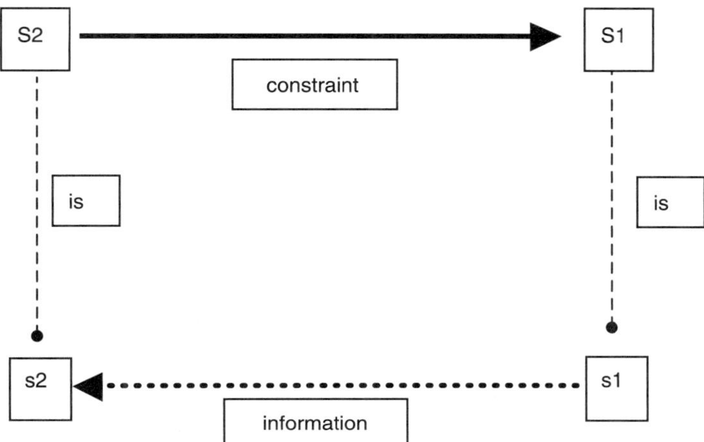

Figure 6.1
The information relationship. Lowercase *s*1 and *s*2 are tokens of capitalized types *S*1 and *S*2, respectively.

those in which there is a dog with a broken leg that visits a veterinarian. Given this, the fact that a situation *x* is of type *X* carries the information that there is a situation *d* (possibly identical to x) of type *D* in which some dog has a broken leg. See figure 6.2.

For our purposes, there are two things to note about this example. First, the constraint between the situation types is doing all the work. That is, the information that exists in the environment exists because of the constraint, and for some animal to use the information the animal must be aware of the constraint.[10] This feature is true not just of the example of the unfortunate dog, but holds generally of information in situation semantics. The second point is that the constraint in the example holds because of a causal regularity that holds among dog bones, x-ray machines, and x-rays. That is, the particular x-ray bears the information about the particular dog's leg because, given the laws of nature and the way x-ray machines are designed, broken dog legs *cause* x-rays with patterns of type *P*. This feature of the example does *not* hold more generally of information in situation semantics. That is, constraints between situation types can hold in virtue of law-governed, causal connections, but they can also hold in virtue of customs, conventions, and other regularities. So a situation with smoke of a particular type can bear information about the existence of fire by natural law, but it can also bear information about the decisions of tribal elders by conventions governing the semantics of smoke signals.

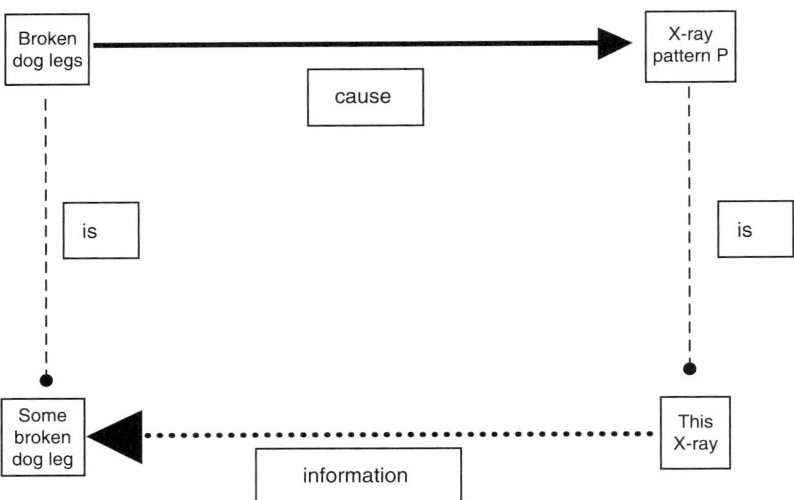

Figure 6.2
Information carried by an x-ray. *This X-ray* is a token of type *X-ray pattern P*; *Some broken dog leg* is a token of type *Broken dog legs*.

Even given this very sketchy description of the nature of information in situation semantics, we can see that this view of information can capture the kind of information that Gibson was interested in. We can see this via an example. Imagine that there is a beer can on a table in a room that is brightly lit from an overhead source. Light from the source will reflect off the beer can (some directly from the overhead source, some that has already been reflected off other surfaces in the room). At any point in the room to which there is an uninterrupted path from the beer can, there will be light that has reflected off the beer can. Because of the natural laws governing the reflection of light off surfaces of particular textures, colors, and chemical makeup, the light at any such point will be structured in a very particular way by its having reflected off the beer can. In situation *s*1, the light at point *p* has structure *a* of type *A*. Given the laws just mentioned, there is a constraint connecting the situations with light-structure type *A* to the beer-can-present situations of type *B*. So the light structure at point *p* contains information about token beer-can-presence *b* (of type *B*). Notice too that, because of conventional constraints governing the relationship between cans and their contents, beer-can-presence *b* being of type *B* carries information about beer-presence *c* of type *C*. Furthermore, the light at some point in the room from which the beer can is visible will contain information about the beer can's affordances. Take some point *p*, which is at my eye height. The light structure available at this point will contain not just information about the beer can and the beer, but also about the distance the point is from the ground, the relationship between that distance and the distance the beer can is from the ground, and hence the reachability of the beer can and drinkability of the beer for a person with eyes at that height.

Note that this example makes clear that on my view, but not Turvey-Shaw-Mace, constraints that connect situations are not limited to lawlike connections but can also be cultural or conventional in nature; the fact that some situation token contains information about some other token does not necessarily entail that the second situation token is factual. For example, the light at my point of observation contains information about the beer can, and the beer can contains information about beer being present. Even though it's possible that, because of some error at the brewery that caused the can to be filled with water, there is no beer in the can, the beer can's presence can still carry information about the presence of beer. But according to Turvey-Shaw-Mace, the connection between the states of affairs must be governed by natural law. So according to the Turvey-Shaw-Mace view, beer can presences don't carry information about beer presences, because the beer can is not connected by natural law with the presence of beer. This is also a feature of Dretske's theory of information (Dretske 1981) and has long been thought to be problematic. Situation theorists have typically argued that constraints need not be lawlike connections between situation types. Barwise and Seligman (1994, 1997), for example, have argued that the regularities that allow the flow of information must be reliable, but must also allow for exceptions. Millikan (2000) makes a similar point. She distinguishes between informationL (information carried in virtue of natural law) and informationC (information carried in virtue of correlation). Because constraints need only be reliable and not lawlike, nonspecifying variables can carry information. Millikan also makes a valuable point concerning just how reliable nonspecifying variables need be. On her view, the correlation between two events need be just reliable enough that some animal can use it to guide its behavior. Thus information-carrying connections between variables can be fully specifying, marginally significant, or anything in between, depending on the type of behavior that the variable provides information for.

This works well with the theory of what it is for perception to be direct, outlined in section 6.3 above. Remember that according to this view perception is direct when it is nonrepresentational, the result of an informational coupling between perceiver and perceived. This says nothing about what kind of constraint allows the information to be available. Since the situation semantics theory of information allows information to be present with merely reliable constraints, constraints that hold only sometimes can underwrite direct perception. So we *can* directly perceive beer-presence, given beer-can-presence, despite occasional mix-ups at the brewery. And we can directly perceive the meaning in the spoken sentences despite the fact that people lie or misspeak. Most important, I think, a child can directly perceive her mother, even though there are no laws of nature concerning individuals.

6.6 Compare and Contrast: On Specification and Symmetry

I have already said that on the views of information and direct perception outlined here, there is information about, and so the possibility of direct perception of, individuals and socially, culturally, and conventionally determined entities and states of affairs. This is already a marked difference between the view I outline and the Turvey-Shaw-Mace view. Even more striking, and perhaps more troubling to some ecological psychologists, is the effect the views I have outlined have on Shaw's principle of symmetry. Remember that the principle of symmetry is that (1) the environment specifies the information available for perception and the information available for perception specifies what is perceived, and (2) what is perceived specifies the information available for perception and the information available for perception specifies the environment. There are, in other words, 1:1 correspondences between the environment and the information available for perception and between the information available for perception and what is perceived. This principle is taken to be the most important part of the Turvey-Shaw-Mace view of information and direct perception. Indeed, as was noted above, information and direct perception are defined in terms of it. On the view described here, however, symmetry does not hold. This is the case because on my situation-semantics-derived view, information does not depend on 1:1 correspondences. To repeat the example, on my view, there could be information about beer at my point of observation because light arriving there has been reflected off an unopened Boddington's can, despite the possibility that there is actually no beer because the can might be full of something else. In fact, according to the view I've outlined, there is an important asymmetry at work here. The asymmetry in question here is partly an asymmetry in what we might call direction of fit. The environment-to-perception fit is at least partly causal, whereas the perception-to-environment fit is primarily normative. The can being the way it is causes the light to be the way it is at my point of observation, which causes me to perceive the beer on the table. But my perception, via the structure of the light, that there is beer in the refrigerator in no way causes there to be beer in the refrigerator. Instead, my perception fails, is incorrect, if there is no beer.

A second way the asymmetry of direction of fit shows up can be brought to light diagrammatically. In situation semantics, constraints connecting types of situations allow tokens of those types to carry information. So, for example, because of various constraints concerning the way light reflects off surfaces, there are causal constraints connecting the type of situation in which my daughter is present to situations in which the optic array is structured in a particular way, and because of the way light interacts with me and my visual system, there will be constraints connecting these optical array structurings and my perception of my daughter. That is, constraint C1 connects Ava-present situation type *E* with Ava-array situation type *A* and constraint C2 connects Ava-array situation type *A* with Ava-perception situation type *P*. Constraints C1 and C2 are, of course, primarily causal. We

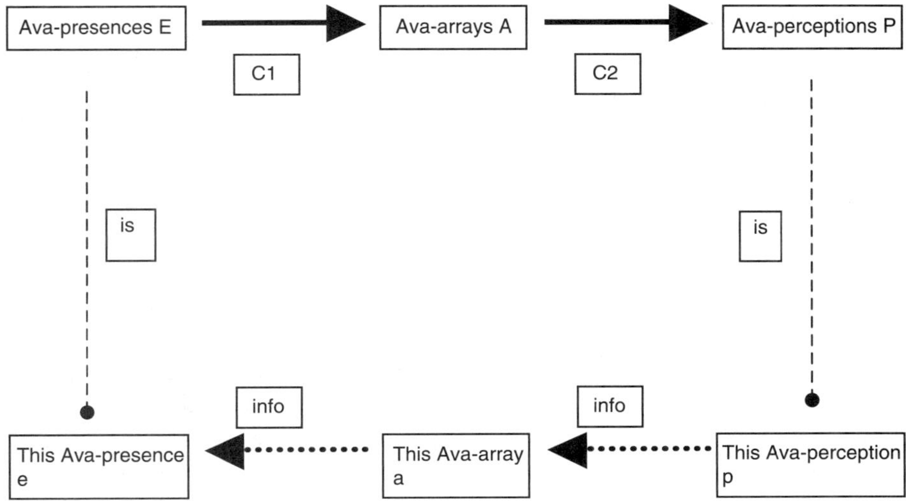

Figure 6.3
Information flow when my daughter is present. *This Ava-presence e, This Ava-array a,* and *This Ava-perception p* are tokens of types *Ava-presences E, Ava-arrays A,* and *Ava-perceptions P,* respectively. The top part of the diagram is analogous to Shaw's E > I > P; the bottom is analogous to his P > I > E.

can see this in the top part of figure 6.3. This part of the figure, and this direction of fit from environment to perception, corresponds to the first part of the symmetry principle, E > I > P. In contrast, consider the lower part of figure 6.3. This depicts the relationship among tokens: this particular Ava-perception token *p* of type *P* is informative about a particular Ava-array token *a* of type *A*, which is, in turn, informative about a particular Ava-presence token *e* of type *E*. This reflects a truism of situation theory: information "flows" among tokens in virtue of constraints among types. This lower part of the diagram corresponds to the second part of the symmetry principle, P > I > E. We can, then, see another way in which the different directions of fit are different: the environment-to-perception direction of fit is due to constraints among types, and the perception–to-environment direction of fit is due to an informational relationship among tokens. On this view, Shaw and McIntyre were right that there is a two-way informational relationship between perception and the environment, but they were wrong in thinking that both directions of the relationship are the same.

6.7 Information All Around

For radical embodied cognitive science to be convincing, more is needed than that ecological information can be coherently defined: it must be ubiquitously available for direct perception, and it must be information of a kind that can guide behavior without requiring mental gymnastics. In other words, it must be argued that the stimulus is not at all impoverished, that all the information required to guide behavior is available in the environment. To begin to make a case for this, I will briefly discuss two different types of research on environmental information: optic flow and visual entropy. Before beginning, I should point out that each of these is a higher-order variable, which is to say that each is relational and takes time to perceive. Most of the variables of interest to ecological psychologists are higher order. The guiding assumption is that perception is an activity involving orienting sensory organs, scanning, and the like, and that activities take time. This means that perception is not just of simple quantities like mass, wavelength, position, and so on, but also of comparatively complex relations, ratios, velocities, and accelerations. There is information available in the environment to perceive each of these properties directly. That is, given the temporal extendedness of the activity of perception one can simply *see*, for example, how fast something is moving, without computing it.

6.7.1 Optic Flow and the Variable τ

Many readers of this book will have seen the documentary film *Winged Migration*. One of the many, many wonderful things to be seen in this film is of direct relevance to us here. The film depicts diving gannets. Gannets, large sea birds that live along colder, northern coastlines, are of interest to us because of the way they fish. Gannets are able to catch fish at much greater depths than other birds typically can, even pursuing them under water, because they dive down to the water from heights of around 100 feet (approximately thirty meters) and reach speeds of up to sixty miles (approximately 100 kilometers) per hour. Such a dive represents an extraordinary coordination problem. Diving gannets must keep their wings spread for as long as possible in order to maintain and adjust their heading toward a target fish in windy conditions. But hitting the water with spread wings would be catastrophic: at sixty miles per hour, wing bones would break. The question here is how gannets manage to retract their wings at the last possible moment, so as to hit the water at the right location and avoid injury. One possibility is that gannets perform a computation: using a stored representation of the expected size of prey fish, compute distance from the surface of the water; then compute time to contact with the surface from this distance, using internally represented laws of motion (mass, acceleration due to gravity, and friction are constants). This, it turns out, is not what gannets do. Gannets rely on *optic flow*, the patterns of motion available at the eyes of any moving observer.

The easiest way to understand optic flow is to remember what happens when one plays a first-person video game. Moving your character around in its virtual environment causes a changing pattern on your monitor that, if the game is well designed, gives you the sensation of actually moving around in the environment. This temporally extended onscreen pattern is a simulation of optic flow. Consider a familiar video game scenario: your virtual car is heading toward a fatal collision with, let's say, a brick wall.

1. As your car approaches the wall, the image of the wall on your monitor expands.
2. When you get close enough, individual bricks will become visible.
3. As you continue toward your virtual crash, the image of the wall will cover the entire monitor, and images of individual bricks will expand.
4. As you get closer to the wall, the images of the bricks will expand so that only a few of them are actually able to fit on the monitor, and they will appear textured.

5. Moving closer still, the images of the texture elements on the bricks will expand as well;
6. Then there is the loud crash noise and the cracked virtual windshield.

Back in the real world and less dramatically, the same phenomenon, called *looming*, happens constantly. As any animal moves about its environment, the images of objects or texture elements that the animal is moving toward will expand at the animal's eyes. This is often described by saying that optic flow is *centrifugal* in the direction of locomotion: texture elements radiate out from the center of your field of view as you move toward an object.[11]

Detecting centrifugal optic flow is very important, of course, but it is not sufficient to guide the gannet in drawing in its wings. David Lee (1980; Lee and Reddish 1981), however, demonstrated that properties of centrifugal optic flow can be sufficient to guide behavior by defining the higher-order optical variable τ. τ is the ratio of the size of a projected image to the rate of change of the image's size. Using a little geometry and calculus, Lee showed that τ, a feature of the optic array available at the eye, is sufficient to guide the gannet's behavior without the use of internal computations. Imagine a situation as pictured in figure 6.4 in which we have a decreasing distance between an object in the world, such as a fish, and an animal's eye.[12] Suppose the distance between the eye and the object is changing at constant velocity V and that at time t the object is at distance $z(t)$. At time t, the object will project an image of a size $r(t)$ proportional to its size R, and as the distance between R and the animal decreases the projected image $r(t)$'s size will increase at velocity $v(t)$. τ is the ratio of size of the image $r(t)$ to rate of change of the size of the image $v(t)$,

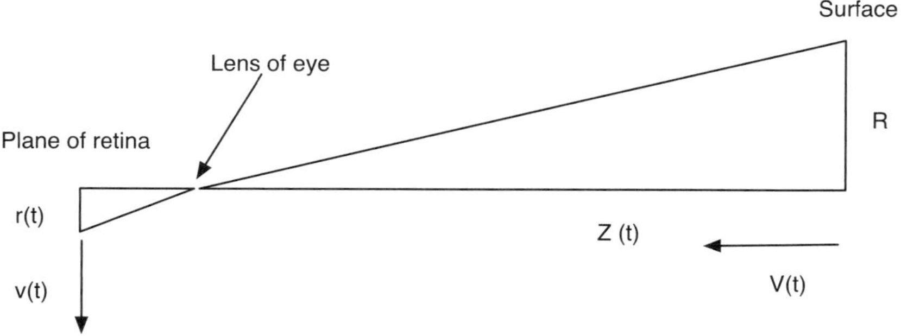

Figure 6.4
The optical expansion at the retina of the image of projected by object R as it moves toward the eye.

$$\tau = r(t)/v(t). \quad (6.1)$$

Because the triangles on each side of the lens in figure 6.4 are similar (and using a little suppressed calculus), we know that $r(t)/v(t)$ is the same as the ratio of the objects distance $z(t)$ and the rate at which it is moving toward the animal V. Thus,

$$\tau = z(t)/V. \quad (6.2)$$

If V is constant,

$$\tau = z(t)/[z(t)/t], \quad (6.3)$$

which simplifies to

$$\tau = t. \quad (6.4)$$

So if V is constant, τ is equal to the time remaining until contact between the eye and the object.

There are several things here worth noting. First note that τ does not give information about the absolute distance of an object. Instead, it gives information about time-to-contact with the object, which is relevant to guiding movement. When you're trying to cross the street, how far away in meters an approaching car is matters much less than how soon it will hit you. Second, note that τ need not be computed by the gannet. It is available at the retina. τ, in other words, can be perceived directly. So, τ provides important information for the control of action in the environment, and it provides that information without requiring mental gymnastics. That is, sensitivity to the ratio of optical angle to the expansion of optical angle is sensitivity to the timing of approaching collision. Third, and most important, Lee and Reddish (1981) show that diving gannets are sensitive to τ and use it to determine when to fold their wings. They filmed diving gannets and showed that the time of wing retraction is better predicted by the hypothesis that gannets pick up information using τ than by the hypotheses that gannets compute time-to-contact or retract wings at some particular height or velocity. Finally, there is evidence that τ and τ-derived variables are used to undertake a variety of visually guided actions. Indeed, Lee's lab alone has shown that τ is used by landing pigeons and hummingbirds, and by humans hitting balls, somersaulting, long jumping, putting in golf, and steering. (See Lee 2006 for an overview.)

6.7.2 Optic Flow and Information Processing

Optic flow has many other features than the sort of expansion in the direction of heading that is captured by τ, and these other features have seemed to many to call mental representations back into the picture. Consider walking toward a destination. Imagine that you are in a parking lot and want to walk toward your car. It would seem that you could use optic flow and the variable τ to do so by walking so that the center of visual expansion is your car. If the only variety of optic flow were this visual expansion, this would be a successful strategy. But in addition to walking toward the car, you will be moving your eyes. So in addition to the optical expansion, you will have rotational optic flow from moving your eyes, and the overall optic flow will be the vector sum of two components: flow from your locomotion and flow from your eye movement. If centrifugal expansion of the object you're walking toward is just one component of your optic flow, it would seem that optic flow is insufficient to determine (and maintain) your direction of locomotion. In fact, it would seem that a mental computation would be necessary to subtract the effect of eye movement on the information available for perception. This sort of worry is the motivation behind motor theories of perception (Grush 1997; Hurley 1998; Ebenholtz 2001; Mandik 2005), the idea in which is that in order to effectively subtract the optic flow generated by eye movements, one uses a mental representation of the eye movement. This representation, sometimes called an *efference copy* and sometimes called *extraretinal information*, can be used to generate a prediction of the optic flow that would be generated by the eye movement, which predicted optic flow can be subtracted from the actual optic flow, leaving behind the optic flow generated by heading. If this is correct, information available in the environment is not sufficient to guide you to your car (or any target); it must be supplemented by mental representations of your eye movements.

Do we need extraretinal information to subtract out optic flow from eye movements to control our locomotion? There is evidence that indicates that we do not. Warren and Hannon (1988; Warren 2004) performed a series of experiments to determine whether optic flow is sufficient to determine the direction of locomotion, or whether extraretinal information is required. Subjects watched a monitor displaying simulated optic flow, and were asked to determine the direction of locomotion. In these experiments two different kinds of optic flow are simulated. In one case, the flow on the monitor simulates motion toward a target. In this case, subjects are also asked to track an object following a continuous path along the monitor. Thus these subjects have optic flow generated by simulated locomotion and their own actual eye movement. In the other case, the flow on a monitor simulates both locomotion toward a target and optic flow generated by eye movements tracking an object on the monitor. So in the second case, the subjects have optic flow generated by simulated locomotion and simulated eye movement. In both cases, the optic flow is the same, but only in the first case (with real eye movement) could there be any extraretinal information or efference copy. If extraretinal information is necessary for perceiving direction of locomotion (i.e., if optic flow is not sufficient), subjects with real eye movements should determine direction of heading much more accurately than subjects with simulated eye movements. In fact, however, both sets of subjects perceived direction of heading equally accurately, which indicates that the environmental information is sufficient and need not be supplemented by mental representations of eye movement. Indeed, many subjects with simulated eye movement reported experiencing illusory eye movements. This is a hint that our awareness of voluntary eye movements comes from the environment and not from internal representations of the movements. That is, perhaps we know what we're doing primarily by seeing ourselves do it.[13]

It seems, then, that we do not need mental gymnastics to use optic flow to tell the direction of our locomotion, but the preceding discussion does supply a sense in which perception involves information processing. The information available in the optical variable τ is only available to animals that are moving. Thus one might say, following Rowlands (2006), that sometimes animals process information by acting in the world. There are countless examples of this sort of information processing via activity, most of which are less exotic than τ. We turn our heads, changing the positions of our ears, to generate differences in the arrival times of sounds and hence information about the direction of the sound. We lean when surveying a scene, and in so doing generate a motion parallax and hence information about the distances of objects. And on and on. This is what radical embodied cognitive scientists mean when they claim that perception and action are tightly intertwined, and that perception is, in part, action. Action changes the information available to an animal's perceptual systems, and sometimes the action actually generates information. Thus there is a sense in which perception-action as studied by radical embodied cognitive scientists involves information processing, but it is a variety of information processing that does not involve mental gymnastics.[14]

6.7.3 Detecting Entropy and Perceiving Sameness

Analogical reasoning has been of special interest in the cognitive sciences, at least in part because it is often taken to be the one uniquely human cognitive ability (e.g., by Lakoff and Johnson 1999). And, indeed, analogical reasoning is taken to require Olympic-level mental gymnastics. It is typically thought that for analogical reasoning to occur, there must be representations of a stored base situation and the current target situation (i.e., the situation to be reasoned about right now). The analogy itself is the represented relation between those two representations. So imagine that you have arrived at an unfamiliar airport, say Charles de Gaulle in Paris, and are interested in finding your luggage. First, you form a mental representation of the current airport, including representations of many of its features. You recall a representation of a familiar airport, say Philadelphia International Airport, one in which you know where the luggage carousel is. You then compare the representation of the familiar airport with that of the unfamiliar airport, putting all the relevant parts of the representations in correspondence.[15] Finally, you adapt the solution in the source representation to fit with the target representation. If the luggage carousel is downstairs at the terminal in Philadelphia, you look for it downstairs at de Gaulle. The difficult part in this, of course, is determining which represented source in memory has enough relevant similarities to the target. There are many sorts of similarities that are relevant. There can be similarities among attributes (both the car and the apple are red), similarities among relations (breakfast is before lunch and the primary is before the general election), and similarities among similarities among relations, and so on. Furthermore, in many cases, it is necessary to ignore lower-order similarities and differences among attributes to attend to higher-order similarities and differences among relations. Thus it would seem that analogical reasoning requires detailed mental representations and complicated procedures for retrieving and comparing them.

Although it does not bear out claims that humans *alone* are capable of analogical reasoning, research by Roger Thompson and colleagues on analogical reasoning in nonhuman primates to suggest that there is a "profound disparity" (Thompson and Oden 2000) between humans and chimpanzees on one hand and monkeys on the other. In a series of studies (Oden, Thompson, and Premack 1990; Thompson and Oden 2000; Thompson, Oden, and Boysen 1997), it was shown that humans and chimpanzees can match pairs of relations and that monkeys cannot. In the studies, adult humans and language-trained chimpanzees are shown to be able to match samples based on the relations among the objects in the samples, while ignoring properties of the individual objects. That is, they would match a pair of quarters (relation = same) with a pair of nickels (relation = same), rather than with a quarter and a dime (relation = different). Furthermore, infant humans and chimpanzees are able to recognize sameness and difference. Capuchin monkeys could do neither. Thompson has used this data to argue that humans and chimps, but not monkeys, have the ability to form the higher-order representations required for analogical reasoning. This is the profound disparity, and it can be seen as giving some comfort to the proponent of radical embodied cognitive science. If only humans and language-trained chimpanzees are capable of matching relations between relations, perhaps only humans and language-trained chimpanzees form representations. A natural hypothesis to explain this is that there is something about learning a public language that imparts representational capacities that were otherwise not there, leaving most cognition of most animals a matter of interaction with their environments. This is the line that Andy Clark (1997, 2003, 2008) takes. Experience recognizing and manipulating public, perceptually accessible symbols leads animals to have new capacities that clearly require representational explanation. These animals internalize the symbols and learn to manipulate them internally in the same way that they did externally.

Things, alas, are more complicated. First, there is mounting evidence that the profound disparity does not hold up, so whatever processes are required in humans and language-trained chimps seem called for in other species. Second, it turns out that analogical reasoning does not require complicated representational processes: pigeons and baboons, at least, can perceive similarity among relations just by picking up information in a higher-order environmental variable. A series of experiments by Ed Wasserman and his colleagues has shown that both pigeons and baboons can perceive sameness and difference in arrays of icons (Young and Wasserman 1997, 2000; Fagot, Wasserman, and Young 2001; Wasserman, Young, and Cook 2004 is a review). Both the baboons and pigeons learned a relational matching task in which they were shown an array of sixteen pictorial icons that are either all identical (sixteen pictures of an ice cream cone) or all different (one picture each of an ice cream cone, a bus, a football . . .), and asked to match them to either a different array of sixteen identical icons or a different array of sixteen different icons. By successfully matching an array of sixteen ice cream cones to an array of sixteen footballs, the pigeons and baboons show that they can ignore surface differences (ice cream cones vs. footballs) and match the arrays according to the relations among them. As Fagot, Young, and Wasserman (2001) point out, successful matching is, in essence, analogical reasoning. The animals must use relevant similarities between two things to guide their behavior, while ignoring both irrelevant similarities and differences, and they must do so by attending to higher-order properties of the arrays (sameness or difference of the entire array of icons) rather than the surface features (the identities of the individual pictures in the array). This suggests that the profound disparity does not hold up, indicating that many animals are capable of analogical cognition.

What lesson should be drawn from the apparent failure of the profound disparity? One possibility is that animals other than humans and language-trained chimpanzees can reason analogically because the mental gymnastics required for analogical reasoning are not the result of learning a public language. Another possibility is that reasoning analogically does not require mental gymnastics. The details of the experiments on pigeons and baboons indicate that the latter of these is the case. As just described, pigeons and baboons are quite capable of learning to match arrays of sixteen icons based on relations. But as one gradually decreases the number of icons in the array from sixteen to fifteen to fourteen and so on down to two, the ability of pigeons and baboons to correctly match arrays drops off, falling to near chance with arrays of four and fewer icons. This should be a surprise to those who assume that this sort of analogical matching requires representation of each of the icons in an array, so that they can be compared with one another to arrive at the representation of the relational property "all the same" or "all different" of the array, which represented relational properties must be stored for comparison with the represented relational properties of the other two icons before a response can be made. If this were the case, it should be more difficult to represent and make comparisons with larger arrays than with smaller ones because larger arrays will present greater computational loads. Yet larger arrays are easier for pigeons and baboons.

To explain this phenomenon, Young and Wasserman (1997) suggest that pigeons[16] are responding to the *entropy* in the arrays. As used here, entropy is an information-theoretic measure of disorder, calculated with this equation:

$$H(A) = -\sum_{a \in A} p_a \log_2 p_a, \tag{6.5}$$

where A is a variable, a is a possible value of that variable, and p_a is the proportion instances of a among observed values of the variable. For the non-mathematically inclined, the key point here is that the maximum possible entropy of a variable increases as the number of bits in the signal increases; while the minimum possible is always 0. For example, when an array has sixteen different icons, the proportion of any icon will be $1/16 = .0625$, so

$$H(A) = -.0625 \times \log_2 (.0625) \times 16 = 4. \tag{6.6}$$

When an array has two different icons, the proportion of any icon will be $1/2 = .5$, so

$$H(A) = -.5 \times \log_2 (.5) \times 2 = 1. \qquad (6.7)$$

Because the $\log_2 (1) = 0$, the entropy of an array of identical items, no matter what size, will be zero. This explains why it is easier for pigeons and baboons to match samples based on sameness and difference when arrays are larger. In arrays of sixteen icons, the animals must discriminate between entropy values of zero (all icons the same) and four (all icons different), but with arrays of two icons, the animals must discriminate between entropy values zero and one. Pigeons and baboons, then, have a hard time with smaller arrays because the differences in entropy on which they make their discriminations are smaller. This accounts for the gradual decrease in performance as the number of icons in the array is reduced, an effect that is counterintuitive if one assumes that the task requires that animals must explicitly represent and compute over the icons in each array to determine whether they are all the same or all different, and then match the results of those computations in order to act appropriately.

The upshot of this is that the higher-order variable entropy carries sufficient information for animals to perceive sameness and difference and to engage in a variety of analogical reasoning, all without mental gymnastics. One might wonder, however, how it is that the higher-order variable entropy can be perceived directly. It is a logarithmic function, after all. Don't animals need to compute it? One way to find out is to use neural network simulations. If entropy can be detected without computations over representations, a neural network without hidden layers ought to be able to make discriminations between entropy levels. A mathematician or computer scientist would say that entropy cannot be detected by a two-layer network. This is the case because, like XOR, entropy is not linearly separable. Indeed, with two icons, entropy is logically equivalent to XOR, and XOR famously requires hidden units. Thus, it might seem that attempting to use a two-layer network to demonstrate the direct perception of entropy is a waste of time. The key to seeing that it might not be a waste of time is to realize that, according to computer scientists, pigeons and baboons cannot make discriminations based on entropy. "Being able to solve a problem" in computer science means being guaranteed to come up with the right answer every time. In contrast, in animal behavior, "being able to solve a problem" means reliably coming up with the right answer at rates significantly greater than chance. So whether a neural network or an animal can solve a problem depends on what you mean by "being able to

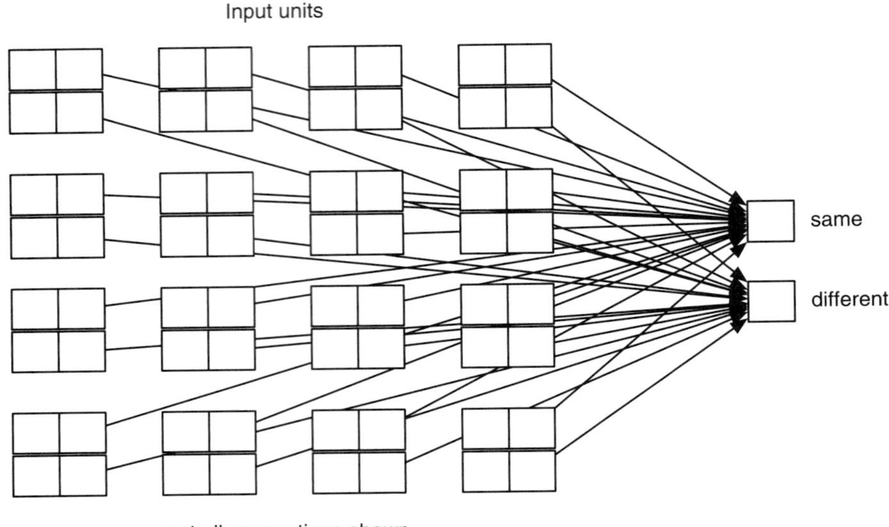

Figure 6.5

solve the problem." Clearly, for the purposes here, the animal behavior criterion is more appropriate.

The question, then, is can two-layer neural networks reliably make discriminations based on entropy at rates significantly greater than chance. We have shown that they can (Silansky and Chemero 2002; Dotov and Chemero 2006). Using MATLAB, we built a neural network with sixty-four inputs (in sixteen sets of four) and two output units. See figure 6.5. Each set of four input units was used to make a binary representation of an icon. Thus, if we wished to present the network an array of sixteen identical icons, the inputs might be sixteen instances of "0010"; if we wished to present sixteen different icons to the network, each set of four would be different. Following the method of Young and Wasserman (1997), we trained the network to distinguish entropy = 0 (all icons identical) from entropy > 0 (at least one icon different from others) and to distinguish maximum entropy (all icons different from one another[17]) from other levels of entropy (at least two identical icons). We trained the network, first, with sixteen icon arrays until further training did not produce improvements in performance. We then repeated this process, gradually reducing the number of icons until there were just two. Our results were qualitatively similar to the data found with pigeons and baboons. In particular, we found that

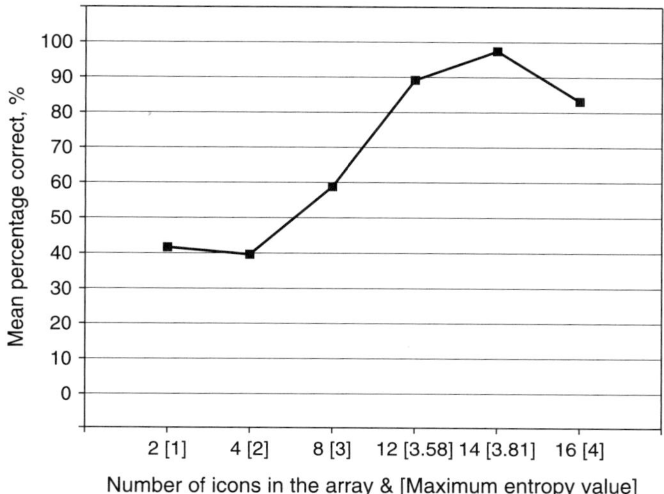

Figure 6.6
Mean percent correct entropy discriminations by six two-layer artificial neural networks as a function of number of icons in the array. Thanks to Dobri Dotov.

the two-layer network could discriminate entropy levels quite reliably with arrays of sixteen icons and that its performance deteriorated gradually as we reduced the number of icons, going to chance and then fluctuating wildly with arrays of five and fewer icons. See figure 6.6.

The simulation results suggest very strongly that pigeons and baboons perceive sameness and difference by directly perceiving entropy. I would argue that they show definitively that it is possible to achieve performance that is qualitatively very similar to that exhibited by pigeons and baboons without manipulating representations. They show, that is, that information about sameness and difference in the form of higher-level variable entropy is available and is sufficient to guide behavior without mental gymnastics.[18]

6.8 Wrap Up

The purpose of this chapter has been to begin to outline a Gibsonian theory of perception and cognition to serve as a background theory for radical embodied cognitive science. So far, I've given a theory of what it is for perception to be direct, and provided a little evidence suggesting that perception might actually be direct. Direct perception is the nonrepresentational use of information in the guidance of behavior. Suggesting that perception is direct involved saying what information is, showing that there's plenty of it around for animals to use, and showing that animals actually do use it. So far so good. But from the point of view of the radical embodied cognitive scientist, the most important information is information about affordances, and I haven't yet said much about what affordances are. This happens in chapter 7.

7 Affordances, etc.

7.1 Direct Perception and Ontology

For radical embodied cognitive science to eschew mental representations, it must take perception to be direct, to be the pickup of information from the environment. Furthermore, animals must be able to use that information to guide action without complex processing, without mental gymnastics. This requires that perception be of affordances, or opportunities for behavior. Animals, that is, must be able to perceive what they can do directly. In the previous chapter, I explained how perception might be direct and gave a theory of the information available for perception. So far, though, I have said nothing about perceptual content, nothing, that is, about what animals actually perceive. This is where affordances come in. Following Gibson, I will maintain that animals perceive affordances directly. This leads to some ontological funny business. To see this, consider that the primary difference between direct and inferential theories of perception concerns the location of perceptual content. In inferential theories of perception, these meanings arise inside animals, based on their interactions with the physical environment. Light, for example, bumps into receptors causing a sensation. The animal (or rather its brain) performs inferences on the sensation, yielding a meaningful perception. In direct theories of perception, on the other hand, meaning is in the environment, and perception does not depend on meaning-conferring inferences. Instead the animal simply gathers information from a meaning-laden environment. The environment is meaning laden in that it contains affordances, and affordances are meaningful to animals. But if the environment contains meanings, then it cannot be merely physical. This places a heavy theoretical burden on radical embodied cognitive science, a burden so severe that it may outweigh all the advantages to conceiving perception as direct. Radical embodied cognitive science requires a new ontology, one that is at odds with today's physicalist, reductionist consensus that says the world just is the physical world, full stop. Without a coherent understanding of what the world is like, such that it can contain meanings and is not merely physical, direct perception is simply indefensible. Thus, like earlier theories that take perception to be direct (e.g., James 1912/1976; Heidegger 1927), Gibson's ecological psychology (Gibson 1966, 1979) includes an ontology, his theory of affordances.

Gibson's first cut at describing affordances is deceptively simple. "The *affordances* of the environment are what it *offers* the animal, what it *provides* or *furnishes*, either for good or ill" (Gibson 1979, 127). An affordance, this seems to imply, is a resource that the environment offers any animal that has the capabilities to perceive and use it. As such, affordances are meaningful to animals—they provide opportunity for particular kinds of behavior. Thus affordances are properties of the environment, but taken relative to an animal. So far, so good. Unfortunately, two pages later, Gibson's valiant, plainspoken attempt to make clear how much his theory of affordances differs from standard physicalist, reductionist ontology ends up just being confusing.

> [A]n affordance is neither an objective property nor a subjective property; or it is both if you like. An affordance cuts across the dichotomy of subjective–objective and helps us to understand its inadequacy. It is equally a fact of the environment and a fact of behavior. It is both physical and psychical, yet neither. An affordance points both ways, to the environment and to the observer. (1979, 129)

This description makes affordances seem like impossible, ghostly entities, entities that no respectable scientist (or analytic philosopher) could have as part of his or her ontology. The purpose of this chapter is to provide a description of affordances that makes them more ontologically respectable, yet still does justice to Gibson's conception and, in so doing, to say how radical embodied cognitive scientists ought to understand affordances.

7.2 Affordances 1.0

Mine is, of course, not the first attempt to develop a coherent theory of affordances. It is worthwhile to say a few things about previous attempts, in order to see what is different about the theory outlined here. Previous (post-Gibson) attempts to set out an ontology of affordances have typically assumed that affordances are properties of the environment (Turvey et al. 1981; Michaels and Carello 1981; Heft 1989, 2001; Turvey 1992; Reed 1996; Michaels 2000).[1] These authors agree that affordances are animal-relative properties of the environment. In particular, affordances are properties of the environment that have some significance to some animal's behavior. To the extent that there is disagreement among these authors it is over two things: what kind of animal-relative properties of the environment affordances are, and what it is about animals that affordances are relative to.

There are two different views concerning the type of animal-relative properties of the environment that are affordances. Edward Reed (1996) argues that affordances are resources in the environment, properties of objects that might be exploitable by some animal, and he links this understanding of affordances to evolution by natural selection. Indeed, Reed takes this linkage between affordances and natural selection to be the most important thing about Gibsonian ecological psychology.

> The fundamental hypothesis of ecological psychology . . . is that affordances and only the relative availability (or nonavailability) of affordances create selection pressure on animals; hence behavior is regulated with respect to the affordances of the environment for a given animal. (Reed 1996, 18)

The resources in the environment are the source of selection pressure on animals, causing them to evolve perceptual systems that can perceive those resources. Those resources that some species of animal evolve the ability to perceive are affordances for members of that species. This selectionist view of affordances, in which they are environmental resources that exist prior to the animals that come to perceive and use them, is also semiendorsed by Stoffregen (2000). (In later work, Stoffregen [2003] does not endorse this view, however.)

In contrast to this selectionist view of affordances, which ties them closely to evolution by natural selection, is the Turvey-Shaw-Mace view, described in great detail by Turvey (1992), in which ecological psychology is tied more closely to physics than to evolutionary biology (see also Turvey et al. 1981)[2]. As discussed chapter 6, according to Turvey, affordances are dispositional properties of the environment. Dispositional properties are tendencies to manifest some other property in certain circumstances. "Being fragile" is a common dispositional property. Something is fragile just in case it would break in certain circumstances, particularly circumstances in which it is struck sharply. Dispositional properties are only conceivable when paired with actualizing circumstances, circumstances in which the disposition becomes manifest—the glass is only fragile if there are possible circumstances in which it might shatter. To say that affordances are dispositional properties of the environment, then, is to say that the environment is such that in some circumstances, certain other properties will become manifest. So, for example, the affordance "being edible" is a property of things in the environment only if there are animals that are capable of eating and digesting those things.

Notice that unlike Reed's view of affordances as resources, Turvey's account of affordances as dispositions is nonselectionist. Dispositions depend on possible actualizing circumstances; for example, nothing is soluble if there are no solvents. If affordances are dispositions, they depend on the possible presence of animals that can actualize them. Affordances, in Turvey's preferred language, must be *complemented* by properties of animals. So, an object can be edible only if there are animals that can eat and digest it. Given this, contrary to Reed's fundamental hypothesis, affordances per se cannot exert selection pressure on animals. Properties of the environment are not affordances in the absence of complementary properties of animals.

Turvey's insistence that affordances must be complemented by properties of animals brings us to the second difference among accounts of affordances: if affordances are animal-relative, we should wonder what it is about animals that affordances are relative to. Turvey (1992) proposes that affordances are complemented by effectivities (Turvey et al. 1981; Shaw, Turvey, and Mace 1982; see also chapter 6 above). Effectivities, like affordances, are dispositions, and as such they must be complemented by properties that lead to their actualization. Effectivities are properties of animals that allow them to make use of affordances. Effectivities and affordances are, thus, inseparable according to Turvey (1992). They complement one another. Claire Michaels (2000) also endorses this view. Another candidate for the aspect of animals to which affordances are relative is body scale. This view of affordances, endorsed by Harry Heft (1989, 2001), is suggested by empirical studies of affordances, which follow Warren's (1984) classic study of stair-climbing affordances in quantifying affordances with π-numbers, which are ratios between measures of body scale and measures of an environmental property.[3] Thus Stoffregen's (2000) discussion of affordances focuses on their relation to body scale. Heft (1989) provides a second reason for taking body scale to be the property of animals to which the affordances of the environment are related. Understanding affordances as body related, Heft suggests, can do justice to the phenomenological insights of Merleau-Ponty (1962) and the profound influence those insights had on Gibson (on which see Heft 2001).

To summarize this brief discussion of some of the previous theoretical work on affordances, we can say the following. First, Turvey, Heft,

Michaels, and Reed agree that affordances are animal-relative properties of the environment. Second, there is some disagreement over whether these properties exist independent of animals. This disagreement comes to an argument over whether affordances are resources that guide natural selection, or dispositional properties of the environment that must be complemented by some property of animals. Third, there is disagreement over whether the relevant properties of animals are abilities (or effectivities) or body scale.

In a paper published a few years ago (Chemero 2003a), I outlined a theory of affordances designed to avoid these two controversies. It did so by disagreeing with the premise on which they are based, the claim that affordances are animal-relative properties of the environment.[4] I argued that affordances are not properties of the environment; indeed, they are not even properties. Affordances, I argued, are relations between particular aspects of animals and particular aspects of situations. As I will explain, I still believe that this is a significant improvement over prior work, but it is nonetheless not sufficient as a theory of affordances.

7.3 A Few Critical Comments Regarding Affordances 1.0

In this section, I will argue very briefly against the idea that affordances are properties of the environment. This argument will have two parts. First, I will argue that affordances are not properties, or at least not always properties. Second, I will argue that affordances are not in the environment.

7.3.1 Affordances and Properties

In "What We Perceive When We Perceive Affordances" (Chemero 2001c), I argued that it is vital to distinguish between features and properties when discussing affordances. The purpose of that discussion was to counter Michaels's claim that perceiving ball-punching affordances (as in Michaels, Zeinstra, and Oudejans 2001) is perceiving something about oneself, not something about the environment. This, I argued, is true only if one fails to realize that there is a more primitive way of perceiving the environment, involving what Strawson called feature placing (Strawson 1959; Smith 1996). Feature placing is easiest to understand in contrast to the perception of objects with properties. Compare, for example, realizing that your car is dented to realizing that it's raining. In the former case, the perception of a property of the car, you must (a) perceive a particular entity; (b) know its identity, that it is your car; (c) know what it is to be dented; and (d) perceive that this particular entity (your car) has this particular property (being dented). In the latter case, the placing of a feature, there is no need to know anything about any particular entity. All that is necessary is the ability to recognize a feature of situations (raininess). To see this, consider that the "it" in "it is raining" is never the same thing; it refers to a situation (what's going on right here, right now) that will never appear again. We can ask what is dented, but we cannot ask what is raining.

Drawing attention to this distinction between placing features and perceiving properties of objects is relevant to the perception of affordances because Michaels (2000) argued that when we perceive ball-punching affordances, we perceive that "it's time to flex the elbow." This, she argues, is perceiving something more about yourself than about the environment. The recognition of feature placing calls this into question. Perceiving that it is time to flex the elbow is like perceiving that it is raining. It is a matter of perceiving that the situation as a whole has a certain feature, that the situation as a whole supports (perhaps demands) a certain kind of action. All of this is to say that perceiving affordances is placing features. And because features are not properties, views of affordances that take them to be properties can't be right.

7.3.2 Affordances and the Environment

If one accepts that affordances are not properties of objects, it is a small step to see that affordances cannot be properties, or even features, of the environment alone. I have just argued that affordances are features of whole situations. Animals are, of course, crucial parts of these whole situations, so perceiving something about the whole situation cannot be perceiving something about the environment, divorced from the animal. Thus, as Stoffregen (2003) suggests, affordances must belong to animal–environment systems, not just the environment. Though I agree with Stoffregen on this point, I'd like to argue for something more specific: that affordances are relations. To see this, consider Harry Heft's (2001) discussion of the relation between Gibson and the American naturalist William James.

In *Ecological Psychology in Context* (2001), Heft argues quite convincingly that Gibson's ecological psychology is a descendent of the radical empiricism of William James. To the radical empiricist, perception is direct because it is an act that includes the thing perceived. This leads to what James called "the problem of two minds." Suppose you and I both perceive the same pint of Guinness. The pint, according to radical empiricism, is part of both my perception and yours. But this leads to a problem of mereology: if the pint is part of both our perceptions, then our minds overlap. This, James thought, is in direct conflict with the (to him) obvious fact that our minds are private. The problem of two minds, then, is as follows. If perception is direct and two individuals can perceive the same object, then how can their minds be truly separate? James struggled with the problem of two minds throughout his later years, never reaching a satisfying resolution. This same problem affects any theory of direct perception, including Gibson's ecological psychology. Affordances are part of the act of perception, so if you and I both perceive the affordance "potability" of the pint of Guinness, our perceptions overlap. Our experiences, and hence our minds, are not private.

The solution to this problem is apparent in another of the main tenets of Jamesian radical empiricism. According to radical empiricism, everything that is experienced is equally real. Among the things we experience are relations between things; so relations are real, with the same status as the things that stand in relations. To solve the problem of two minds, suppose that perceivables are relations between perceivers and aspects of situations. If that is true, you and I can both perceive the potability of the Guinness, without our perceptions overlapping. You will perceive the relation between you and the pint, while I will perceive the relation between me and the pint, and our perceptions can remain private. The key to this solution, though, is that what we perceive, the affordance potability, is not in the environment alone. It is, instead, the relation between the perceiver and the environment. This point, that affordances are *relations*, is the key to the theory of affordances I will describe in the following sections.

Here, I call the view of affordances I am about to describe, the one which I set out in the 2003 paper mentioned above, "Affordances 1.1." In section 7.5, I argue that it resolves the issues I have been pointing to for Affordances 1.0. However, I have come to believe that Affordances 1.1 is not, in itself, sufficient as a theory of affordances. In section 7.6, I use Affordances 1.1 as the basis for a sketch of Affordances 2.0, a theory of affordances that meshes well with dynamical systems explanations and, hence, is more appropriate for radical embodied cognitive scientists.

7.4 Affordances 1.1

I have said several times that affordances are relations between animals and features of situations. I will now spell out in detail what that means. To begin, here is the basic logical structure of affordances, which will be expanded later.

Affords-ϕ (environment, organism), where ϕ is a behavior.

Translated literally into English, this means "The relation 'affords-ϕ' holds between 'environment' and 'organism'"; translated more loosely and colloquially, this means "The environment affords behavior ϕ for the organism." To get an idea of what this means, and what it means to say that affordances are relations, compare it to a more familiar relation.

Taller-than (Shaquille, Henry).

This says that Shaquille is taller than Henry. Notice first that the only objects in this relation are Shaquille and Henry. The taller-than relation is not inherent in either of them, but depends on both of them for its existence. Affords-ϕ is like taller-than in this respect: it is neither of the person, nor of the environment, but rather of their combination. Second, the affordance is not an extra thing in any of the usual senses of "thing." Yet it exists nonetheless, and, like the fact that Shaquille is taller than Henry, it is directly perceivable. (Remember the discussion of entropy in chapter 6.) Taking affordances to be relations, despite the fact that they are not things in the usual sense, is quite plausible in light of Heft's (2001) account of Gibson as a Jamesian radical empiricist (Chemero 2003c). As noted above, according to the radical empiricist relations are perceivable, and anything perceivable is real.

The formal definition of affordances as relations between organisms and environments is incomplete. In the next few section, I will fill it out.

7.4.1 The Environmental Relata

As discussed above, perceiving affordances is placing features, seeing that the situation allows a certain activity.[5] Thus the environmental relata in affordances must be features, not properties. The only further comment here is that this is in direct disagreement with Turvey, who pronounces that "There are only propertied things" (1992, 176). Situations are not things; features are not properties.

7.4.2 The Organismal Relata

Ever since Warren's (1984) groundbreaking experiments on stair climbing, it has been (tacitly) assumed by experimentalists that the aspect of animals that determines what the environment affords, the organismal relata in the affordance relation, are aspects of body scale. Warren, in attempting to quantify affordances for stair climbing, quantified them as unitless π numbers, the ratio between leg length and riser height. The affordance climbability is then identified as this ratio. Subsequent experiments identified affordances similarly, as ratios between body scale and some bit of the environment measurable in the same units. (See, e.g., work on gap crossing by Mark 1987; Burton 1992, 1994; Jiang and Mark 1994; Cornus, Montagne, and Laurent 1999; Mark et al. 1999.) Many experimentalists, I suspect, have not given much thought to this fact, simply assuming that what they are measuring just are affordances. Given the discussion above, it might seem natural to say that the affordance is expressed as the following relation:

affords-climbing (my leg length, riser height),

which is perceivable whenever the ratio of my leg length to the riser height is within a certain range. Doing so is a mistake: it must be remembered that body scale is just an easily quantifiable stand-in for ability. Most theoretical work on affordances does not make this mistake, pointing out that the animal-side counterparts of affordances are effectivities (e.g., Turvey 1992; Reed 1996; Stoffregen 2000; Michaels 2000; see above for discussion).[6]

Although body scale is easily measured, it is only occasionally a good placeholder for ability. In most cases, there is not a tight relation between body scale and ability. Indeed, recent research seems to be calling even the paradigm cases of body-scaled studies of affordances into question. Consider, for example, research by Cesari, Formenti, and Olivato (2003) on stair-climbing affordances. The experiments they report indicate that subjects perceive stair-climbing and descending affordances not as the ratio between leg length and riser height (as Warren 1984 holds) but rather as a relation between stepping ability and riser height. In the Cesari et al. study, subjects were asked to determine the highest step they could climb; this variable was called "perceived riser height." Subjects were then asked to (1) approach the steps from a distance of four meters as if they were going to climb them, (2) stop, and then (3) climb the stairs. The important variable here was distance from the subject's foot to the stair bottom when the subject stopped. It was found that different types of subject (children, young adults, older adults) had the same optimal ratio of distance from step to riser height, which is to say that they had the same ratio for the highest step they could climb. This ratio is a function of stair-climbing ability, not leg length. To see this, consider further results from the same set of studies. First, there was an important difference between older adults, on the one hand, and younger adults and children, on the other: older adults maintained the optimal ratio of distance from step to step height for steps as much as 10 percent shorter than the maximum steps they could climb, whereas in younger subjects the ratio changes significantly for steps 10 percent shorter than the maximum climbable height. Finally, Cesari et al.

found that older adults are significantly less flexible than younger adults and children.

Put together, Cesari et al.'s results indicate quite strongly that the relevant animal-side variable for stair-climbing affordances is climbing ability. First, there is an optimal ratio of height to distance for stair climbing, and all subjects used this information to determine the tallest step they could climb. Less flexible older adults maintained this ratio even for steps lower than their highest climbable steps; young adults and children did not. Given the flexibility results, older adults have different stair-climbing abilities than young adults and children. They also use the ratio differently, choosing to maintain the optimal ratio even for situations in which they can climb stairs relatively easily. So, the ratio, which is the aspect of the environment perceived in determining climbability, is perceived in terms of ability.

Two more experiments, done in my lab, show similar results for gap-crossing affordances. In the first, we (unpublished data from experiments discussed in Chemero, Klein, and Cordeiro 2003) asked subjects to stand on a platform and judge whether or not they could step across a series of differently sized gaps onto another platform. We then measured the subjects' leg length and the length of an actual step they took on the floor (not on the platform). We calculated two π numbers: one is the ratio of leg length to the maximum gap size subjects judged they could cross; the second is the ratio of step length to the maximum gap size subjects judged they could cross. We found first that subjects perceived gap-crossing affordances very accurately: the ratio of step size to maximum gap judged crossable was equal to one. Second, we found that step size was much more highly correlated with maximum gap judged crossable than leg length was. In fact, partial regression revealed that the correlation between maximum gap judged crossable and leg length, with the effect of step length subtracted, was zero. So our subjects perceived gap-crossing affordances very accurately, and they did so in terms of their stepping abilities, not leg length. In another experiment (Fox and Chemero, unpublished data), we compared the perception of gap-crossing affordances by college students and senior citizens. As in the prior study, we measured leg length and step size, and determined the maximum gap the subjects judged they could step across. We found that the mean leg lengths for college students and senior citizens were the same, but that college students stepped farther and judged that they could cross larger gaps. For both groups, step size was highly correlated with maximum gap size judged crossable. But only college students had significant correlations between leg length and maximum gap judged crossable. Like the Cesari et al. experiments, these studies show that if one can separate body scale and ability, it becomes clear that affordances are functions of, and perceived in terms of, ability.

Affordances, then, are relations between abilities and features of the environment. Affordances, that is, have this structure:

Affords-ϕ (feature, ability).

7.4.3 Affordances, Abilities, and Dispositions

Thus far, I have been using the words "ability" and "effectivity" more or less interchangeably. There are two things about effectivities as they are typically discussed that makes them different from abilities, however. First, effectivities are defined as the organismal complement to affordances *qua* dispositional properties of the environment (Turvey et al. 1981; Shaw, Turvey, and Mace 1982; Warren 1984; Turvey 1992). I have been arguing that affordances are not properties of the environment; thus there is no need for the complementing property in the organism. Second, effectivities are defined as dispositions. Abilities are not dispositions.

The problem with seeing abilities as dispositions is that when coupled with the right enabling conditions, dispositions are guaranteed to become manifest. The soluble solid sugar will always dissolve in water in suitable conditions. This is not true of abilities. Having the ability to walk does not mean that one will not fall down even in the ideal conditions for walking.[7] This is to point out that there is something inherently normative about abilities. Individuals with abilities are supposed to behave in particular ways, and they may fail to do so. Dispositions, on the other hand, never fail; they simply are or are not in the appropriate circumstances to become manifest. A better way to understand abilities is as functions. Functions depend on an individual animal's developmental history or the evolutionary history of the species, both of which occur in the context of the environment. Given this, it is actually more appropriate to understand abilities, like affordances, as being inherent not in animals, but in animal–environment systems. That is, like affordances, abilities are relations.[8] Abilities come to play the role they do in the behavioral economy of the animal because, at some point in the past, they helped the animal (or its ancestor) to survive, reproduce, or flourish in its environment. Yet even in identical circumstances to those in which they were helpful in the past, abilities can fail to become manifest; there can, that is, be a malfunction. By taking abilities to be functions, we can account for the fact that even on a firm surface, with no wind, while perfectly healthy and sober, I may fail in my attempt to climb a step that affords climbing for me. This is inconceivable in the case of dispositions, which necessarily become manifest whenever their actualizing circumstances are present.[9]

This analysis of abilities, as functions and not as dispositions, has a further noteworthy consequence. Since functions depend on evolutionary history and affordances are partly constituted by functions, affordances are tied to evolution. This makes ecological psychology a branch of biology, and a truly ecological science (Withagen and Chemero 2009). But notice that it does so without being selectionist in the way Reed's (1996) understanding of affordances is.[10] That is, it does not assume that affordances are resources that exert selection pressure. I take it that being evolutionary and ecological but not selectionist is a positive feature of the theory of affordances outlined here. First, there are (admittedly highly controversial) reasons from theoretical evolutionary biology to be skeptical of selectionist views of evolution.[11] And, indeed, radical embodied cognitive scientists should align themselves with nonselectionist, developmental systems approaches in biology (Griffiths and Gray 2001; see section 7.6 below for more on the connection between radical embodied cognitive science and these approaches in biology). Second, a selectionist view of the relationship between affordances and animals fails to do justice to the mutuality of animal and environment (Gibson 1979). If it is affordances that exert selection pressure, it cannot be, as Gibson suggested, that animals imply niches (sets of affordances—see below) and vice versa. Rather, on the selectionist view, it is affordances that are in the driver's seat, and animals must conform to them over evolutionary history. On the view being offered here, there is true animal–environment mutuality. Affordances, which are the glue that holds the animal and environment together, exist only in virtue of selection pressure exerted on animals by the normal physical environment. They arise along with the abilities of animals to perceive and take advantage of them.

7.4.4 Perceiving Affordances

Any account of the ontology of affordances requires a story about perceiving affordances. Perception for the radical embodied cognitive scientist is direct and can be conceptualized as a relation between the perceiver and what is perceived. On the account of affordances outlined here, this relation looks like this.

Perceives [animal, affords-ϕ (feature, ability)].

This is the act of perception that is studied by the psychologist, from a third-person perspective. Typically, though, an animal is consciously aware only of the affordance relation, and not the constituent relata. That is, from the point of view of a behaving animal, the structure of the perception of affordances will be this:

Perceives [animal, affordance-for-ϕ].

This is surely the usual phenomenology of humans. I am normally not aware of anything about my climbing abilities or riser heights when I perceive that I can climb a step. Humans, however, can—with training and when so inclined—perceive things about their abilities and features of the physical environment. I suspect that most nonhuman animals are incapable of this.

7.5 Ecological Ontology

Affordances 1.1 are neither properties of the animal alone, nor properties of the environment alone. Instead they are relations between abilities and some feature of a situation. They are not kickable and often not easily localizable physically, but they are nonetheless perfectly real and perfectly perceivable. There are still unanswered questions about affordances. In the next sections, I will answer three of them.

7.5.1 Affordances and Niches

Gibson (1979) points out that a niche is the set of affordances for a particular animal. Different animals, with different abilities, may have physically colocated but nonetheless nonoverlapping niches. For example, a human and a bacterium may share a physical location (as when a bacterium is inside a human), but their niches will not overlap. As noted above, Gibson also suggests that this is the way to make sense of the mutuality of animals and environments. An animal's abilities imply an ecological niche. Conversely, an ecological niche implies an animal. Given the relational definition of affordances, we can make sense of these facts about niches.

Start by taking organisms to be sets of abilities. These abilities will be interconnected, of course. An animal cannot have the ability to run if it cannot maintain its posture, nor will it be able to climb a tree if it cannot affix itself to things (with suction, by grabbing, etc.). As Reed (1996) points out in his revealing analysis of action systems, all other abilities will depend on basic orienting abilities, abilities to maintain posture, and the like. There will also be a nested structure of abilities, in which larger abilities will be composed of smaller-scale abilities. Each of an animal's abilities will have a set of situations in which it can be exercised. But no larger-scale ability will be exercisable in situations in which its component smaller-scale abilities can't be exercised; similarly no ability will be exercisable in situations in which a more basic ability on which it depends cannot be exercised. Thus, if walking is leg swinging, falling, and catching yourself, walking will be impossible in situations in which one cannot swing a leg, or fall, or catch oneself. Walking will also not be possible in situations with no gravity, or too much gravity, or in which the atmosphere is in flames, because the basic orienting system on which walking depends is inoperable in these situations.

All this said, we can define an animal's niche as the set of situations in which one or more of its abilities can be exercised. To put this formally, start with the set of all possible situations, S. For each ability a_i there is a subset of S, s_i in which that ability can be exercised. Suppose an organism has abilities $a_1 \ldots a_n$. That organism's niche will be the union of $s_1 \ldots s_n$, for each ability $a_1 \ldots a_n$ that the organism has. This collection of situations forms the organism's cognitive, behavioral, and phenomenological niche.

7.5.2 Affordances and Events

In his 2000 paper "Affordances and Events," Stoffregen argues that events, conceived as changes in the physical layout, are not perceivable according to ecological psychology. This is the case, he argued, because what we perceive are affordances, and events and affordances are of different ontological kinds. In response, I (Chemero 2000b) offered a different understanding of events, an understanding according to which event perception is not problematic for ecological psychology. Perceivable events, I argued, are changes in the layout of affordances. A later paper by Chemero, Klein, and Cordeiro (2003) provides experimental evidence that events so described can be perceived. I will discuss these data in chapter 9. Here, I will limit discussion to how the definition of affordances outlined here impacts the theory of events just described.

Assume that affordances are relations between abilities and features of environmental situations and that events are changes in the layout of affordances in the animal–environment system. How, then, do events happen? Equivalently, how do affordances change? Most changes in relations between the abilities of animals and environmental situations will be changes in environmental situations. Most events, that is, will result from changes in the physical environment. If the glass of water spills, the affordance drinkability disappears because my drinking abilities are not appropriate for spilled water; once the apple falls from the tree it is edible, because my being able to grasp the apple is a necessary condition for my being able to eat it. In cases such as these, there are events, changes in affordances, without changes in abilities. There can also be changes in affordances without changes in the features of the environment. The very same stair no longer affords climbing to an individual whose stepping abilities have decayed as a result of aging. Since abilities typically change more slowly than the environment, these events will happen less frequently than events that result from changes in the environment.

7.5.3 Do Affordances Exist without Animals?

For all the noise ecological psychologists make about being realists, it is not obvious at the outset that ecological psychology is not a form of idealism, in which perceivables exist only when they are perceived. It is a small step from this to a global idealism, in which the world disappears whenever I close my eyes. (See chapter 9 for a more general discussion of realism and radical embodied cognitive science.) Reed's (1996) conception of affordances as resources that exert selection pressure avoids this issue by making it the case that affordances exist unproblematically, even without animals capable of perceiving them. Other understandings of affordances must face this problem. For Turvey et al. (1981), Warren (1984), Turvey (1992), and Michaels (2000), who claim that affordances must be complemented by the effectivities of animals, the status of affordances is unclear in the absence of animals. Similarly, if affordances are relations between abilities and situations, as in Affordances 1.1, affordances depend in some sense on animals. The questions that must be answered are: In what sense do affordances depend on animals? Do affordances exist without animals?

As a first pass at answering these questions, I will once again coopt some terminology from Dennett (1998). Dennett distinguishes between things that are lovely and things that are suspect. To see the distinction, consider that a female hippopotamus in a zoo might be lovely, even if no male hippopotamus has ever seen her. She is lovely just in case if a male hippopotamus were to see her, he would find her to be so. The key is that being lovely depends on a potential observer, not an actual act of observation. Compare this to being suspect. To be suspect, something actually has to be under suspicion. Being suspect requires an actual observer. Whether affordances exist without animals is a matter of whether affordances are lovely or suspect. Affordances, we can see, are lovely. A feature of some situation might exist just as it is even if there are no animals. There will be affordances in which that feature takes part as long as some animal exists with the appropriate ability. This is the case even if that animal is nowhere in the vicinity of the situation that affords something to it.

Affordances do not disappear when there is no local animal to perceive and take advantage of them. They are perfectly real entities that can be objectively studied and are in no way figments of the imagination of the animal that perceives them. So radical embodied cognitive science is not a form of idealism. But affordances do depend on the existence of some animal that could perceive them, if the right conditions were met. Because affordances, the primary perceivables according to ecological psychology, depend in this way on animals, the ontology of ecological psychology is not a simple form of realism. It is a form of realism about the world as it is perceived and experienced—affordances, which are inherently meaningful, are in the world, and not merely projected onto it by animals. I will say a lot more about how this can be true in chapter 9.

7.6 Affordances 2.0

When considered within the confines of the ongoing theoretical debate among ecological psychologists about the nature of affordances, the theory of affordances just outlined seems to me to be a significant improvement over prior attempts to give a formal theory of affordances. (Of course, it would seem that way to its author.) In retrospect, however, it seems inadequate to the practice of radical embodied cognitive scientists. It is inadequate because radical embodied cognitive scientists are dynamicists, and in their actual experimental practices they understand affordances dynamically. Yet the formal theories of affordances offered by Gibson and later ecological psychologists (Affordances 1.0) and my attempt to improve on them (Affordances 1.1) define affordances statically. Perhaps this occurred because the view of affordances that forms the basis for this discussion was originally formulated by Turvey et al. (1981) at a time before dynamical systems modeling had so thoroughly infected ecological psychology. Now, however, it seems clear that we (ecological psychologists, radical embodied cognitive scientists) need a theory of affordances that is dynamical root and branch. My Affordances 1.1 is not that. Radical embodied cognitive science requires Affordances 2.0, a dynamical theory of affordances.

To formulate Affordances 2.0, start with Affordances 1.1, according to which affordances are relations between abilities to perceive and act and features of the environment. Then consider the interaction over time between an animal's sensorimotor abilities, that is, its embodied capacities for perception and action, and its niche, that is, the set of affordances available to it. This is depicted in figure 7.1. Over developmental time, an animal's sensorimotor abilities select its niche—the animal will become

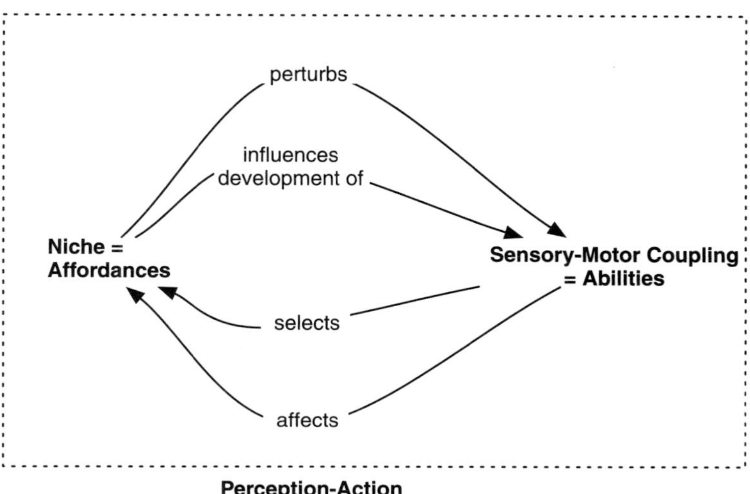

Figure 7.1

selectively sensitive to information relevant to the things it is able to do. Also over developmental time, the niche will strongly influence the development of the animal's ability to perceive and act. Over the shorter time scales of behavior, the animal's sensorimotor abilities manifest themselves in embodied action that causes changes in the layout of available affordances, and these affordances will change the way abilities are exercised in action. The key point here is that affordances and abilities are not just defined in terms of one another as in the dispositional and relational views discussed above, but causally interact in real time and are causally dependent on one another.

There are three noteworthy consequences of the shift to Affordances 2.0. First, this is not so much a new way of understanding affordances as a critique of prior attempts to come up with a *definition* of the term "affordance." Ecological psychologists have always been aware of, indeed keenly interested in, the interaction of affordances and abilities in real time. As noted above, radical embodied cognitive scientists (including ecological psychologists) study perception and action dynamically. Affordances 2.0 is an attempt to develop a theoretical understanding of affordances that is more in line with the experimental and explanatory practices of ecological psychologists. (See Chemero 2008.)

Second, notice that this reconceptualization of affordances is a variety of niche construction that occurs over shorter time scales and in which the constructed niche is an animal's individual behavioral, cognitive, and phenomenological niche. In more standard biological niche construction, the activity of some population of organisms alters, sometimes dramatically, the population's own ecological niche as well as those of other organisms (Odling-Smee, Laland, and Feldman 2003). These animal-caused alterations to niches have profound and wide-reaching effects over evolutionary time. And, indeed, the population of organisms and the niche are so tightly coupled that Griffiths and Gray (2001) recommend that they form a unified developmental system that is to be modeled with just one variable *Œ*. The dynamics of this variable are specified in the following equation

$$dŒ_{pop}/dt = f(Œ_{pop}, E) \qquad (7.1)$$

in which $Œ_{pop}$ is the coupled organism–niche system for the population and E is the physical environment. The variety of niche construction sketched in Affordances 2.0 is an equally tightly coupled animal–environment system. It differs from the much-discussed biological case in two ways. First, the constructed niche is for an individual organism, not for a population. Second, it occurs over shorter time scales—an animal's activities alter the world as the animal experiences it, and these alterations to the phenomenological-cognitive-behavioral niche, in turn, affect the animal's behavior and the development of its abilities to perceive and act, which further alter the phenomenological-cognitive-behavioral niche, and on and on. Affordances 2.0, therefore, emphasizes the connections between radical embodied cognitive science and its natural allies in biology, that is, developmental systems and niche construction.

Third, this reconceptualization of affordances is explicitly formulated to make the natural, but largely unmade, connections between ecological psychology and another form of radical embodied cognitive science: the burgeoning enactivist movement in the cognitive sciences (Varela, Thompson, and Rosch 1991; Thompson 2007). Figure 7.2 is an expanded version of figure 7.1, expanded to show the connection between organisms and sensorimotor coupling, as understood by enactivists, and Affordances 2.0. Enactivists view the organism as a self-organizing, autonomous, autopoietic system. In this system, the nervous system generates neuronal assemblies that make sensorimotor abilities possible, and these sensorimotor abilities modulate the dynamics of the nervous system. Combining Affordances 2.0 with enactivist studies of the organism makes radical embodied cognitive science a fully dynamical science of the entire brain–body–environment system: nonrepresentational neurodynamic studies of the nervous system and sensorimotor abilities (Cosmelli, Lachaux, and Thompson 2007;

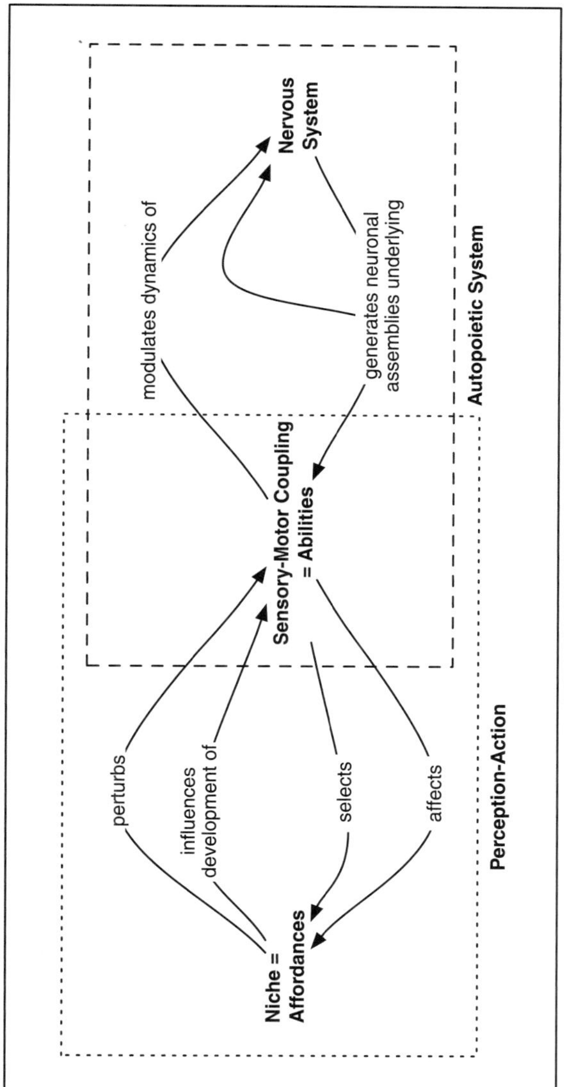
Nervous
System
modulates dynamics of
generates neuronal
assemblies underlying
Autopoietic System
Sensory-Motor Coupling
= Abilities
perturbs
influences
development of
selects
affects
Niche =
Affordances
Perception-Action
Animal-Environment System

Figure 7.2

Thompson and Varela 2001) match up with ecological psychological studies of affordances and sensorimotor abilities. Obviously, much more work is required to genuinely integrate ecological and enactive cognitive science under the banner of radical embodied cognitive science. These two approaches have more in common than their proponents realize. Combining them could make radical embodied cognitive science a much more significant force in the cognitive science community than either the ecological or enactive movements are separately.

7.7 Information about Affordances

So far I've given some details about what affordances are, how they relate to other important pieces of an ecological ontology, and how they ought to be understood dynamically. But I haven't directly addressed what Gibson called the central question for the theory of affordances: "The central question for the theory of affordances is not whether they exist and are real, but whether information is available in the ambient light for [directly] perceiving them" (1979, 140). I have already discussed several cases that imply that there is information available in the ambient light for the perception of affordances without mental gymnastics. For example, τ and its temporal derivatives provide information about affordances for locomotion, pursuit, and collision avoidance. (See also the discussions of gap-crossing and stair-climbing affordances in this chapter.) In this section, I will discuss one more piece of evidence that there is information in the environment that enables the direct perception of affordances: perception of moveability by dynamic touch. I will discuss dynamic touch (a.k.a. haptic perception) here for three reasons. First, it is an area of very active research in ecological psychology, but is not well known to most cognitive scientists. Second, cognitive scientists and philosophers tend to focus too narrowly on visual perception, ignoring the other senses. Third, perception by dynamic touch is a temporally extended process, which shows the value of a dynamic conception of affordances.

7.7.1 Perception by Dynamic Touch

Right now, you are holding a book.[12] You can see the book, but if you were to close your eyes, you would still have considerable information about the book. The book is exerting mechanical pressure on the portions of your fingers that are touching it. If you move your fingers along the surface of the book, you can feel its texture. Notice that only a small portion of the book is actually in contact with only parts of your fingers. Yet, even with your eyes closed, you can tell how big the book is: not just how heavy, but also how long, wide, and thick. You can also tell its orientation. (Is it parallel to the floor? Perpendicular? At some other angle?) This is possible because your muscles are working so that you can hold the book. You are applying pressure with your fingers to keep the book from slipping through them, and you are also working with your wrist and the rest of your arm to fight gravity and keep the book in place, in a position where you would easily be able to see it were your eyes open. This is dynamic touch.

Dynamic touch is *action*. Holding the book takes work from your muscles, and this work causes pressure and deformation to muscles and tendons, stimulating mechanoreceptors just as light stimulates retinal cells. This stimulation is the primary source of information for dynamic touch. (See Gibson 1962, 1966; Turvey 1996; Carello and Turvey 2000.) Notice too that to perceive the book by dynamic touch, you have to heft it; that is, you have to intentionally move it around, actively exploring the way it exerts forces on the muscles of your hands, wrists, and arms. As you move the book, the forces it exerts on your body change, which changes the way you experience the book and the affordances for continued active exploration of the book.

Solomon and Turvey (1988) studied the perception of length by dynamic touch.[13] Subjects were seated, placed their arm on a table so that they could move only their wrist and hand, and asked to grab the end of a rod occluded by a curtain. They judged the rod's length by moving a visible object (a block of wood on wheels) to the distance of the rod's length with their other hand. Subjects were quite good at this task, but what information were they using? Length per se cannot be perceived by dynamic touch, because length cannot affect mechanoreceptors. Solomon and Turvey showed that the length of rods is perceived by sensitivity to their rotational inertia, their resistance to turning about the wrist. Mathematically speaking, rotational inertia is quantified as the primary moment of inertia, which is approximately

$$I_1 = 1/3\ m \cdot L^2, \tag{7.2}$$

where m is the mass of the rod and L is its length.[14] Solomon and Turvey's results suggest that this moment of inertia is the higher-order variable that provides information about the length of a wielded rod, and it does so in a form that mechanoreceptors are sensitive to. But think again about the book you're holding. If you hold it in just one hand and use just your wrist, you can rotate it up and down, side to side, and you can twist it. That is, you can rotate it in three dimensions. Notice too that it will resist your attempts to move it differently in different directions. So just one moment of inertia will not provide enough information to determine an object's length. Instead, one must use the *inertia tensor*, a three by three matrix that can be used to determine three principal moments of inertia, called eigenvalues. These three moments of inertia are the source of information for perception by dynamic touch (Turvey 1996). In fact, the values of these three moments of inertia define an ellipsoid, a three-dimensional virtual shape that resembles the shape of a wielded object. For example, a sphere generates rotational inertia so that the three principal moments of inertia are equal. Burton, Turvey, and Solomon (1990) showed that subjects could use this information to perceive shape: their subjects could visually select objects that matched occluded objects they wielded (by holding a stick attached at the base, so they could not feel the object's shape).

Later work on dynamic touch showed that subjects could perceive a wide variety of properties of objects based on the inertial tensor. For reviews, see Turvey 1996; Pagano and Turvey 1998; and Carello and Turvey 2000. Remember, though, that the issue for ecological psychology is whether there is information available for affordances, and so far I have been discussing object properties such as mass, length, and shape. I will now briefly discuss research showing that there is information for perceiving affordances by dynamic touch.

7.7.2 Dynamic Touch and the Size-Weight Illusion

One of the riddles I remember from when I was a child went as follows: Which is heavier, a pound of feathers or a pound of lead? An eight-year-old who thinks he is smart will quickly answer that the pound of lead is heavier. Most eight-year-olds will make this mistake only once. When asked to make this judgment by touch rather than by knowledge of the materials, however, they will continue to make the mistake.[15] This is called the *size-weight illusion* (Charpentier 1891; Murray et al. 1999). Given two objects of equal mass, people (both children and adults) judge the one with a smaller diameter to be heavier. That is, they judge a comparatively small pound of lead to be heavier than a comparatively large pound of feathers. This illusion has typically been taken to be the result of mental gymnastics: one judges an object's size and uses this judgment to (erroneously) correct one's judgment of weight.

To investigate the size-weight illusion, Amazeen and Turvey (1996) created what are called *tensor objects*. Tensor objects are composed of two rods connected to form a "plus" sign, with a third rod attached perpendicular to the point at which the two rods forming the "plus" sign intersect. Metal

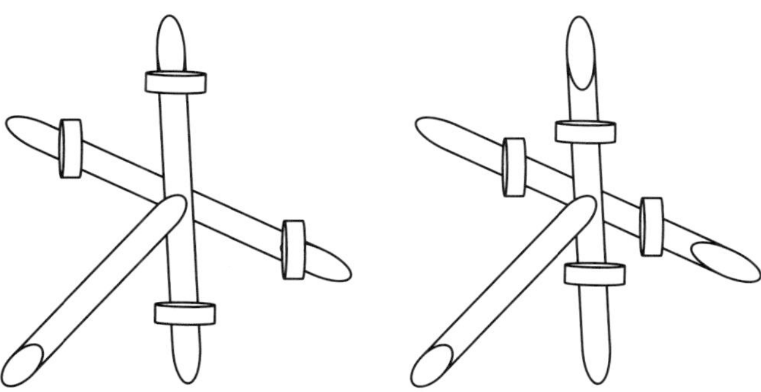

Figure 7.3
A tensor object (Amazeen and Turvey 1996).

rings are attached at different locations on the rods on the object so as to create tensor objects with different weight distributions. (See figure 7.3.) Different weight distribution means different moments of inertia (i.e., different pressures felt at the wrist joint). These tensor objects allowed Amazeen and Turvey to construct a series of objects of identical size and weight, but with different moments of inertia designed to mimic the stimuli typically used in experiments that produce the size-weight illusion. They found that subjects judged the heaviness of these tensor objects as predicted by their inertia tensors, despite the fact that they were the same size and weight. This occurred both when subjects wielded the objects occluded behind a curtain and when they could see the objects (covered tightly with paper to make their volume apparent but hide the distribution of the metal weights). Thus, Amazeen and Turvey showed that subjects do not perceive the weight of objects by judging their size (whether by touch alone or by vision and touch) and mentally combining that judgment with their felt force due to gravity. Instead, they use the information available at the wrist, as determined by the object's inertial tensor.

The point of the above is that humans do not misperceive weight by mentally calculating it, computationally combining size and force due to gravity. Instead, they correctly perceive the information in the inertial tensor, which does not carry information about weight alone. (Remember from formula 7.1 that the principal moment of inertia is a function of both length and mass.) What, then, is the information in the inertial tensor about? More recent work by Shockley, Carello, and Turvey (2004) indicates that these subjects perceive the affordance *moveability*. In particular, they showed that subjects who misjudge the weight of an object when falling prey to the size-weight illusion make nearly identical judgments about whether the object is moveable. That is, the question "On a scale of 1 to 100, where 50 is the control object, how heavy is this object?" gets the same answer as "On a scale of 1 to 100, where 50 is the control object, how easy is it to move this object?" So the size-weight illusion occurs because subjects are actually basing their judgments on perception of moveability, not weight, and their judgments about moveability are accurate. Indeed, it makes perfect sense that moveability is what subjects perceive by dynamic touch. Many, many experiments have confirmed that an object's inertial tensor is the source of the information for dynamic touch. As noted above, the eigenvalues of an object's inertial tensor carry information about the object's rotational inertia, which is to say they carry information about the object's tendency to resist rotation in a particular direction, which is to say they carry information about how difficult it is to move the object.

There is, then, information about the affordance moveability available for direct perception. I have also provided descriptions of empirical investigations into the directly perceivable information available for affordances for climbing, gap crossing, guidance of locomotion, and analogical reasoning. The answer to Gibson's central question is clearly "Yes": information about affordances is available in the environment.

7.7.3 Is Dynamic Touch a Special Case?

I have just described a case in which one can perceive affordances using dynamic touch.[16] I could just as easily have described another line of research in which one perceives the affordances of tools by dynamic touch (Carello et al. 1999; Cooper, Carello, and Turvey 1999; Wagman and Carello 2001, 2003; Wagman and Taylor 2004). In fact, the majority of the experimental research on perception of affordances done in recent years has been dynamic touch research. It is worth pausing to consider why that is the case. On the face of it, it might seem that perception by dynamic touch is a special case. Perception by dynamic touch is a matter of detecting information that centers on the wrist. This information is picked up by mechanoreceptors in the muscles and tendons of the hand, wrist, and arm. So in perception by dynamic touch, the information for perception is centered on the location of the action that is to be undertaken. Furthermore, because the eigenvalues of the inertial tensor carry information about resistance to rotation, the information available at the wrist is already "formatted" for use in action. Dynamic touch is the ideal kind of perception to call upon if one wants to explain links between perception and action without resorting to mental gymnastics. Because of the colocation of receptors and effectors and because no transformations are needed, the information available at the wrist is directly usable for controlling action.

The worry one might have at this point is that dynamic touch is the *only* kind of perception in which this is true. Compare dynamic touch with vision. It would seem that we see with our eyes and act on visual information with the rest of our bodies. This would put some distance between visual perception and action, leading to the worry that dynamic touch is a special case. There are two ways in which dynamic touch seems special. First, the information gathering and action occur at the same location of the body. Second, the information is correctly formatted for action. We have seen already that this second feature of dynamic touch does not differentiate it from vision: visual information *can* be in the right format for guiding action (e.g., τ and collision, discussed in chapter 6). Furthermore, if one understands vision correctly, it is simply false that vision and visually guided action happen at different places in the body. To see this, consider the distinction Gibson made between sensory modalities and perceptual systems (Gibson 1966). A sensory modality is defined anatomically, in terms of a collection of energy-specific receptor cells that make it up and the brain areas they are connected to. Perceptual systems, on the other hand, are defined functionally, in terms of information-gathering activity. Perceptual systems include energy-specific receptors and brain areas as proper parts, but also include parts of the organism that adjust, modify, or orient the receptors in active exploration. The human visual system, for example, includes the eyes and the canonical visual neural pathways along with the muscles and brain areas involved in eye movements and orientation of the head and neck, not to mention the head and neck themselves—all the parts of a human that take part in the activity of exploring the environment by looking around. In fact, Reed (1996) argues that perceptual systems are a variety of action system. Vision, the act of looking and seeing, is carried out by the entire visual system—an action system whose function is looking—and not merely by the visual sensory modality.

Understanding that perception is accomplished by perceptual systems, not sensory modalities, makes clear that dynamic touch is not a special case and not the only sense for which the information pickup and information-guided action are colocated. The same is true of the visual system, which uses information available in light to direct saccades and scan, focus, and track with the eyes, but also to control squinting, turn and rotate the head and neck to point both eyes at something of interest, crane to see over or around something, and so on. So information pickup by looking and the activity of looking *do* happen at the same place, but that place is the multipart visual system.

The haptic system, the system whose functions include dynamic touch, is not a special direct-perception-friendly perceptual system, but there is a way in which it differs from other perceptual systems. The difference, though, is in the sensory modalities commonly associated with the systems. The energy-specific receptors of the visual, auditory, and gustatory-olfactory systems are localized in organs on the head (in humans). In contrast, the receptors commonly associated with the sensory modality touch (the nerves in the skin, mechanoreceptors), are spread across the body. Furthermore, for these receptors to be activated, you have to actually be in contact with the object, usually acting upon it. This spatial diffuseness of the sensory modality and the fact that its receptors are only stimulated by contact with objects being sensed makes the tight connections between perception and action more obvious for dynamic touch than for other senses. But these special features of touch are special features of the sensory modality, not the perceptual system of which the sensory modality is a proper part, and it is perceptual systems, not sensory modalities, that pick up information about affordances.

7.8 Part III, Outro

This ends our introduction to Gibsonian ecological psychology, which I recommend as a nonrepresentational guide to discovery for radical embodied cognitive science. I have sketched a picture of animals as active agents, interacting with a world replete with information, and indeed generating information with their actions, including information about affordances. Perception and action, on this view, are tightly interconnected. Indeed, perception is a variety of action, and a good deal of action is done in the service of perception. The coupling of perception and action and the availability of information about affordances allow animals to guide their behavior without resorting to mental gymnastics. As noted in chapter 5, this theory of the nature of animals and their activity meshes perfectly with dynamical systems theory as a modeling tool. Again, as noted in chapter 5, this is unsurprising, given that dynamical systems theory was introduced as a modeling tool for psychology by ecological psychologists.

Here, then, is radical embodied cognitive science: Animals are active perceivers of and actors in an information-rich environment, and some of the information in the environment, the information to which animals are especially attuned, is about affordances. Unified animal–environment systems are to be modeled using the tools of dynamical systems theory. There is no need to posit representations of the environment inside the animal (or computations thereupon) because animals and environments are taken, both in theory and models, to be coupled.

In the final part of the book, I will examine how radical embodied cognitive science interacts with some traditional philosophical problems.

IV Philosophical Consequences

"Hurry—this way!" Everyone was converging on McTaggart Hall, the headquarters of the Metaphysics Department, whose storm-cellar was known throughout the region as the roomiest and best-appointed such refuge between Cleveland and Denver. The mathematicians lit gas-mantles and storm-lamps, and waited for the electric light to fail.

—Thomas Pynchon, *Against the Day* (2006)

8 Neurophilosophy Meets Radical Embodied Cognitive Science

I've spent the first seven chapters of this book explaining the nature of radical embodied cognitive science, both as a theory of what cognition is and as a set of tools for explaining it. In this, the last part of the book, I will discuss the way that this theory of cognition and set of explanatory tools should make us think about a few philosophical problems. In this chapter, I will talk about the mind–body problem. As one might expect, antireductionist conclusions follow pretty directly from radical embodied cognitive science. In chapter 9, I will address more general metaphysical issues. It has been argued several times, including once by me (Chemero 1998a), that irrealist conclusions follow from embodied cognitive science, radical or not. In chapter 9, I will argue that these conclusions do not, in fact, follow and that they are based on hidden premises that fans of embodied cognition ought not embrace. I will also, in chapter 9, say how radical embodied cognitive scientists ought to think about consciousness.

Before I start in on this spurt of philosophizing, it is worth pausing to comment on the character of the arguments I will be making. My attempts to develop positions on these classical philosophical problems will not be based on distinction mongering, thought experiments, or fanciful case studies. I will not be talking about Martians, varieties of supervenience, or zombies. I take it that it is an obsession with things like this that causes (many) cognitive scientists to view philosophers as boring know-it-alls who are out of touch with reality. It also leads (many) philosophers to view cognitive scientists as failing to address "the real problems." This situation is especially dangerous to philosophers, who seem increasingly irrelevant to colleagues outside their departments. Indeed, even some philosophers view their own colleagues as irrelevant. To take two recent examples, Churchland (2002) mocks those who do not apply findings in neuroscience to philosophical problems as "no-brainers"; Bickle (2003) mocks anyone with traditional philosophical concerns, including "naturalistic philosophers of mind." Though (in most moods) I do not endorse the name calling, I do think that Churchland and Bickle are on the right track about the kinds of arguments that philosophers ought to be making. So in what follows, I will address philosophical problems and develop philosophical positions using experiments and data, as opposed to trying to imagine the properties of the c-fibers of Martian zombies.

On, then, to this chapter's big philosophical issue: the mind–body problem. The astute reader will have noticed that I have, thus far, said very little about brains. This is surprising in an age in which a good deal of highly regarded research in cognitive science and psychology is the repetition of prior experiments, but this time with magnets strapped to the heads of the subjects, and when any self-respecting philosopher of mind can tell you something about the function of the lateral geniculate nucleus. One of the initiating causes of the recent philosophical fondness for neuroscience was Patricia Churchland's *Neurophilosophy* (1986). This book began a movement bearing its name, one that truly came of age in 1999 when Kathleen Akins won a million-dollar fellowship to begin the McDonnell Project in Philosophy and the Neurosciences. The McDonnell project put neurophilosophy at the forefront of philosophy of mind and cognitive science, yielding proliferating articles, conferences, special journal issues, and books.

In this chapter, I will look at neurophilosophy and reductionist claims made by neurophilosophers from the perspective of radical embodied cognitive science.[1] An analysis such as this one is especially important as proponents of radical embodied cognitive science focus primarily on environmental information, perception, and action, and have (sometimes correctly) been taken to be no-brainers, denying the importance of the brain in understanding cognition. Given the ascendancy of neuroscience and neurophilosophy, such an attitude toward the brain simply will not do. In this chapter, I will recommend a way for radical embodied cognitive scientists to come to terms with the undeniable importance of neuroscience and neurophilosophy, showing that it is possible to resist brain-obsession without becoming a no-brainer.

8.1 Reduction, Ruthless and Otherwise

I take it that readers of a book like this one do not need a detailed discussion of reductionism. I will, therefore, describe reductionism only briefly, focusing specifically on reductionism as it relates to the mind–body problem. The first point to make is that, following Nagel (1961), I will be interested in intertheoretic reduction, as opposed to ontological reduction. (See Silberstein 2002 for a discussion of both styles of reductionism.) That is, as I will use the word, reduction is a matter of accounting for the facts, generalizations, and laws of one theory, the reduced theory, in terms of the facts, generalizations, and laws of a second, more general theory, the base theory, along with some bridge principles. In a successful reduction, the base theory and the bridge principles entail the reduced theory. Nagel's basic formula has been modified many times over the years (e.g., by Hooker 1981a,b,c; Churchland 1985, 1989), but it will suffice for present purposes. A key feature of reductionism so conceived is that the base theory must be a more general theory of the same slices of space and time. That is, you have to be able to use the base theory to account for activity in the same regions of space that the reduced theory accounts for, and others to boot. Physics, then, is a good candidate for a base theory because its laws and generalizations are thought to apply always and everywhere.

In the arena of the mind–body problem, the ultimate goal of reductionists may be to use physics as a base theory, but only via intermediate theories and only in the very long term. In today's discussions the proposed reduction is from cognitive science to neuroscience. The guiding metaphor of computational cognitive science actually encourages the reduction of cognitive science to neuroscience. Computationalists present cognitive science as guided by an analogy between the mind and computer programs. The basic idea is that the mind is to the brain as the program is to the computer that is running it. So despite a good deal of antireductionist rhetoric on the part of computationalist cognitive scientists and philosophers thereof it is open to the would-be reductionist to accept the analogy and argue as follows: any explanation of the operation of a computer program would be entailed by an analysis of the computer itself, along with some bridge principles (among which would be a story about how the program is compiled, and so on). So too for the science of the mind and the science of the brain. Ultimately, reductionists will argue, the neurosciences will account for the generalizations, laws, and facts of cognitive sciences. And indeed, many philosophers of mind and cognitive science have made these arguments. The most common strategy employed here is to argue that cognitive science is reducible to cognitive neuroscience. This is a natural way to proceed: computational cognitive scientists view mental processes as computational manipulations of representations; cognitive neuroscientists view neural processes as computational manipulations of representations. Paul and Patricia Churchland have been the most famous proponents of such a reduction (P. S. Churchland 1986, 2002; P. M. Churchland 1979, 1989[2]), but see also Bickle 1998 and Bechtel and Mundale 1999. I take it that this style of reductionism is familiar.

As mentioned above, John Bickle (2003) has argued in favor of a different sort of reductionism, which he calls *ruthless reductionism,* in which cognitive science is reduced to *molecular,* rather than cognitive, neuroscience. To avoid a raft of problems that would attend such a reduction, including nitpicky issues over the exact nature of reductionism and questions of the content of cognitive states (what happens to it?), Bickle advocates what he calls *new wave metascience.* In new wave metascience, one trusts neuroscientists, who understand neuroscience much better than philosophers after all, to know what their work has accounted for. So rather than focus on the *n*th-level objections and replies to philosophical accounts of intertheoretic reduction, a new wave metascientist focuses on the claims made by scientists themselves, and lets the neuroscientific results speak. Such views might seem strange coming from Bickle, a philosopher who has contributed substantially to the debate over the exact character of intertheoretic reduction, so it is worth pausing briefly to look at ruthless reductionism in action. Bickle's demolition of multiple realizability arguments provides a good window. Looking at multiple realizability here serves another purpose: it will allow us to draw a stark contrast between the antireductionism of traditional philosophers of mind and the antireductionism that comes with radical embodied cognitive science.

The basic idea behind multiple realizability arguments is that because cognitive things could be made of material other than brain-stuff, cognitive things are not identical to neural things. (Putnam 1975 includes several of his arguments for multiple realizability.) That angels and ghosts without material brains, robots with metal and silicon brains, and Martians with brains much different from ours could in principle feel pain shows that pain is not identical to a type of brain state. So no reduction of the cognitive realm, ontological or intertheoretic, to the neural is possible. My (admittedly fallible) sense is that most philosophers believe that the cognitive is multiply realizable, and hence not reducible to the neural. Bickle's ruthless reductionist response to multiple realizability comes in two parts. First, the neuroscientist and the new wave metascientist don't care about multiple realizability, about whether angels or aliens might have differently implemented minds. The issue that matters to the (new wave meta-) scientist is whether real minds on Earth are multiply realized. The issue is not imaginable multiple *realizability*, but actual multiple *realization*. Of course, the data concerning whether mental states are multiply realized on Earth are not all in, but some are. For example, the current sense among the neuroscientific community is that long-term memory in mammals is identical to long-term potentiation. Bickle uses this consensus to argue that our cognitive scientific theory of long-term memory (including the consolidation of short-term memory and the storage of memories) is reducible to the neuroscientific theory of long-term potentiation. He then shows, in great detail, that the very same molecules and mechanisms at work in mammals during long-term potentiation are also at work in long-term potentiation in houseflies and sea slugs. Bickle takes this surprising identity of molecular mechanisms in these evolutionarily distant species to indicate that long-term potentiation and long-term memory are realized in *exactly one* way on planet Earth. So long-term memory, at least, is not multiply realized. Whether this holds of the cognitive in general is an empirical matter, one that has nothing to do with thought experiments. The ruthless reductionist bets that other capacities of interest to cognitive scientists will be accounted for as long-term memory has been, that is, in terms of very low-level molecular and genetic processes that do not vary in their instantiation in living things on Earth.

As might be obvious by now, I prefer Bickle's ruthless reductionism to other brands of reductionism for a variety of reasons. First, as should be abundantly clear, I mistrust the representational and computational assumptions of both cognitive science and cognitive neuroscience. Second, I cautiously approve of Bickle's "new wave metascience" approach. I like the cleanliness with which it cuts off many kinds of debate, particularly a priori philosophical arguments that such-and-such a theory can never account for so-and-so a subject matter. (See chapter 1.) I find these arguments even more deplorable than idle speculations about Martian physiology. Third, and perhaps most important, Bickle shines a philosophical light on the *rest* of neuroscience, the noncognitive majority that focuses on cellular, molecular, and genetic mechanisms. Fourth, I should point out that—new wave metascience aside—Bickle's reduction of the cognitive to the molecular is fully in line with the goals of other reductionists; it just goes a step further, casting cognitive science in terms of genetics and biochemistry, which is more general than cognitive neuroscience.

So: Three cheers for ruthless reductionism, which I think is the best hope for the reduction of the cognitive to the neural. I also think Bickle is correct that most neuroscientists are ruthless reductionists. But I also think that, in some cases at least, this ruthless reductionism is actually bad for neuroscience. I will argue for this via a review of research in molecular neuroscience, psychopharmacology, and behavioral genetics that uses object exploration by rats and mice to assess the role of particular brain areas, neurotransmitters, genes, and drugs in learning, memory, and intelligence, and then by describing an experiment with object exploration that I did with Charles Heyser (Chemero and Heyser 2005, 2009). The point will be to show that object exploration experiments are potentially confounded precisely because those who perform them are ruthless reductionists. This is something that should bother ruthless reductionist philosophers. I will also make recommendations concerning how one might correct these confounds. These recommendations will amount to an argument against both ruthless reductionism and regulation, nonruthless reductionism. They will also amount to an argument for radical embodied cognitive science.

Because the case against reductionism is based on the details of experimental practice (as opposed to the results of experiments), this chapter will have more detailed descriptions of experiments than we have seen in previous chapters.

8.2 Object Exploration

One of the most commonly used behavioral methodologies in animal research is the study of exploratory behavior (Renner 1990; Hughes 1997). Unfortunately, in current practice, exploratory behavior is typically assessed by observing animals in an empty open field and recording only the number of line crosses and/or rears. Although undeniably useful, this is a highly restricted view of "exploratory behavior." The normal case for animals, especially rodents, is to be in environments cluttered with objects, with many more opportunities for exploration. Many researchers, therefore, have begun to study exploratory behavior in environments that contain objects (e.g., Chen et al. 2000; Renner and Rosenzweig 1986; Roullet, Mele, and Ammassari-Teule 1997). There are many advantages to the object exploration task. For one, there is no explicit need for any food or water restriction. For another, in addition to allowing the study of object exploration per se, the task is useful for the study of various forms of learning (e.g., habituation and recognition memory).

The general procedure for this task involves a bounded open field and multiple objects. Either identical objects are used or sets of different objects are used within each trial. In either case, the set of objects is presented repeatedly, and the behavior of the animal is recorded. After a number of presentations, either an object is replaced with a novel object or the spatial configuration of the objects is changed. One can infer recognition memory from the animal's behavioral response to the environmental change. This inference is based on two aspects of behavior. First, rats and mice tend to seek out and explore novelty (as long as the novel feature is not too stressful or aversive). Second, with repeated presentation, animals become familiar with a certain set of objects. Therefore, changes in the environment should result in preferential exploration of the newly substituted object or spatially rearranged objects. Experimenters assume that in order to respond to these changes, the rat must recognize either the familiar objects or the novel spatial change. Change in the pattern of exploration of the objects, then, is taken as a measure of an animal's recognition memory.

Matt Rosen, Charles Heyser and I (Heyser, Rosen, and Chemero 2003) initially used the object exploration task to assess recognition memory in rats (Renner and Rosenzweig 1986; Roullet, Mele, and Ammassari-Teule 1997; Save et al. 1992). More specifically, we were interested in examining the effects of ethanol withdrawal on recognition memory in rats. Surprisingly, these results showed that ethanol withdrawal did not impair recognition memory. In fact, ethanol-withdrawn rats reacted with an increase in exploration of novel objects when compared to controls (nonwithdrawing rats). Initially, we concluded that perhaps ethanol withdrawal affects the habituation process in these animals. This would have been a striking finding. Imagine being continuously drunk for four weeks,[3] then finding an improved recognition memory during the first few hours of withdrawal. In other words, our data indicated that severe hangovers improve recognition memory. Unfortunately, after closer examination of the data, it became clear that the findings were greatly influenced by the properties of the objects, with rats preferring objects they could climb on to those they could not. That is, the rats showed a preference for objects that have affordances for a common rat activity.

8.3 Recent Work on Object Exploration

The results of this initial study led Charles Heyser and I to investigate whether other studies had reported similar results. In reviewing a portion of the published neuroscience literature that uses object exploration/recognition, we found that very little detail is provided about the nature of the objects selected for these tasks. Perhaps most disturbing is the fact that there is little or no discussion of why or how the particular objects were selected for use in these experiments. This lack of detail concerning the objects used in studies is unsurprising, for two reasons. First, consider the discussion of the objects used in the first modern object exploration paper, Ennaceur and Delacour 1988. This paper, which has been cited hundreds of times, has only the following as a description of the objects used: "The objects to be discriminated were made of glass, plastic or metal and existed in duplicate. Their weight was such that they could not be displaced by rats" (48). This description of the objects is repeated verbatim (or nearly verbatim) in all of the object exploration studies done by Ennaceur (and various colleagues), one or more of which is cited by nearly every object exploration study we have seen. Second, researchers who use the object exploration task are typically molecular neuroscientists, behavioral geneticists, and psychopharmacologists; that is, they are exactly the types of neuroscientists who, as Bickle points out, tend to be ruthless reductionists. Yet in spite of this lack of concern for to-be-explored objects, the nature of the objects used in these studies may be critical to the behavior observed (i.e., initial exploration, response to novelty, and recognition memory), in that different objects afford different activities. For example, some objects can only be touched or reared on, whereas other objects can be climbed onto and into, leading to potentially qualitatively and quantitatively different exploratory behaviors (Renner and Rosenzweig 1986).

Heyser and I (with help from our student Chris Silansky) reviewed 116 recent papers on object exploration published in neuroscience journals.[4] For each article, we attempted to determine the age(s) and species of animal used and the properties of the object used. We used this information to determine what the affordances of the to-be-explored objects were for the animals in the studies. Crucially for the literature review, we can also determine whether different objects used in individual studies have equivalent affordances.

For the review, we assumed that objects have equivalent affordances whenever the relationship between an animal's abilities and the objects are sufficiently similar that the animal can perform the same stereotypical behavior with respect to the object. We also assume that "same behavior" is read very broadly, so that climbing (pushing, hiding in, etc.) of any kind is the same behavior. To take one relevant, illustrative example, any two objects that

(1) are sufficiently sturdy to support the full weight of the animal without deformation, and
(2) have a surface that is
(a) parallel to the ground,
(b) at a height less than the full length of the animal (tail excluded),
(c) at least as wide as the distance between the animal's left and right feet, and
(d) at least as long as the distance between the animal's front and back feet

afford the same behavior, namely, climbing on. This rather loose individuation of behaviors, and hence affordances, allows us to say that a CD case and a notebook, but not a beer bottle or a ping-pong ball, afford climbing on for mice and rats. This understanding of being climbable does not make a distinction between the different sequences of muscle movements required to get the animal onto these objects.

The main results of the literature survey were as follows. Of these 116 articles, 52 (approximately 44 percent) gave little or no information concerning the specific objects that were given for exploration, and 64 (approximately 56 percent) provided detailed descriptions of the objects. Of the 64 articles that included descriptions of the objects used in the experiments, 32 (approximately 28 percent of the total) used sets of objects with nonequivalent affordances for the species of animal under study. (For example, several studies compared exploration of objects that could be climbed by rats with objects that could not be climbed.) Only the remaining 32 studies used objects with similar affordances for the animals under study.[5]

This leads to the following evaluations of the current state of research on object exploration. Approximately 72 percent of the research papers we reviewed may have the same methodological problem we found in our initial work, making the results difficult to interpret and virtually impossible to generalize across experiments. Call these the *potentially confounded studies*. The majority of these potentially confounded studies (44 percent of the articles we surveyed) do not give enough information about the objects used, and so fail to meet one of the primary goals of scientific research: these studies are *not replicable*. The remaining potentially confounded studies are *suspect*, because their results could be skewed by the comparison of exploration of objects that have different affordances. In these studies, there seems to be the attitude that it doesn't really matter what the objects are, as long as one or more of them are novel or their spatial arrangement is changed. The objects were either deemed not worth describing or were simply things that happened to be around the lab (e.g., soda cans are popular).

This rather pessimistic evaluation led Heyser and I to do a series of experiments on object exploration and affordances. These experiments are designed to explore the relationship between the affordances of objects and the ways that animals (mice in our case) explore them. The pessimism of our evaluation is unfounded if our experiments show that animals explore objects similarly, whether or not they have different affordances. The experiment also has consequences for ruthless reductionism. If scientific experiments suffer because ruthlessly reductionist neuroscientists attend to neurochemicals to the exclusion of other behavior-relevant issues (e.g., the affordances of the objects they use), it would seem that ruthless reductionism among neuroscientists is counterproductive. This is a problem for ruthless reductionism.

8.4 Are All Objects Equal?

Heyser and I have done a series of studies with mice specifically looking at object selection and its impact on performance in the object exploration task. (We describe the experiment reported here, and several others in more detail, in Chemero and Heyser 2009.) For the study described here, we used adult male and female mice,[6] randomly assigned to two groups. The first group (TOUCH) was tested with objects that could not be climbed. That is, the objects did not meet the criteria for affording the behavior climbing-on described above. The second group (CLIMB) was tested with objects that did meet these criteria. Testing was conducted in a large circular arena (large, that is, for a mouse—1.2 meters in diameter) and consisted of four six-minute trials, with a three-minute intertrial interval between each trial. There were no objects in the arena during trial 1, which served as a baseline/familiarization period to the novel environment. In trial 2, we placed four different objects in the open field. For mice in the TOUCH group, these objects consisted of a glass bottle, a metal rectangular can, a set of plastic stacking squares, and a plastic toy barrel. These objects were all of sufficient height and weight that they could not be climbed or moved. In addition, the objects did not afford chewing and were washed between trials. For mice in the CLIMB group, the objects were a plastic square, a rectangular bottle on its side, a cardboard box, and a plastic object with a hole in the center. All these objects were of a size that they could be climbed on, but were too heavy for the mice to move them. We washed the objects between trials. The objects were positioned equidistant from the walls and from each other. The same four objects remained in the open field during trials 3 and 4. Several behaviors were recorded during trials 2 through 4 including: line crossing, rearing, grooming, the frequency and duration of contact with each object, and latency to make first contact with each object within a given trial.

We found clear differences in exploratory behavior as a function of the type of object. First, mice in the CLIMB group spent significantly more time in contact with the objects, when compared with duration scores in the TOUCH only group. Furthermore, males in the TOUCH group, but not the CLIMB group, explored objects longer than females (see figure 8.1). Thus objects that could be climbed on were explored longer and masked a

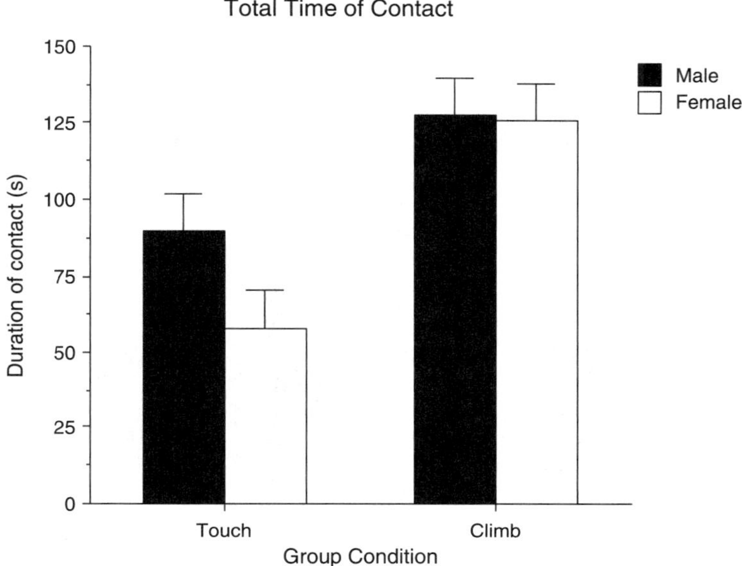

Figure 8.1
Total time of contact with objects across trials by male and female mice in the TOUCH and CLIMB groups.

sex difference that is apparent with object that cannot be climbed. The type of object also influenced the rate of habituation. Specifically, the mice in the TOUCH group showed faster habituation (as defined by a decrease in the duration of exploration over time) than mice in the CLIMB group (see figure 8.2).

Put simply, this experiment shows that all objects are not created equal: their affordances really do affect the way animals explore them. This means that the assumption—common among molecular neuroscientists, behavioral geneticists, and psychopharmacologists—that studying neurochemicals can be a replacement for studying behavior is misleading, at least when one uses the object exploration methodology.

8.5 Conclusions from the Study

There are several lessons to learn from this experiment, some neuroscientific and some philosophical.

First, the experiment shows that object exploration studies cannot use just any objects. It also shows that our earlier pessimistic evaluation of the

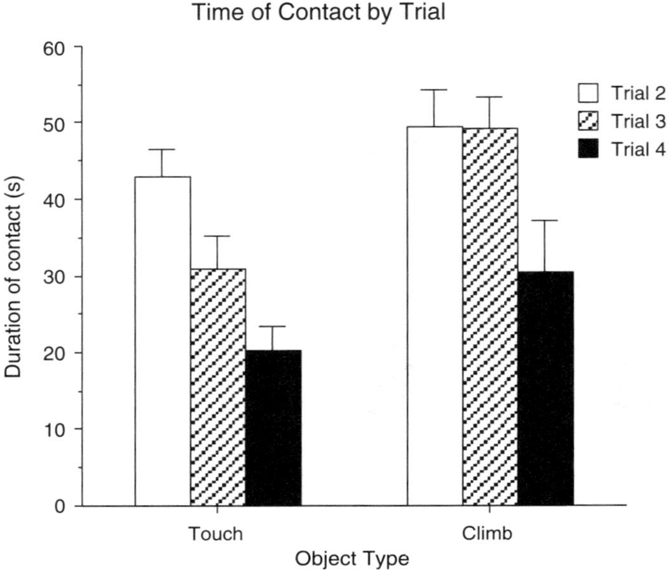

Figure 8.2
Habituation rates in the TOUCH and CLIMB groups.

current literature on object exploration does in fact hold up. The differences in the exploratory behavior that mice display given the affordances of the objects to be explored indicate that at least 32, and as many as 84, of the 116 articles we surveyed report results that should be seen as potentially confounded. There are, of course, more than 116 published articles on object exploration, but there is no reason to think that these numbers will not hold up for all of the papers on object exploration. If we're right, nearly 3/4 of the literature on object exploration is at least potentially confounded. This is not to say that the data obtained in these studies are not "real." However, given that these studies rely on a simultaneous presentation of multiple objects, it is possible (even highly likely) that the behavior of the animal is not only influenced by the affordances of a specific object but also by the interaction of all available objects. This point is most problematic in situations where the objects are explored differently (i.e., when the affordances of the objects are not equivalent). Therefore, although the data from these experiments are not flawed per se, the conclusions drawn from these experiments may be suspect and at the very least give rise to alternative hypotheses.

Second, the problem with the extant research on object exploration is methodological, but a conceptual issue also lurks behind the scenes. The problem is that neuroscientists tend to ignore the animals attached to the brains they are interested in studying. The solution to this problem is to adopt an understanding of animals that insists on studying brains, perception, memory, cognition, and the like only in terms of their relation to behavior. Radical embodied cognitive science, according to which one cannot understand perception or cognition separately from action, solves this problem. The literature review and experiment described above are an example of the benefits that might come with adopting a radical embodied perspective. Failing to attend to the species-typical behaviors of mice and rats and whether or not the objects to be explored afford any of those behaviors has led to a series of results that could be artifacts of the experimental setup. A mouse or rat may recognize that some object is novel, indicating that it remembers what objects were present before, but may not explore that object because it lacks affordances for species-specific behaviors. Although no one has done the same sort of systematic literature review or experiment on any other research methodology, there are likely similar artifacts in other experimental paradigms, such as gaze preference in human infants and nonhuman primates, that make generalizations about learning (or cognition or memory) based on the amount of time an animal spends attending to something. In these fields as well, radical embodied cognitive science—particularly, careful attention to affordances—could turn out to be essential.

Getting now to the more philosophical conclusions, our results indicate that ruthless reductionism can lead to bad neuroscience. Work on object exploration may have suffered because experimenters were not as concerned about the nature of the objects they used, despite the fact that those objects can have profound effects on exploratory behavior. Clearly, the molecular neuroscientists, behavioral geneticists, and psychopharmacologists thought that the objects did not matter. I attribute this neglect to the attitude among these researchers that studying molecules *is* studying cognition; that is, I attribute the choice of objects in these experiments to the experimenters' ruthless reductionism. This is a serious problem for the ruthless reductionist. A philosophical attitude toward science that leads to bad science is not an attitude that scientists ought to hold. Remember that ruthless reductionism is connected with new wave metascience, in which philosophical attitudes toward scientific research take their cues from the attitudes of the scientists whose work it is. Our literature review and experiment indicate that neuroscientists who use object exploration may need to reflect on and empirically validate the process of object selection, and realize that behavior and affordances matter. So ruthless reductionism is an inappropriate position for neuroscientists to hold because ruthless reductionism can lead to questionable experimental methodology. Ruthless reductionism, this means, is also inappropriate for philosophers of science.

Finally, the methodological changes required to improve object exploration experiments have consequences for reductionism about cognition more generally. As noted above, computational cognitive science encourages reductionism by taking the mind to be software running on the brain. Spatially, then, the object of study of cognitive science and neuroscience is the same; these two theories just focus on different "levels." But our recommendation for fixing the methodological problems with object exploration research involves adopting an approach to cognition in which the object of study is spatially larger than the brain. According to radical embodied cognitive science, the object of study for cognitive science is the nonlinearly coupled animal–environment system. To the extent that radical embodied cognitive scientists study brains, they study them only as parts of behaving animals in information-rich environments. This makes a reduction of cognitive science to neuroscience (cognitive or molecular) out of the question. Researchers in lower-level theories such as neuroscience depend on those in higher-level theories such as cognitive science to help them decide what needs explaining. For example, we can only reduce long-term memory to long-term potentiation if we have a reasonable theory of long-term memory to guide research on brains and to be reduced to a theory of long-term potentiation. Neuroscientists and reductionists, in other words, need cognitive scientists to get things (roughly) right. But getting things even roughly right in cognitive science (and neuroscience for that matter) requires knowing about affordances. And there is the rub. For in an intertheoretic reduction, the base theory must be a more general theory that applies to the same regions of space and time as the reduced theory. But no theory of the brain alone will be applicable to the combined brain–body–environment system. The base theory in this case is not a more general theory of the same subject matter, for there are no genes or neurotransmitters in the majority of the system under study. So a reduction of cognitive science to neuroscience will fail.

Before moving on to consider the relationship, in general, between radical embodied cognitive science and neuroscience, I would like point to a possible limitation to the conclusions just presented. A reductionist might sensibly point out that the literature review and experiment have only shown a problem with one sort of experiment, and that reductionism has served neuroscientists very well in other settings, for example, in the work on memory that Bickle cites. But to turn this into a defense of reductionism, it must be argued that the work reviewed above on object exploration is an exception to otherwise methodologically unimpeachable work done by other ruthlessly reductionist neuroscientists. Then one could argue that, in general, neuroscientific work is not aided by expanding the focus of inquiry to include nonneural (so nonneurochemical) things such as bodies and affordances. The only argument for this would be careful study and defense of other methods used by molecular neuroscientists. Both neuroscience and neurophilosophy would benefit if philosophers were to pay this sort of close attention to additional experimental methodologies. Indeed, I would be happy to have this work done, even should it be the means by which reductionism is vindicated in general, and radical embodied cognitive science pushed to the margins.

8.6 Neither No-Brainers nor Brain Obsessed

I've just argued that reductionism can lead to methodological problems in neuroscience and that one can solve these problems by taking the object of study, even in neuroscience, to be the combined brain–body–environment system. This suggests, of course, that neuroscientists should be radical embodied cognitive scientists. I have said nothing, however, about how radical embodied cognitive scientists ought to respond to the explosion in neuroscience of the last few years. What, then, should the radical embodied cognitive scientist say about the undeniably good and important work done by neurophilosophers and by the neuroscientists whose experiments they cite?

The main strategy here must be to insist cognition, though not magical or nonnatural in any way, is not confined to the head. This leads to significant disagreements with reductionist neurophilosophers. First, for psychology to be reducible to neuroscience, the psychological must be entirely in the head. That is, it must be internalist; radical embodied cognitive scientists disagree with internalism. Second, if the mental is all in the head, the way for the environment to have an impact on the mind is by being mentally represented; radical embodied cognitive scientists deny representationalism. But the radical embodied cognitive scientist can deny both internalism and representationalism without deserving the epithets "no-brainer" or "a priori philosopher of mind."

Since the 1970s, there have been a priori arguments that internalism about the mental is problematic. Putnam and Burge, for example, famously argued that "meaning ain't in the head." The arguments they used are thought experiments, though, and we should not expect neurophilosophers to give up internalism based on a priori considerations. Radical embodied cognitive scientists, however, insist that psychology acknowledge a causal and explanatory spread outside the skull of the animal being studied. But to have any hope of convincing the neurophilosopher, or at least not provoking scorn, one must develop an empirical case against internalism. This has been the point of much work in radical embodied cognitive science. The experiments that Charles Heyser and I have done are part of this case, as is most of the research described in this book. There is, then, a substantial empirical case against internalism.

Internalists tend to be representationalists, but so do nonradical embodied cognitive scientists. This entire book has been making the case that representationalism is optional when explaining coupled animal–environment systems. It is also optional when doing neuroscience, despite claims by prominent neurophilosophers to the contrary. Consider, for example, Patricia Churchland's excellent neurophilosophy textbook *Brain-Wise* (2002). Churchland's focus on cognitive neuroscience (i.e., on neural information processing) commits her strongly to representationalism. As such, issues of representation are at the center of her work, and explanations of how the brain might represent are crucial parts of her accounts of the self and of knowledge. These accounts rely heavily on Grush's emulation theory of representation. As discussed in chapter 3, according to the emulation theory of representation (Grush 1997), the most basic representations are forward models that provide the organism with a prediction of the outcome of its current action. Because they provide information about an animal's own body, emulators are especially appropriate for Churchland's discussion of self-knowledge, and she uses them to great effect there. Furthermore, there is evidence that something like emulators really are at work in the control of behavior in many species. (See, e.g., Webb 2004.) This might seem to be a problem for radial embodied cognitive scientists, who deny that representations are required in motor control. But, as also discussed in chapter 3, it is far from obvious that emulators, though they may be ubiquitous in action control throughout nature, really are representations. Representations, traditionally, are about the external world, whereas emulators are control structures that are about the body. If one is not a very strong internalist, taking the mental to be confined to the central nervous system, one can quite naturally understand emulators as simply an element in the system they are controlling. Compare: the gears of a clock control the motion of its hands without being a representation of that motion. Emulators are similarly attached to the body parts they control.

Though I expect that Churchland, who clearly does believe that cognition is restricted to the central nervous system, would not accept this interpretation of emulators, she is open to the possibility that representationalism may not be the future of neuroscience. She mentions (though does not follow up) the possibility that dynamical systems theory might be a more appropriate language for neuroscience. The radical embodied cognitive scientist must embrace this possibility. Dynamical systems theory is not only an appropriate language for understanding the activity of the nonlinearly coupled brain–body–environment system, there is mounting evidence that it is also the key to understanding the brain, and not in terms of representations. Recent work by Bressler and Kelso (2001), Thompson and Varela (2001), Varela et al. (2001), Bressler (2002), and Kelso and Engstrøm (2006) makes this point vividly. In all of this work (and much more), dynamical systems models are shown to work both in brain-only explanations and in brain–body–environment ones. Furthermore, decades of work by Walter Freeman (e.g., Freeman 1975, 1999; Skarda and Freeman 1987) show that dynamical systems theory can also provide nonrepresentational explanations of internal brain processes.

The point of this section is that it is perfectly respectable, even in the face of rapid advances in neuroscience and its philosophy, for radical embodied cognitive scientists to acknowledge that brains are important, but insist that they are far from whole story. I hope to have made it convincing that one can easily resist the pull of the neurophilosophical wave without thereby being a no-brainer. To accomplish this feat, I offer the following three-step program for radical embodied cognitive scientists: First, admit that brains are important; second, embrace dynamical systems modeling as the brain-friendly, but still noninternalist, means of explaining the activity of brain–body–environment; third, do not, under any circumstances, make arguments based on Twin Earth, inverted qualia, or Martian psychology. Radical embodied cognitive scientists can take results in neuroscience in stride by showing that they are best interpreted as shining light on a proper part of the larger brain–body–environment system. This is in part the point of figure 7.2 in chapter 7. Indeed, radical embodied cognitive scientists can develop an attractive counter to reductionism by modeling the nervous system as a dynamical system with its own intrinsic dynamic. This intrinsic dynamic both determines and is determined by the way the brain is coupled to the rest of the body and the way the body is coupled to the environment. This extended coupled brain–body–environment system is what radical embodied cognitive science is all about.

9 The Metaphysics of Radical Embodiment

Given the historical pedigree of radical embodied cognitive science, it should not be surprising that endorsing it leads one to need to address core issues in metaphysics. I claimed in chapter 2 that radical embodied cognitive science is a direct descendent of the pragmatism of American naturalists William James and John Dewey. Now that I have described radical embodied cognitive science in some detail, this is much easier to see. I'm not the only one who thinks so. For example, Teed Rockwell (2005) argues that a roughly Deweyan conception of the mind leads one to view cognitive systems as spanning animal–environment boundaries and to use dynamical systems theory to understand them. Harry Heft (2001) shows that James Gibson's ecological psychology is the transformation of William James's radical empiricism into a scientific psychology. Thus both key components of radical embodied cognitive science have pragmatist pedigrees, which means that both have some metaphysical explaining to do. To see this, consider Heft's casting of Gibson as a radical empiricist and neutral monist. Neutral monism is the view that the mind and the world are composed of "pure experience," which is in itself neither mental nor physical. Rockwell's "behavior fields" have the same neither mental nor physical character. And so, of course, do affordances. From the point of view of today's cognitive scientists and philosophers thereof, neutral monism seems just plain odd. Today, for those who think about metaphysics at all, the primary arguments are over whether the entities in the world are exhausted by those that can be described by the laws of physics or whether there are also qualia. For the vast majority, though, any questioning of physics-based realism is a waste of time. But neutral monism does indeed have all the trappings of antirealism, in particular because it runs metaphysics and epistemology together. If the animal and the environment—the thinking and the thought about, the perception and perceived—are taken to be an inseparable unity, one cannot first try to understand what the world is like and then, given that, work on how animals know about it. These questions must be understood simultaneously, or, worse from the point of view of realism, by beginning with understanding the nature of the cognitive system. This is, indeed, the ordering in Gibsonian ecological psychology. First, understand that perception is direct, then figure out what the environment must be like for that to be true. So the radical embodied cognitive scientist has some metaphysical explaining to do.

In fact, this is a problem for both radical embodied cognitive science and its representationalist cousin. Varela, Thompson, and Rosch (1991), Cussins (1992), Smith (1996), Chemero (1998b), Keijzer (2001), and Rohde and Stewart (2008), among others, have made the case that embodied cognitive science, radical or not, is out of line with metaphysical and scientific realism. For the most part in this chapter, therefore, I will refer to "(radical) embodied cognitive science" to indicate that I mean both views. The primary purpose of the chapter is to show that the arguments that (radical) embodied cognitive science is not in line with realism are not to be trusted. (Radical) embodied cognitive science is compatible with at least one variety of realism. A fair portion of my argument for this will consist in showing that my own argument that embodied cognitive science is incompatible with realism shouldn't be trusted. The problem with that argument comes to light most obviously if one replays a bit of the debate between Jerry Fodor (1984, 1988) and Paul Churchland (1988) over the theory ladenness of perception.

Here, then, is the plan. In section 9.1, I'll go through two arguments that purport to show that (radical) embodied cognitive science is incompatible with realism. In section 9.2, drawing on Churchland and Fodor, I'll show that embodied cognitive scientists can be realists after all. In section 9.3, I'll recommend a particular variety of realism, a slight modification of Hacking's entity realism (Hacking 1982, 1983), as especially appropriate for (radical) embodied cognitive science. After making the case that (radical) embodied cognitive scientists can, and should, be realists, I will say a few things about how this affects phenomenology and consciousness. When I do so, I will go back to talking about just "radical embodied cognitive science" (without the parentheses), because the claims I make about phenomenology and consciousness depend on denying that cognition is computation, and hence are only licensed by radical embodied cognitive science.

9.1 Embodied Cognition and Realism

Ever since the current focus on embodiment in cognitive science began, there have been arguments that the approach is somehow inconsistent with realism. However, the inference from (radical) embodied cognitive science to irrealism is highly controversial. Many proponents of (radical) embodied cognitive science are steadfast realists (Turvey et al. 1981; Mandik and Clark 2002) or don't want to be bothered by metaphysical concerns in the first place (Clark 1997; along with nearly every nonphilosopher). Yet others have argued that understanding cognition as necessarily embodied, and hence limited by the nature of our sensory systems, profoundly affects our abilities to know about and interact with an animal-independent world. Here I will look at two arguments from (radical) embodied cognitive science to irrealism: Varela, Thompson, and Rosch's argument in *The Embodied Mind* (1991) and my own published in 1998 (Chemero 1998b). I will ultimately argue that (radical) embodied cognitive scientists can be realists. Before doing any of this, though, I should point out that the unmodified word "realism" has so many uses as to be almost empty. By realism, I mean the coupled claims that (1) at least some of perceptions/thoughts/theories are accurate, and (2) that the objects of our accurate perceptions/thoughts/theories exist in an animal-independent world.

In their book *The Embodied Mind*, Varela, Thompson, and Rosch (1991) take Brooks's robots to be a paradigmatic case of their enactive approach to cognition. Brooks's (1991) robots, Varela et al. say, are *structurally coupled* to the environment, which is to say that robot and environment are not separate. Instead, they are mutually specifying in that the robot's behavioral abilities and sensory systems determine what its environment is, which in turn determines what the robot does. So, for example, the robot Allen has a ring of twelve sensors, which it uses to determine the distance to the nearest object at each "hour" around its body. With just these twelve sensors, Allen can wander around most cluttered environments successfully. The only things that can perturb Allen—that is, influence its behavior—have sufficiently large surfaces that reflect pulses from its sensors. According to Varela et al., only these things are part of Allen's world. This makes Allen closed in an important sense: only very particular stimuli can elicit a reaction from Allen, and the way Allen reacts determines the significance of those stimuli for Allen. This is what it is for Allen to enact, or "bring forth" a world. Varela et al. take Allen as a model for all animals. All animals are closed as Allen is, structurally coupled to a world composed of very specific stimuli; all animals enact or bring forth a world that is determined by the nature of their sensorimotor systems, which in turn determine the significance of the perturbations.

This sounds suspiciously like old-fashioned idealism. Animals have their own worlds, determined by what they are capable of sensing. But Varela et al. reject this interpretation:

> It is precisely this emphasis on mutual specification that enables us to negotiate a middle path between the Scylla of cognition as the recovery of a pregiven outer world (realism) and the Charybdis of cognition as the projection of a pregiven inner world (idealism). These two extremes both take representation as their central notion: in the first case representation is used to recover what is outer; in the second it is used to project what is inner. Our intention is to bypass entirely this logical geography of inner versus outer by studying cognition not as projection or recovery but as embodied action. (Varela, Thompson, and Rosch 1991, 172)

By rejecting representationalism, which is to say, by being radical embodied cognitive scientists, Varela et al. claim to stake out a position that is neither realist nor idealist. On their view, animals and worlds are not separate, so there is no need for animals to represent the world. Without representations, there is nothing besides the world for the animal to interact with, but the worlds that animals—including humans, including philosophers and physicists—interact with are strictly limited, and are determined by sensorimotor capabilities.

Andy Clark, toward the end of a book that outlines and defends nonradical embodied cognitive science, dismisses this as a mere distraction:

> Varela et al. use their reflections as evidence against realist and objectivist views of the world. I deliberately avoid this extension, which runs the risk of obscuring the scientific value of an embodied, embedded approach by linking it to the problematic idea that objects are not independent of the mind. My claim, in contrast, is simply that the aspects of real-world structure which biological brains represent will often be tightly geared to specific needs and sensorimotor capacities. (Clark 1997, 173)

This dismissal is far too glib. We might try to get a handle on Clark's reasoning by noting that he also dismisses Varela et al.'s antirepresentationalism (less glibly, with argument). If animals are representing, we can ask what they are representing, whether what they are representing exists, and whether they are representing it accurately. We can also wonder whether there is anything beyond the representations. So, to repeat a mixed metaphor, Clark's representationalism puts us off Varela et al.'s middle path and back into Odysseus' boat. Once there, Clark chooses Scylla (realism) because, well, it's not a distraction. As much as one might argue with the philosophical probity of such a move, it is easy to see its point. Clark, perhaps more than anyone else, has worked to separate embodied cognitive science from radical embodied cognitive science, and to define embodied cognitive science as a modest revolution, one that treats both babies (realism, representation) and bathwater (Cartesianism) appropriately. So, Clark hopes, nonradical embodied cognitive science can avoid the metaphysical distractions that beset radical embodied cognitive science.

It is, alas, not so easy. In a review of Clark's book (Chemero 1998b), I argued that Clark's representationalism doesn't save embodied cognitive science from worries about realism. (This paragraph and the next are a paraphrase of that argument.) We can see this by considering that the representations involved in embodied cognitive science are action oriented. As Clark describes them, action-oriented representations (see chapter 3) are representations that *both* describe a situation *and* suggest an appropriate reaction to it; they are essentially representations of affordances. Action-oriented representations are doubly indexical, in that they are both local and personal: they are local in that they relate to the circumstances currently surrounding an animal; they are personal in that they are related to the animal's needs and the skills that it has. Nonradical embodied cognitive scientists take action-oriented representations to be the basis of human cognition and, quite probably, the only representations available to most nonhumans. From here, it is a few small steps to worries about realism.

Start by realizing that humans' and other animals' action-oriented representations will concern only the actions they undertake. Animals, that is, will represent only affordances for animals like themselves. And given the differences in the activities of animals of different species, we should expect the affordances perceived by animals of different species, or animals of the same species at different developmental stages, to be widely divergent and even contradictory. (Indeed, this is a central point of the idea of affordances. See Michaels and Carello 1981.) This is to be expected if one assumes, as (radical) embodied cognitive scientists do, that perceptual systems evolved to guide behavior. Neither humans nor beetles have action-oriented representations that represent the animal-independent world exactly correctly. Indeed, representing the animal-independent world is not what action-oriented representations are supposed to do; they are supposed to guide action. So the set of human affordances, that is, action-oriented *representeds*, is just as tightly geared to specific human needs and sensorimotor capacities as those of any other type of animal. This leaves us with a multiplicity of conflicting sensorimotor systems, each of which is appropriate for guiding the adaptive behavior of animals whose systems they are.

This multiplicity of differing, conflicting, sets of action-oriented representeds is a problem for realism. Because there is no reason to assume that there is any criterion for correctness of action-oriented representations other than appropriately guiding behavior, there is no reason to think that humans, but not beetles, have action-oreiented repersentations that reflect animal-independent reality. This becomes a problem when one adds the premise, common among proponents of embodied cognitive science, that distinctively human "higher thought" (language use, theorizing, science, etc.) is based on action-oriented representations. Indeed, many (Deacon 1997; Clark 1997; Christiansen and Chater 2008) have suggested that public language evolved to fit facts about our prelinguistic brains. So, because action-oriented representations are tightly geared to needs and sensorimotor capacities and hence are not accurate reflections of mind-independent reality, so too will be language-based higher thought. If both our everyday perceptual categories and the categories of our sciences are built on a skewed foundation, they too will be skewed. Essentially, action-oriented representations don't map the animal-independent world because they aren't supposed to; our theories don't map the animal-independent world because they are built from our action-oriented representations. We must, then, reject one part of realism as defined above. Although we may be justified in believing that there is an animal-independent external world, we have no justification to believe that our perceptions, thoughts, and theories are accurate reflections of it.

This leaves us able to believe in what Putnam (1985) calls *internal realism* at best.[1] In internal realism, one believes the entities of a theory to be real as long as one understands them as theory bound, and not elements of an independent reality. And though not everyone agrees as to whether internal realism is a kind of transcendental idealism (Putnam 1985; Millikan 1993) or a kind of nominalism (Hacking 1983), everyone does agree that it is not a kind of realism.

So Varela, Thompson, and Rosch argue that nonrepresentational radical embodied cognitive science is inconsistent with realism. I've argued that representational embodied cognitive science is inconsistent with realism. The controversies that Clark wanted to sweep under the rug are leaving an unseemly lump. Must (radical) embodied cognitive scientists give up on realism?

9.2 The Joys of Plasticity

In this section, I argue that, for reasons specific to embodied cognitive science, the argument just presented, despite its initial plausibility, is not to be believed. (See Mandik and Clark 2002; Anderson 2006 for different responses to these arguments.) To make this case, I will replay an argument made by Paul Churchland in a somewhat different context. The context in question is the debate between Churchland (1988) and Jerry Fodor (1984, 1988) over the theory ladenness of perception (Hanson 1958; Kuhn 1962;

Churchland 1979). Though the debate over theory ladenness is most directly about objectivity, whether perception is theory laden is directly relevant to realism. If perception is theory laden, the theories we believe affect what we perceive. How, then, can theory-laden perception can be of theory-independent reality? Kuhn (1962), for example, has argued that holders of different theories perceive different (at least partly theory-determined) worlds. Attempting to head these worries off, Fodor (1984) argues that, because perception is modular, perception is not theory laden. Perceptual mechanisms, Fodor (1983, 1984) argues, are modular, that is, innately structured and informationally encapsulated. Because perception is informationally encapsulated, theories (not handled by perceptual modules) do not change perceptual mechanisms or the output of perceptual modules. Therefore, Fodor argues, perception is not theory laden. Furthermore, because perceptual modules are innately structured, they're the same in all (normal) humans. There is, then, no sense in which humans who believe different theories perceive a different world. Their perceptual mechanisms produce the same output given the same input. Although they may hold different theories about what they perceive, they perceive the same thing. So, Fodor holds, the modularity of perceptual and cognitive systems makes perception a neutral basis for theoretical disputes, and this can form the basis for objectivity and scientific realism.[2]

In a reply to Fodor, Churchland (1988) argues that the modularity of perceptual mechanisms does not get Fodor what he wants, which is *theory-neutral* perception. A perception is theory neutral "just in case its truth is not contingent upon the truth of any general empirical assumptions, just in case it is free of potentially problematic assumptions" (Churchland 1988, 170). Innate perceptual mechanisms are not free of empirical assumptions; their empirical assumptions are simply hardwired by evolution. Churchland points out that having innate, informationally encapsulated perceptual models "merely dooms us to a single point of view, a point of view that is epistemologically just as problematic as the infinity of other sets of empirical assumptions that might have been hard-wired into us instead" (ibid.). Furthermore, Churchland continues, because these mechanisms are hardwired and encapsulated, we are stuck with them, no matter how faulty we might learn that they are. Far from getting us theory-neutral perception, that is, modularity gets us instead "universal dogmatism" in which all humans have perceptual systems that share the same, probably false, but unshakeable assumptions. Swinging this around to meet up more directly with the arguments of section 9.2 above, what Churchland shows is that Fodor's argument is not an argument for theory neutrality at all. Rather, we end up exactly where section 9.2's arguments left us, with evolutionarily hardwired, hence action-oriented, hence anthropomorphically biased, empirical assumptions built into our perceptual systems. This leads to grave doubts that our perceptions are of a human-independent world, to internal realism at best. Indeed, some evolutionary psychologists have reached the same conclusions from their devotion to innately structured, evolved, perceptual modules: both Plotkin (1993) and Boyer (2001) embrace nonrealist conclusions.

Although Churchland's argument—not surprisingly—rolls right off Fodor's back (see Fodor 1988), it does lead to worries about the argument from embodied cognitive science. First, Fodor, Plotkin, and Boyer are not good company for (radical) embodied cognitive scientists. If (radical) embodied cognitive scientists are agreeing with them, something must be terribly wrong. And something has gone terribly wrong. We can see what it is by reminding ourselves of something that Fodor, Plotkin, and Boyer agree on, in opposition to Churchland and—as far as I know—all (radical) embodied cognitive scientists. Fodor and evolutionary psychologists are *nativists*. In contrast, situated, embodied cognitive scientists follow Churchland in fully embracing neural, perceptual, behavioral, and conceptual *plasticity*. And embracing plasticity is fatal to the argument outlined in section 9.2. To see this, we can continue replaying Churchland's (1988) arguments. Churchland points out that the uniformity of innate perceptual mechanisms (and universal dogmatism) only lasts until a mutant shows up, with a different but equally good (or better) perceptual mechanism.

> In fact, we begin to become such mutants or aliens ourselves, when we change our sensory modalities by augmenting them with unusual instruments such as phase-contrast microscopes, deep-sky telescopes, long-baseline stereoscopes, infrared scopes, and so forth. And the metamorphosis is completed when, after years of professional or amateur experience, we begin to see the world appropriately and efficiently with these new senses. (Churchland 1988, 171)

The point of all these examples of perceptual augmentation is not merely that we can augment our perception. Though interesting, mere augmentation doesn't get us out of the argument described in section 9.2. If the action-oriented foundations for our perceptual systems are crooked, making the building taller won't help. More important for our purposes is the metamorphosis of perceptual systems.[3] Churchland argues that plasticity in our perceptual systems allows them to reorganize in order to take full advantage of technological extensions.[4]

There is every reason to think that our perceptual systems can be reorganized. First, no matter what you think about (radical) embodied cognitive science, pick up any neuroscience textbook to see that our brains are exceptionally plastic. Second, for (radical) embodied cognitive scientists, consider the centrality of cognitive artifacts in cognition. Our brains, behavior, and perception must be capable of transformation if we are to take advantage of such artifacts. Indeed, Clark (2003) argues that the ability to take advantage of perception-transforming technology (including public language) is the most distinctively human feature of our brains. If this is correct, then there is every reason to think that we can realign our perceptual foundations and adjust our perceptions to deal with new situations, despite our biased action-oriented representations. Indeed, the action-oriented representations themselves can be linguistically, theoretically, and technologically altered, potentially moving closer to alignment with an animal-independent world. So if we assume plasticity in our perceptual systems, we can avoid the nonrealist conclusions of section 9.2.

Before concluding this section, a few caveats are in order. First, my calling on plasticity above is no guarantee of realism. It just shows that my own (comparatively) youthful argument from embodied cognitive science to irrealism need not be believed, and neither should Varela, Thompson, and Rosch's argument from radical embodied cognitive science. Second, this is a *local* issue in two senses. It is local in that it only concerns the particular purported connection between (radical) embodied cognitive science and the untenability of realism. If you worry about defending scientific realism from general, empiricist arguments, I haven't helped your case here. The point here has been to show that there is no *special* reason to be antirealist relating to (radical) embodied cognitive science. The issue is also local in that the help I've offered against the realist only applies in the embodied neighborhood in cognitive science, where we believe that cognition is embodied and that perceptual systems are plastic. The points raised in this section concerning plasticity do not affect those who live across town and believe in evolved, innately structured perceptual modules. If you deny that perceptual systems are highly plastic, as evolutionary psychologists and other nativists do, you probably ought to believe in universal dogmatism and/or some kind of nonrealism (internal realism, etc.). Plotkin and Boyer agree.

9.3 But What Sort of Realism?

OK, so (radical) embodied cognitive scientists can be realists. That is, they can believe that there is an animal-independent world, and that some of our perceptions and thoughts get it right. But to say that is to say very little, considering the wide variety of realisms on the market. In this section, I'll outline one variety of realism that is particularly appropriate for (radical) embodied cognitive science; there are no doubt others that will do the trick. Before saying what kind of realism is appropriate, it's worth commenting on one that isn't appropriate. The argument that allows (radical) embodied cognitive scientists to be realists is one that Churchland offers in a different context, and it depends on the plasticity of our perceptual systems. Since (radical) embodied cognitive scientists are also committed to plasticity, it might seem that Churchland's own realism, described in *Scientific Realism and the Plasticity of Mind* (1979), would be just the right kind of realism. Why not, after all, let Churchland solve all our problems for us? Alas, it's not that easy. Churchland's own single-sentence description of his scientific realism makes this plain. "Excellence of theory emerges as the fundamental measure of all ontology" (1979, 2). Because Churchland thinks *all* knowledge is theoretical, this serves as a means to secure realism about both the unobservable entities that natural scientists talk about and, in those cases where our theories are appropriate, the middle-sized objects that populate our everyday environment. But this is plainly inappropriate for (radical) embodied cognitive science, which is founded on the claim that most cognition is interaction with the environment, and has nothing to do with theory. Indeed, (radical) embodied cognitive science is wholeheartedly opposed to the idea that minds are, or are analogous to, theories.[5,6] So Churchland's scientific realism is not the right realism.

(Radical) embodied cognitive science, with its focus on action, needs a realism that moves away from theory to focus on *practice*. Ian Hacking's entity realism (Hacking 1982, 1983), suitably modified, will do the trick. Hacking's realism moves debates over scientific realism out of the realm of scientific theory and into the lab. The existence of theoretical entities, Hacking argues, is secured by our ability to manipulate them during experiment. His primary example is electrons. Experimentalists are justified in believing in electrons because they can build equipment that exploits the properties of electrons to investigate something else (e.g., neutral bosons). When electrons become tools in the experimenter's kit, their reality is on a par with all the rest of the experimenter's tools (glassware, computers, etc.). Hacking writes:

> The more we come to understand some of the causal powers of electrons, the more we can build devices that achieve well-understood effects in other parts of nature. By the time that we can use the electron to manipulate other parts of nature in a systematic way, the electron has ceased to be something hypothetical, something inferred. It has ceased to be theoretical and has become experimental. (1983, 262)

Theoretical entities are real when they become part of the practice of the experimentalist. This, Hacking insists, is independent of whether the experimentalist has a true theory of electrons. Two important caveats. First, although Hacking's theory has been the subject of considerable debate (Shapere 1993; Resnik 1994; Reiner and Pierson 1995; Clarke 2001; Massimi 2004), for now I will simply assume that entity realism is tenable and explain how it can be fit to (radical) embodied cognitive science. Second, some readers will react to my call upon entity realism thus: "That's not what *I* mean by 'realism.'" And it is surely true that Hacking's realism is not standard scientific realism. Entity realism, I am about to argue, seems especially appropriate for (radical) embodied cognitive science. But note that the previous section argued that there are no special reasons that (radical) embodied cognitive science leads to irrealism. So, if you want to be a realist, but entity realism is not for you, there is no in principle reason that some other form of realism might not also work. That said, onward.

The source of the problem with realism for embodied cognitive science, radical or not, is that at root animals perceive affordances, and affordances are animal dependent. Given this animal-dependence, in what sense are we justified in taking affordances to be part of the basic furniture of the universe? There are two ways to apply Hacking's entity realism to these particular entities. The first way is to expand Hacking's position from scientific to a more general realism. The second is to stay within Hacking's area of concern, and apply entity realism to affordances as theoretical entities. We will look at these in turn.

9.3.1 Expanding Entity Realism

Hacking makes very clear that his entity realism is about scientific entities, a position in the debate over the existence of theoretical entities, entities that are observable only with specialized equipment or not at all. (See Hacking 1983, chapter 7.) He takes for granted the more general realism, about the things we perceive, that was called into question by the arguments outlined above. It is easy to see, though, how to expand entity realism to fit affordances and the middle-sized objects of the environment. The key is to realize that experimental practice is just one kind of practice. Just as experimentalists are justified in believing in electrons because they can use them in their investigations, the rest of us are justified in believing in entities that we use in our successful practices. I see no reason to think that this extension is untenable. Such an extension applies immediately and obviously to affordances. We perceive affordances and guide our actions based upon them. This behavior is successful even though humans are rarely able to report accurately, or at all, on what they perceive that allows them to behave successfully. (What are you perceiving, right now, that allows you to maintain upright posture in your chair as you read? What are you perceiving while driving that allows you to brake successfully, avoiding collision, while coming up to a stop light? Hint: It's not your car's speed. See Owens, Chiang, and Muller 1996.) Humans most assuredly don't have true theories of the affordances they are using, yet they use them successfully in their practices. According to entity realism, then, affordances are real and we are justified in believing in them. Our perceptions are of affordances, which really exist, even though we often can't say anything true about them.

This focus on practice also makes entity realism an appropriate response to Varela, Thompson, and Rosch's (1991) nonrepresentationalist irrealism. Varela et al. claim that the question of realism versus idealism only comes up if one is a representationalist. Entity realism, though, does not depend on representations. It depends not on what one thinks or theorizes but on what one does. Indeed, like Varela et al., Hacking (1983) is skeptical of the idea that thoughts and sentences are representations. Entity realism is appropriate for radical embodied cognitive science.

9.3.2 Affordances as Theoretical Entities

Discussing affordances as theoretical entities might seem a bit odd. Affordances, after all, are what animals are supposed to perceive. If animals perceive affordances, in what sense are they unobservable, theoretical entities? There are two reasons to think of affordances as unobservable. First, the sense of "observation" relevant to the philosophy of science involves describing, recording, and reporting what is perceived. That is, perception is very rarely observation. (See, e.g., Torretti 1986.) But as noted above, humans are rarely able to report that they perceive affordances. Furthermore, even when we are able to report that we perceive affordances, we can almost never describe them. (Again: try to describe what you're perceiving that allows you to maintain your posture as you're reading this.) If humans are generally unable to describe or report on affordances they perceive, affordances are not observable in the sense relevant to the philosophy of science. Feyerabend puts the point this way: "There is no use appealing to observation if one does not know how to describe what one sees, or if one can offer one's description with hesitation only, as if one had just learned the language in which it is formulated" (1975, 59)[7]. Second, affordances per se do not reflect light and cannot be detected by laboratory instruments. Typically, ecological psychologists in the lab measure physical properties of animals and environments and record the responses of animals. They then use this data, along with theoretical premises, to infer the presence and qualities of affordances. For example, Warren (1984) measured the leg length of his subjects and their energy consumption while climbing stairs of different heights, and recorded their judgments about which steps were climbable. This information was combined with premises about the nature and perceivability of affordances to determine characteristics of affordances for stair climbing. Given this, it is appropriate to think of affordances as unobservable, theoretical entities.

9.3.3 Affordances as Experimental Equipment

In entity realism, one is justified in being a realist about theoretical entities when one can use them as tools in experimental investigations of other entities. I will now describe three lines of research that use known, stable properties of affordances to study some other phenomenon: an experiment I did with Colin Klein and William Cordeiro (Chemero, Klein, and Cordeiro 2003) on affordances and event perception, research by Dennis Proffitt and his colleagues on affordances and distance perception, and research by Krista Casler and Deborah Kelemen on the perception of function by children.

9.3.3.1 Affordances and events As noted in chapter 7, I have argued that perceivable events are changes in the availability of affordances. Colin Klein, Will Cordeiro, and I used affordances related to gap crossing to study the perception of events related to gap crossing. Humans and other animals often have to step, hop, or jump over discontinuities or breaks in the ground. In recent years, a good deal of research has explored the combination of environmental and animal properties that determine whether gap-crossing affordances are present. In particular, experiments have shown that stable, repeatable relationships among anthropomorphic measures (eye height, leg length, flexibility, gait), postures (sitting, standing, walking, running), and environmental properties (gap size, gap depth, ground stability) determine the presence and perceivability of gap-crossing affordances. (See Mark 1987; Burton 1992, 1993, 1994; Jiang and Mark 1994; Mark et al. 1999; Cornus, Montagne, and Laurent 1999; Chemero, Klein, and Cordeiro 2003.) These findings allowed us to manipulate gap-crossing affordances in order to determine whether humans can perceive behaviorally salient gap-crossing events. In particular, based on what we know about gap-crossing affordances, we were able to make gap-crossing affordances appear and disappear in real time and measure the way in which subjects responded. We predicted, and found, that subjects would be able to accurately perceive behaviorally salient events. (See Chemero, Klein, and Cordeiro 2003 for details.)

9.3.3.2 Affordances and distance perception Dennis Proffitt and his students have published a series of papers in which they manipulate affordances to test judgments of distance. For example, Witt, Proffitt, and Epstein (2004) manipulate affordances for action along with the intentions of subjects in order to study how subjects judge distance. Subjects who were given balls that were less throwable judged the distance of targets to be farther away than when they were given balls that were easily throwable, but only when they were expecting to actually throw the ball at the target. This effect was not seen when subjects were expecting to walk the ball over to the target: when they were not expecting to throw the ball, the degree of throwability did not affect distance judgment. The same effect on distance judgment is seen when the ability to walk by the subjects is manipulated. In another experiment reported in the same paper, Witt, Proffitt, and Epstein had subjects walk on a treadmill until fatigued, which affected the extent to which various distances afforded walking by the subjects. They found that subjects who had walked on the treadmill overestimated the distance of targets when they were expecting to walk a ball to them, whether or not the ball was easily throwable. In contrast, subjects who were expecting to throw the ball at the target did not systematically overestimate distance after walking on the treadmill. A number of similar studies have been done in the Proffitt lab, in which affordances for walking are shown to affect perception. For example, age, fitness, health, fatigue, and carrying heavy loads, all of which determine to what extent a distance affords walking, affect judgments of geographic slant (Proffitt et al. 2003; Bhalla and Proffitt 1999). In another example, Stefanucci et al. (2005) show that steep uphill and downhill slants also lead to overestimations of distance. In each of these cases, affordances for walking and throwing are manipulated in order to examine effects on the perception of physical features of the environment. That is, affordances are manipulated in experiments on something else; affordances are part of the experimentalists' toolkit.[8]

9.3.3.3 Affordances and perception of tools A third kind of research that uses affordances to study something else is work done by comparative and developmental psychologists on tool use. In developmental work, Casler and Kelemen (2005, 2007) showed two-year-olds, three-year-olds, and college students tools with very similar affordances, but only demonstrated that one of them could be used for a task (poking a ball from a tube). Two- and three-year-olds saw the tool whose affordances were demonstrated for them, but not the other similar one, as having the function of ball poking. Children also resisted using the tool they perceived as a ball-poker for other functions, despite the fact that it afforded those functions. (College students had the same tendencies as the children, but were less fixed in their attributions.) In these studies, affordances of tools are manipulated in order to explore how children attribute functions to objects. In the Casler and Kelemen case, the manipulation was a matter of purposefully keeping the relevant affordances fixed.

Each of these lines of research uses affordances as a tool to study something else. The very possibility of such an experiment is justification for Hacking-style realism about affordances. This is true even though there are several competing theories of just what affordances are. (See chapter 7.) Yet despite this widespread theoretical disagreement, all parties agree about the basic experimentally determined properties of affordances. Whatever affordances are, they are real and have well-known properties that can be used in experiments. We are justified in believing in affordances.

These three applications of entity realism to affordances show that entity realism is an appropriate stance to take regarding the objects of interest to (radical) embodied cognitive scientists, even the contested, animal-dependent ones. We can be (radical) embodied cognitive scientists and realists.

9.4 Phenomenological Realism

This discussion of realism about affordances allows us to address conscious experience.[9] Doing so in terms of radical embodied cognitive science, however, does not involve addressing the problem of qualia: the problem of qualia does not arise in radical embodied cognitive science. The main reason for this is that radical embodied cognitive science rejects computationalism, in which it seems as if there are two mind–body problems, not one. The results of computability theory show that a merely physical device (a computer) can have states that are about the world. That is, computability theory, particularly the completeness results, shows that a merely physical device can house *meaning* or *intentionality*. Thus we are invited to imagine that the laptop on which I'm writing this sentence has states in it that that represent features of the environment in exactly the same way that my thoughts do, and the transformations of those representations in a computer might perfectly mirror inferences in my thoughts.

The second mind–body problem, which Jackendoff (1987) calls the mind–mind problem, arises because of the intuition that, despite the fact that both my laptop and I can have states representing my appointments, my computer cannot have the vivid sensation of looking forward to an upcoming weekend trip. A metal and plastic machine, that is, may have states that are about my vacation, but it can't have *experiences* of anticipating. This bit that's left out in the case of the computer is qualia, which are what is left when you subtract the intentionality from an experience. So a computer that has a representation of my kitchen as being a particular shade of green will still lack the experience of what this particular shade of green looks like, what it feels like to see that shade. This mind–mind problem arises because of the way philosophers of mind have solved the first meaning–body problem, namely, via computational cognitive science. There is a widely shared intuition that understanding meaningful cognition as computation leaves the experience out. This is why David Chalmers's (1996) thought experiments about qualia-free zombies have gained so much traction among computationalist philosophers of mind. The ground for this traction, however, does not exist in radical embodied cognitive science. If one rejects the claim that the mind is a computer, all of scientific psychology is aimed at explaining experience, and our experience of the world as being meaningful is inseparable from our experience of it as looking (sounding, smelling, etc.) particular ways. To make claims like this, as Dennett (1991), Gallagher (2005; Gallagher and Zahavi 2008), Hutto (2005), Noë (2005), and Thompson (2007) have, is not to say that out experience is not real, vivid, and wonderful.[10] Rather it is to explain that experience in such a way that qualia do not come up.

So radical embodied cognitive scientists do not need an account of qualia. (See box 9.1 for another long-standing philosophical problem that does not bedevil radical embodied cognitive science.) This does not, however, excuse the radical embodied cognitive scientist from saying something about conscious experience. I argued in section 9.3 that we are justified in taking affordances to be genuinely existing aspects of animal–environment systems, as real as polka dots and pencils. This allows us also to say that conscious experiences are genuinely existing aspects of animal–environment systems. Michael Silberstein and I have called this view *phenomenological realism* (Chemero 2008; Chemero and Silberstein 2008a; Silberstein and Chemero, under review). I should point out that it is here that it is most clear that enactivism is a variety of radical embodied cognitive science. (See also section 7.6.) Indeed, Thompson and Varela (2001) have used the term "radical embodiment" to describe their view of the

Box 9.1
Mental Causation and Radical Embodied Cognitive Science

The most obvious objection to Cartesian dualism is the problem of interaction: how does the immaterial soul cause the material body to act? Since almost no one is a Cartesian dualist anymore, one would think that the problem of mental causation would have faded away. Alas, it has not. In today's philosophy of mind, nearly everyone is a materialist of some kind (except perhaps about causally impotent qualia), yet they still need to worry about mental causation. This is because of the focus among philosophers of mind on "levels." Dennett (1987), for example, distinguishes three levels at which we might explain a cognitive system. We might explain behavior at the *personal* level, in terms of folk psychology; we might explain it in terms of information processing at the *cognitive* level; or we might explain it in terms neurotransmitters and the like at the *physical* level. The debate in the philosophy of mind throughout the 1980s was about the relationship among these levels. But whatever you think about whether the personal level is identical to, supervenes on, or independent from the physical level, you still have the problem of explaining how folk-psychological states as such have any real causal power. That is, just as with Cartesian dualism, one has to explain how personal-level beliefs and desires can cause changes to neurotransmitters at the physical level and cause bodies to move. If my belief that I am almost finished with the proofreading is identical to or supervenes on some neuron and neurotransmitter activity, then it is really the neuron and neurotransmitter activity that has the causal power, not the belief *as such*. The case is even worse if the belief is taken to be relatively independent of things at the physical level.

The general problem is often referred to as the problem of *mental causation* or *downward causation*. How can something at a higher level of organization (e.g., a thought) causally impact something at a lower level (e.g., a neurotransmitter) when the lower level is causally complete? A level is causally complete just in case all of the behavior at that level is a result of the entities and laws of nature at that level. None of this is a problem for radical embodied cognitive science because radical embodied cognitive science uses dynamical systems theory to explain cognition. In dynamical explanations, the behavior of a system is typically explained in terms of *collective variables* (Kelso 1995; Kelso and Engstrøm 2006). A collective variable describes the emergent, coordinated activity of the parts that compose a dynamical system, and in some cases this collective variable is causally responsible for the component parts. Consider finger wagging and the HKB model discussed in chapter 5, for example. In that system, the relative phase of the fingers *b/a* is a collective variable whose state determines the behavior of the system. At any moment, the value of this collective variable is determined by the relationship between the moving fingers. At the same time, the value of the collective variable constrains the

Box 9.1
(continued)

activity of the fingers. Relative phase, in other words, is a higher-level entity, which is composed of lower-level entities, but also controls the behavior of those very same lower-level entities. This sort of explanation implies that the lower level is not causally complete, but is subject to constraint from the higher-level collective variable. (Rayleigh-Beynard convection is a more dramatic case of this. See Chemero and Silberstein 2008a.) This is exactly what philosophers of mind need in order to show that mental causation is possible (Thompson 2007). That is, it is a high-level (i.e., cognitive) entity that acts causally on the lower-level (i.e., physical) phenomena that make it up. Of course, this solution to the problem of mental causation is only available to those who explain cognition dynamically.

neuroscience of conscious experience. Thompson and Varela (2001) argue that work on the neuroscience of consciousness that begins by looking for the neural events that act as necessary and sufficient conditions for conscious experience, so-called *neural correlates of consciousness*, is bound to fail because the physical substrate of conscious experiences spans brain, body, and world. Noë and Thompson (2004) point out that the problem here is largely due to assumptions that neural states are representations. As one might expect, having read this far, I couldn't agree more. Experiences do not happen in brains. Even though it is perfectly obvious that *something* has to be happening in neurons every time an animal has an experience, for the radical embodied cognitive scientist, as for the enactivist, this something is neither identical to, nor necessary and sufficient for, the experience.

To see how this could be true, recall the discussion of Affordances 1.1 from chapter 7. First, according to ecological psychologists, affordances are what we perceive; they are the content of experiences. Second, affordances are relations between what animals can do and features of the environment. Thus although affordances are animal dependent, they are perfectly respectable ontologically. Third, the perception of affordances is also a relation; it is a relation between an animal and an affordance. Combining these three points with the realism about affordances I argued for in section 9.3 gives us phenomenological realism. This is the case because realism about affordances is realism about what is experienced *as such*, and not just realism about the features of the environment that make up the environmental end of the relation. The affordance for the climbing of a step, that is, doesn't disappear when no one with the right abilities is home. (Affordances are "lovely," not "suspect." See chapter 7 and Dennett 1998.) The same is true for the sorts of affordances more commonly discussed when talking about consciousness: the affordance for appearing red doesn't go away when no one with the right visual system is around to take advantage of it. What we perceive, which is to say what we experience, are relations between ourselves and our environments. Our perception of affordances, which is to say our perceptual experience, is also a relation, this time between ourselves and our affordances. The upshot of this is that our experiences are not things that happen in our heads; they happen in animal–environment systems. Conscious experiences, that is, are what happen when animals pick up information about affordances.

The same point can be made in terms of the more dynamical Affordances 2.0. Recall from chapter 7 that an animal's phenomenological-cognitive-behavioral niche is the set of affordances available to that animal; recall also that Affordances 2.0 shows the place of affordances in the ongoing developmental and behavioral unfolding of coupled animal–environment systems: an animal's activities alter the phenomenological-cognitive-behavioral niche (i.e., the world as the animal experiences it), and these alterations to the phenomenological-cognitive-behavioral niche, in turn, affect the animal's behavior and development of its abilities to perceive and act, which further alters the phenomenological-cognitive-behavioral niche, and so on. To see how this works, consider a case of perceptual learning by human infants. From birth, infants engage in exploratory actions that allow them to change their environment and in so doing change their experience of the world. For example, even very young infants kick their legs spontaneously, one at a time in a manner not unlike the way they will move their legs when they learn to walk. Rovee-Collier and Sullivan (1980) showed that two-month-olds with one leg connected to a visible mobile can learn to kick the connected leg in order to make the mobile spin. Later, Thelen (1994) took three-month-olds who had been trained to spin a mobile by kicking and rubber-banded their legs together, making it difficult to spin the mobile by kicking with just one leg. These infants very quickly learned to kick both legs simultaneously, an unnatural activity for infants, in order to spin the mobile. For current purposes, these studies are important for two reasons. First, they demonstrate that even very young children actively explore their environments in order to discover affordances. Second, these studies show that infants make changes to their behavioral repertoire in order to alter their environment and, in so doing, to alter their phenomenology.

Figure 9.1 is the animal–environment system as understood in Affordances 2.0, redrawn from chapter 7. We can trace the activity of the infant-plus-mobile as a phenomenological-cognitive-behavioral animal–environment system through the diagram, starting at the right of the diagram, and over behavioral time. At point 1, the infant's nervous system has an endogenous, intrinsic dynamic, which generates transient patterns of activity (point 2). Sometimes these transient patterns of activity result in a spontaneous leg kick (point 3). If the infant's leg is mechanically coupled to the mobile, this leg kick will cause the mobile to spin (point 4). The spinning mobile alters the infant's experienced environment (point 5). This change to the experienced environment changes the information available to the infant (point 6), which impacts the infant's sensorimotor coupling to the niche (point 7), which in turn perturbs the endogenous dynamics of the infant's nervous system (point 1), and again and again back through the loop. This trace through the infant-plus-mobile phenomenological-cognitive-behavioral system is in one important way deceptive. Tracing the activity this way makes the system seem as if it progresses in a series of discrete steps, when in fact each of these points in the diagram is simultaneously active. That is, the infant's niche is constantly and continuously affected by the infant, and the infant is constantly and continuously being affected by its niche. This aside, tracing the activity through the infant–mobile system demonstrates the phenomenological realism described above. The entire extended phenomenological-cognitive system, including environment as experienced, is required to account for the infant's conscious experiences and the ways it changes its activity in order to generate experiences. That is, we need the whole system to explain the infant's phenomenology, cognition, and behavior.

It might seem like I'm pulling a fast one here. Am I not conflating perceptual content with conscious content? Isn't only the latter properly phenomenological? This is not a fast one; it is a positive position. According to ecological psychology and radical embodied cognitive science, you experience affordances when you perceive them, even though they are often difficult to describe. All adaptive activity by animals involves experiencing the environment. To put this in philosophy of mind lingo, the point here is that intentionality and consciousness are inseparable. That is,

(1) perceiving something as being a particular way

is inseparable from

(2) experiencing it as being that way.

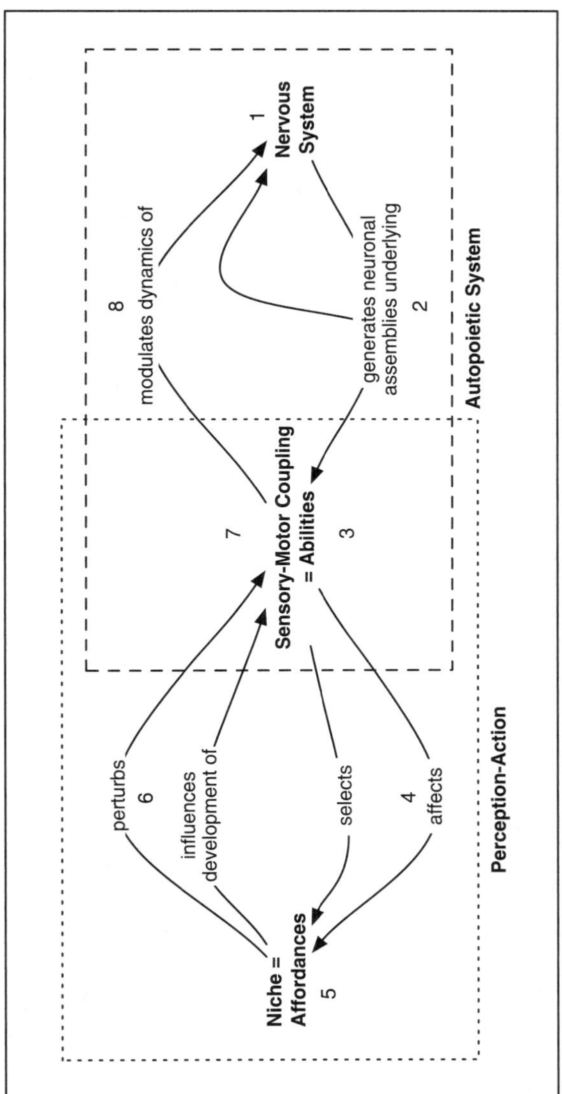

Figure 9.1
Phenomenological realism, depicted as a trace through the animal–environment system.

Frankly, it seems to me that it takes years of study of the philosophy of mind and computational cognitive science to believe that there is a difference between (1) and (2). Moreover, it seems to me that the distinction between (1) and (2) loses its already limited plausibility when we consider perception done on the service of real-time activity, that is, in the cases of central interest to radical embodied cognitive scientists.

As an example, consider maintaining upright posture while standing (Balasubramaniam and Wing 2002). To maintain your standing balance, you use visual and mechanical information in a very subtle and complex way, in real time, to maintain an unstable equilibrium among your slightly swaying body, gravity, your visible surroundings, and the surfaces that are supporting your weight. Doing so requires perceiving the relevant affordances. We don't have words to describe most of these affordances, of course, and perhaps partly because of this we rarely purposely attend to them or report on them in conversation. But this does not mean that we do not experience them. If you think that these affordances are not experienced, I invite you to ask someone who has practiced meditation seriously. Or, even better, the next time you have to stand in line for a few minutes, do not distract yourself with a silent monologue about how annoying it is. Instead, try to direct your attention to how things look and feel as you stand there, swaying gently and adjusting the felt pressures on different parts of your feet. You will notice these felt changes to the pressures—accomplished by flexing and relaxing the muscles of your feet, legs, and torso—come along with with the slight optical expansion and contraction of the hairs on the back of the head of the person in front of you in line. You are seeing that person's head move slightly closer and then slightly farther away, which is seeing both that you are falling toward (or away from) the person and the affordance for leaning backward (or forward) slightly to keep your body upright by applying pressure with different parts of your feet. Once you have attended carefully to this experience, ask yourself whether it seems plausible to say that your (1) tightly coupled perception of and action upon these affordances could take place without them (2) appearing the way that they do. Or, put differently, is there something to the way these affordances seem to you that exceeds your use of them in maintaining your balance?[11]

The point of the preceding is that, taken out of the context of the computationalism and put into the context of the use of affordances for guiding adaptive action in real time, the case for a distinction between perceived and conscious content seems anemic. Thus I submit, following Gibson, Dennett, Reed, and the enactivists mentioned above, that perceiving—guiding ongoing activity by using information about affordances—is nothing more nor less than experiencing. It may seem that I am deflating an important topic and am failing to do justice to a vast literature on dancing qualia, a-consciousness vs. p-consciousness, and formerly color-blind neuroscientists. In response, I remind you that from the perspective of radical embodied cognitive science, none of these problems arise—they all depend on separating use of information from conscious experience. In radical embodied cognitive science, using information to perceive affordances and guide behavior in real time just is having conscious experiences. When we have explained how animals use information to directly perceive and act in their niches, we will also have explained their conscious experience. We are, of course, miles away from having satisfactorily explained how information is used to perceive and act, but the headway that has been made is also headway toward explaining consciousness.

10 Coda

I began this book in chapter 1 by trying to say what philosophical argument should not do. Philosophers should not make the naive assumption that Feyerabend made in his youth: "We also assumed, at least initially, that a complicated issue involving major conceptual revisions could be solved by a single clever argument." No philosophical argument, no matter how clever, should derail an empirical research program. Luckily, they never do. The rest of this book is an implicit argument concerning what philosophers *can* do for the sciences: show that something is possible by clearing up conceptual muddles, show that views are coherent, place current concerns in historical perspective, and show how research bears on philosophical issues. Whenever possible, philosophers of science should participate in the science itself. This is the only way to really understand what's going on.

I have argued that radical embodied cognitive science is part of the American naturalist tradition in psychology, and that it is not just a provocative form of more vanilla, more acceptable embodied cognitive science. Radical embodied cognitive science, that is, is not just embodied cognitive science plus antirepresentationalism. Rather, embodied cognitive science is radical embodied cognitive science plus computationalism. Nonetheless, the primary difference between these two views is over the explanatory value of representation. I also argued that radical embodied cognitive scientists should not waste their time in arguments over whether their models *really* have representations, and they should not try to change the definition of "representation" so that the term is less widely applicable. Instead they should use theories and explanatory strategies that treat animal–environment systems as unified entities and so do not license the invocation of representation and mental gymnastics. The theory and explanatory strategy I have recommended come from two comparatively small, progressive (in Lakatos's [1970] sense), and partly overlapping research programs in cognitive science: Gibsonian ecological psychology and dynamical systems modeling. Although these can be deployed separately, they work best together. Gibsonian ecological psychology is the best theory of the nature of animal–environment systems for radical embodied cognitive science; dynamical systems theory is the best modeling tool to put the hypotheses generated by ecological psychology in touch with actual data. That both these research programs are progressive should be evident from the empirical research I have described throughout this book. Although they have not called themselves by this name, radical embodied cognitive scientists have been extending the scope of their research program by applying their theoretical conceptions to new domains, and they have been corroborating these extensions of the theory by careful experimentation. Radical embodied cognitive science is a progressive research program.

I have not shown that radical embodied cognitive science is the one true story about the mind or cognition or even perception-action. No clever philosophical argument can do that. Indeed, I don't believe radical embodied cognitive science is the one true story, because I doubt there is any one true story. It is, though, a promising step in our ongoing attempt to naturalize cognition, to see human experience as part of the natural order. And I think that it is the best way to do cognitive science right now. My greatest hope is that over the course of this book I have convinced a few readers of that.

Notes

Preface: In Praise of Dr. Fodor

1. The term "radical embodied cognition" is introduced in Clark 1997. He argues against radical embodied cognition.

2. I am quite certain that Fodor would hate the cognitive science described here. When this book was in the last stages of editing Fodor's book, *LOT 2* (2008) appeared. In it, he blames all the foibles of the cognitive sciences on the sort of ideas behind a work like this. I cannot respond to Fodor at length here, though I will point out that it seems to me that Fodor mistakenly believes that cognitive scientists are concerned with issues in the philosophy of language. They are not, and ought not be. For more on this, see chapter 1.

3. I make this point too forcefully in Chemero 2001a, a review of Fred Keijzer's *Representation and Behavior*. It now seems to me that my criticism of Keijzer's space-making arguments against computationalism overshadows my discussion of his own positive theory, which is quite good.

1 Hegel, Behe, Chomsky, Fodor

1. A warning for those readers who are professional philosophers. My experience suggests that the material in this chapter tends to make some professional philosophers angry: some philosophers seem to view the arguments made as not just mistaken, but also somehow evil. To head off any misinterpretations, I will point out that I do not, as one former teacher worried, hate philosophy. Indeed, I hope that this book will be taken as exemplifying a way that philosophers of science can play a role that is genuinely philosophical, constructive, and actually valuable to practicing scientists.

2. I hereby acknowledge the possibility that this is not the best way to understand Hegel's *Habilitation*. This is the best I could do in terms of reconciling Hegel's text with the oft-repeated (analytic) philosophical story about Hegel and the planets. Beaumont (1954) offers a similar reading. In any event, I apologize to Hegel scholars if I've got it wrong.

3. "Similarly it seems quite beyond question that children acquire a good deal of their verbal and non-verbal behavior by casual observation and imitation of adults and other children" (Chomsky 1959, 416). Furthermore, it is worth noting that there is now significant evidence against premises (1) and (2) of Chomsky's argument. See, e.g., Goldstein, West, and King 2003 and Reali and Christiansen 2005.

4. Thanks, Adam Kovach.

5. For some reason, the vast majority of philosophical arguments about "the nature of the physical" and "the nature of the mental" display a blissful ignorance of both physics and psychology.

6. My lumping of Chomsky, Pylyshyn, and Fodor with Behe is intended to poke fun at three giants in the cognitive sciences. Recent evidence, however, suggests that Fodor wishes to place himself firmly in Behe's camp. (See Fodor 2007.)

7. Reading an earlier draft of this chapter, Ken Aizawa raises two related issues concerning Fodor and Pylyshyn's evidence for systematicity. First, he suggests that asking for experimental evidence for the systematicity of language is akin to asking for empirical evidence that dogs have tails. Second, he worries that I am setting up a possible infinite regress of evidence: one can ask for empirical evidence for every premise in an argument; then one can ask for further empirical evidence that the originally cited evidence is actually evidence for the premise it justifies, and on and on. I actually do think that one should be able to demand evidence for any empirical premise in an argument, and in some cases, one might wonder whether the evidence actually supports the premise. But don't be surprised if doing so irritates people. More importantly, though, an argument like Fodor and Pylyshyn's is a *scientific* argument, and it is perfectly reasonable to expect that premises in a scientific argument have systematically gathered evidence supporting them. Fodor and Pylyshyn cite exactly one empirical study, which they misinterpret.

8. This section was inspired by a discussion I had with Pete Mandik.

9. See Reynolds 2001 for a lively discussion of the multiplication theory. What follows is drawn from that article and from Paul Spade's wonderful, but still unpublished, *A Survey of Medieval Philosophy*, a.k.a. *The Course-in-a-Box*.

10. Bechtel (1988) suggests that psychology is not an immature science, and that computational cognitive science is a genuine Kuhnian paradigm. Leahey (2001) disputes this. For what it's worth, I'm on Leahey's side here. The claims I make about Hegelian arguments work whether cognitive science is immature or in crisis (as Bechtel suggests). See below.

11. Indeed, what I say below should hold up mutatis mutandis even if one rejects the specifics of Kuhn's story about the history of science, in favor of Lakatosian research programs (Lakatos and Musgrave 1970), Feyerabend's (1975) anarchism, or Laudan's (1977) research traditions. In each case, there will be multiple competing

paradigms (programs, traditions), at any point in time. Given this, we ought to expect Hegelian arguments from adherents of paradigm A against paradigm B, and we should expect the proponents of paradigm B to ignore them.

12. In fact, the reliance on commonsense evidence is, as we see in the arguments by Chomsky and by Fodor and Pylyshyn above, is one of the hallmarks of immature science.

13. Thus Fodor (2008) writes the following about what he calls "pragmatism," a blanket term that includes the sort of views promoted in this book: "So, to repeat, pragmatism can't be true: In the order of explanation, thinking about being painted blue is part and parcel of acting so as to get yourself painted blue *and not vice versa*. That is, as one laughingly says, a conceptual point; so *pace* Churchland once again, it must hold 'from an evolutionary point of view' as from every other. (Or maybe it's not a conceptual point; maybe it's a metaphysical point. The same conclusion follows on either assumption.)" Fodor's whole book is a series of Hegelian arguments against anything he perceives as a threat to computational cognitive science as he sees it, which is apparently different from the way most practicing computational cognitive scientists see it.

14. Jonathan Tsou (2003) points out that Feyerabend's anarchism differs only linguistically from his earlier, much more highly respected pluralism. The only real difference between the respectable Feyerabend and the anarchist Feyerbend is that in the latter the word "anarchism" replaces the word "pluralism."

2 Embodied Cognition and Radical Embodied Cognition

1. Thanks, Ken Aizawa.

2. This sort of work is sometimes called "mental chronometry," and was first done by Donders in the mid-nineteenth century. Note, not coincidentally, that experiments of the same form are done by cognitive psychologists, e.g., Shepard 1982. The same thinking is at work in many neuroimaging studies.

3. The word "embedded" is often used to describe this variety of cognitive science. It is roughly a synonym of "situated."

4. See footnote 1 of Barwise and Perry 1981.

5. Perhaps inadvertently so. Brooks does not cite Gibson, but Kirsh (1991) argues convincingly that the theory of action Brooks outlines just is Gibson's.

6. Brooks has softened his antirepresentationalism in the years since 1991. See the essays collected in Brooks 1999.

7. Harry Heft (2001) does an excellent job of bringing the James–Gibson connection to light. Teed Rockwell (2005) uses Dewey to argue for a position somewhat similar to radical embodied cognitive science.

8. Adams and Aizawa (2008) argue that defenders of the sort of view of cognition that I am defending here need to give a definition of "cognition." In comments on a draft of this chapter, Ken Aizawa suggests that I am defining "cognition" as "intelligent behavior," which definition Aizawa points out is almost surely circular. I do not intend such a definition, and I disagree that proponents of radical embodied cognitive science actually require a definition of "cognition." That aside, I will say a few things about what I mean by "cognition." I take it that cognition is the ongoing, active maintenance of a robust animal–environment system, achieved by closely coordinated perception and action. This understanding of the nature of cognition is intended to reflect claims by radical embodied cognitive scientists in philosophy, psychology, AI, and artificial life. (See Maturana and Varela 1980; Reed 1996; Beer 2003; Thompson 2007.) Note, finally, that these brief remarks are not intended to supply a set of necessary and sufficient conditions, or criteria for what Adams and Aizawa call the "mark of the cognitive." In chapters 6 and 7, I lay out a Gibsonian theory of perception, action and cognition. This also does not provide criteria for the "mark of the cognitive." There is no such thing.

9. Note that Beer 2003 is an extended dynamical analysis of the research initially discussed in Beer 1996.

10. Actually, Heidegger picks out several others as well. Philosophers of mind, however, only focus on these two.

11. Mason Cash suggests that not all critics of radical embodied cognitive science will find the Van Rooij et al. task to be satisfyingly representation hungry, and not therefore an instance of "real cognition." This, he points out, is the result of a mistaken belief that if something is explicable dynamically, then it cannot be real cognition. Case 8 in chapter 5.1 should put a definitive end to this mistaken belief. So should the perusal of any of the papers listed at the end of 4.3.

3 Theories of Representation

1. Of course, many philosophers have found fault with teleosemantics. Among the most worrisome problems with teleosemantics are those raised by Mason Cash (2008a,b).

2. The discussion of oscillators in this chapter draws heavily on Chemero and Eck 1999, where similar arguments are made in full mathematical dress.

3. Nitpicky detail: Thelen and Smith use true mass-spring oscillators in their models; Schoner and Kelso explore the dynamics of moving masses (fingers) with different (non-mass-spring) oscillators.

4. Note that this is not a criticism of adaptive oscillator models of rhythm. They make good predictions about where downbeats occur in rhythmical signals and are considerably simpler than some other candidate models. Given that they were not

designed to be used in large groups, their instability in such a context should be forgiven.

5. It will become clear later that my philosophy of science runs toward Hacking's experimental realism (Hacking 1982, 1983), according to which the best reason to believe in theoretical entities is our ability to use them to explore other phenomena.

6. Ramsey does not see these representations this way. S-representations, for "structural" or "simulation" representations, are features of maps or models, which maps are isomorphic to what they represent and allow "surrogative reasoning." This sounds like it requires decouplability, but it does not. This is the case because Ramsey explicitly claims that he is not fussy about what counts as a simulation/map. Ramsey's only restriction is that the representation must be part of a map (or must itself be a map) and must be used in virtue of its being isomorphic to what it represents. This lack of fussiness allows nearly everything to count as a map. In particular, the represented target might be always present. This is just the same as Millikan's view, and it is even expressed in the same language. So Ramsey's s-representations are a variety of traditional representation.

7. Haugeland rejected this as a reading of his views on representation while reviewing an earlier version of this material.

8. Bickhard's interactivist theory of representation (Bickhard 1993, 2003) and Rosenberg and Anderson's guidance theory of representation (Rosenberg and Anderson 2004; Anderson and Rosenberg 2008) in a sense go much further than Smith. Rather than requiring that it be possible for something to decouple, these views require a representation to always be decoupled. Representations, on these views, are representations of possible future actions. As such, what they stand in for cannot be physically present.

9. It is worth considering to what extent emulators are necessary for actual reaching. Though it may be true that proprioceptive feedback arrives too slowly to aid in controlling a ballistic reach, it is not the primary source of information we use in directing reaches. We primarily control our reaches *visually*, and visual information does arrive quickly enough to help in guiding reaches. Think of how differently you reach for things in the dark. So it doesn't seem that emulators are actually necessary for guiding reaches.

10. At least temporarily. In another paper, coauthored with Michael Wheeler (Wheeler and Clark 1999), Clark moves back to a view that allows nondecouplable systems to represent their targets. He has, however, continued to endorse the idea of emulators as representations (Clark 2008).

11. Ramsey (2007) tries this, while arguing that his view of representation is closer to the nonphilosophical meaning of the term. So, while we share skepticism about representationalist cognitive science, our strategies are quite different. Ramsey argues that, if only cognitive scientists used the word "representation" correctly, they

would realize that cognition is largely nonrepresentational. As will become evident in the next chapters, my strategy is to say look at the way cognitive scientists actually do use the word "representation," and to argue that it doesn't help them to explain cognition. Ramsey (1997) used to prefer my current strategy.

4 The Dynamical Stance

1. This chapter and the next are based upon Chemero 2000a.

2. The spindle is the representation producer in the Watt governor *qua* representational system. (This satisfies criterion R1 of the definition.)

3. Bechtel (1998) has also argued that the Watt governor is representational, and he argues that the Watt governor is computational as well. Bechtel and I disagree here because we have different views of what computation is. Bechtel makes a distinction between "processes operating on representations" and "representations figuring in processes." Either case, he thinks, counts as computation. I follow Haugeland (1985) in thinking that only the former of these is computation: having representations figure in processes is not enough.

4. Haselager, de Groot, and van Rappard (2003) reach a similar conclusion from a different starting point. That is, they also conclude that the debates over whether there are representations in models of cognitive systems are fruitless. They reach this conclusion by arguing that there are no agreed upon, operationalizable criteria for whether there are representations in a system. I hope to have shown that there are such criteria.

5. Wheeler (2005) agrees with me that it is possible to view these robots as having action-oriented representations. He now thinks that this is because the systems really are representational.

6. A covering law explanation is one in which a fact is explained if and only if the statement of that fact is deduced from other statements, at least one of which is a general scientific law. Note also that according to the covering law model of explanation (and dynamical models of cognition), prediction is the dual of explanation: a fact is explained if and only if it could have been predicted. See Hempel 1966.

5 Guides to Discovery

1. Perhaps the most obvious unifying model in cognitive science is artificial neural networks (ANNs). Some have argued that ANNs are best understood as dynamical systems (van Gelder 1998); some have even argued that they are nonrepresentational dynamical systems (Ramsey 1997). In many ways, ANN research has dovetailed with radical embodied cognitive science (see, e.g., the Beer robots discussed in chapter 2 and the Sussex robots discussed in chapter 4). I will not take this up here.

2. The Tuller et al. (1994) model discussed in chapter 2 is also a potential function.

3. Information will be discussed at length in chapter 6.

4. In other, so-far-unpublished studies by this group (which includes J. Dixon, Damian Stephen, Rebecca Boncoddo, James Magnuson, and Rob Isenhower), they have replicated these results with preschool and school-age children and with eye trackers rather than finger tracking. Thanks to Damian Stephen for helping me to get the description of this research right.

5. This respect for theories does not rule out what Winsberg (2006) calls falsifications, assumptions in models that are counter to the tenets of the theory.

6. Note that this makes explicit that I reject the *semantic view of theories*, according to which theories just are collections of models (Suppes 1969; van Fraassen 1980). I agree with Cartwright (1999) and Morrison (1998, 2007) that this misplaces the role of models in science. In particular, I believe that Morrison (1998) is correct that models are autonomous.

6 Information and Direct Perception

1. The theory of information I will describe in this chapter was first outlined in Chemero 2003b, on which this chapter draws heavily.

2. I should also point out that I owe them a personal debt. Though I was never formally a student of Shaw, Turvey, or Mace, each has been patient corrector of my misinterpretations and has even encouraged me in the development of my competing views. They still think I'm wrong.

3. Reed (1996) also tries to give a philosophically sound account of Gibson's theory of information and affordances. This chapter is an attempt to improve on Reed's work.

4. Note that there is still stimulation of retinal cells in this case. Stimulation is necessary, but not sufficient for perception.

5. Fodor and Pylyshyn (1981) agree with this point about the relational nature of information as Gibson understands it. They disagree with more or less everything else in Gibson 1979.

6. The exact nature of the relationship between height and other aspects of body scale and affordances is a matter of dispute. See Chemero 2003a and chapter 7 below.

7. A quick note on Edward Reed: Although Reed was an author on the paper on cognition and spent his career working on a philosophically sound version of Gibson's ecological psychology, I think it makes more sense to speak of the Turvey-Shaw-Mace view and not the "Turvey-Shaw-Reed-Mace view." This is because after working on the 1981 paper, Reed developed views that diverged both from that presented in

the 1981 paper and from the one I'm presenting here. See Withagen and Chemero 2009.

8. Warren, a student of Shaw and Turvey, spells out the Turvey-Shaw-Mace view clearly and in detail in his "Direct Perception: The view from here" (2005). Warren (2006) also presents a very clear description of the Turvey-Shaw-Mace view of information, and links it to dynamical systems explanations of action. Philosophers of science should be more appreciative when practicing experimentalists take time to produce theoretical work as careful and detailed as that done by Turvey, Shaw, Mace, and, more recently, Warren. It makes our jobs much easier.

9. I should point out that there are some who would argue that there are mental representations involved, even in effective tracking. Chapters 3, 4, and 5, I hope, show that this is unhelpful.

10. Awareness is intended very thinly here. An animal is aware of a constraint when it guides its activity as if the constraint holds.

11. Though it is not directly relevant here, it is worth pointing out that optic flow is centripetal in the direction you are moving away from. Think about looking out the back of a moving car: the image size of objects decreases as you move away from them, which is to say that texture elements move toward the center of your field of view.

12. This demonstration and the accompanying figure are based on Bruce, Green and Georgeson (2003) and differ slightly from Lee 1980.

13. It must be noted that there is also evidence that subjects fail to judge heading accurately when the simulated eye movements are comparatively large. This would seem to indicate that extraretinal information is necessary, at least for large eye movements. But in the sort of simulations used in these experiments, optic flow with large, simulated eye movements is consistent with what one would see if one were following a curved path without eye movements. The "errors" subjects make in perceiving heading with simulated eye movements are consistent with correctly perceiving following a curved path, and subjects in experiments with simulated large eye movements often report that they are moving along a curved path. (See Warren 2004 for a review.) Thus it seems that there are two kinds of responses to optic flow with simulated eye movements: when the simulated eye movements are small, subjects perceive that they are following a straight path and that they've moved their eyes; when the simulated eye movements are large, subjects perceive that they are following a curved path and have not moved their eyes. Neither response indicates that extraretinal information or efference copy is necessary.

14. This shows that Clark (2008) is incorrect when he says that dynamical approaches err in that they "obscure the specifically intelligence-based route to evolutionary success. That route involves the ability to become apprised of information concerning our surroundings and to use that information as a guide to present and

future action. As soon as we embrace the notion of the brain as the principal (though not the *only*) seat of information-processing activity, we are already seeing it as fundamentally different from, say, the flow of a river or the activity of a volcano" (Clark 2008, 25). The discussion in 6.6.3 shows that dynamics can and does account for information use in control of action, yet it does so without taking the brain to be the seat of information processing activity. Information processing in something that we do by acting in the world.

15. The word "relevant" in this sentence (well, not this very sentence, but the one to which this footnote is attached) should make you worry about the frame problem. If it does not, read Dennett 1984 immediately. If you think connectionist networks are the right way to solve the problem, read Haselager 1997 or Haselager and van Rappard 1998.

16. Fagot, Wasserman, and Young (2001) use entropy to explain similar performances by baboons.

17. The actual value of the maximum entropy varies depending on the number of icons in the array.

18. It must be admitted that I interpret these simulations differently than some animal cognition researchers. Mike Young, in personal communication, has argued that our simulations do not match pigeon and baboon behavior, but merely curve fit the training set. Although he studies pigeons and baboons, the basis for his argument is from computer science: the problem is not linearly separable, so it is impossible in principle for a two-layer network to solve it. Pigeons and baboons, Young believes, are performing computations. Also in a personal communication, Roger Thompson, who studies pigeons, monkeys, chimps, and humans, suggests that our simulations do accurately model pigeon and baboon behavior and are evidence in favor of the profound disparity. Pigeons and baboons that learn to perceive higher-order sameness and difference do so by directly perceiving entropy. Humans and chimps, on the other side of the profound disparity, reason about sameness and difference.

7 Affordances, etc.

1. There are also views that take affordances to be varieties of mental representation (Vera and Simon 1993; Millikan 2000; Sahin et al. 2007). These are inappropriate for radical embodied cogntive science, so merit no further consideration here. See also Chemero and Turvey 2007a,b.

2. Because Turvey (1992) goes well beyond Turvey et al. 1981 in its discussion of affordances, I will refer primarily Turvey's paper in this chapter. I believe that Shaw and Mace endorse the content of that paper, so comments I make about it also apply both the Turvey et al. 1981 and what I called "Turvey-Shaw-Mace" ecological psychology in chapter 6.

3. Heft (1989) also draws on Merleau-Ponty to derive a theory of the role of culture in affordances. I will not address this aspect of Heft's theory here.

4. Stoffregen (2003) agrees. He claims that affordances are emergent properties of animal–environment systems.

5. Note that environmental situations can be formalized in terms of situation semantics (Barwise and Perry 1981, 1983; chapter 6 above).

6. Warren, who is responsible for the introduction of π-numbers into ecological psychology, agrees that body scale is just an easily measurable substitute for ability (personal communication). Saying so, of course, in no way downplays the importance of Warren's studies and, more generally, π numbers.

7. Millikan 2000 makes this point forcefully; the remainder of this paragraph is based on her analysis of abilities. See also Millikan 1984 and Stoffregen 2003.

8. In fact, I have argued elsewhere that abilities are best understood as relations between *affordances* and actions. This makes the definitions of both "affordance" and "ability" circular. Although I think that this interdefining of these terms is appropriate, it is not something I wish to defend here. For one thing, defending it requires defending circular definitions, and this is not the place to do that. The necessity of circularity for understanding natural, complex systems is defended at length in Chemero and Turvey 2007a and in Chemero 2008.

9. Notice that this solves the problem that Rowlands (2006) thinks makes representational explanation necessary. Rowlands argues that unless we understand actions as representation guided or even as representations themselves (he calls these "deeds"), we cannot account for the normativity inherent in human perception and action. Affordances, which are only comprehensible in terms of norm-laden abilities, are themselves normative.

10. It is worth noting that Reed's overall views are not selectionist.

11. For some reasons, see Lewontin 1994; Griffiths and Gray 2001. For more on the connection between radical embodied cognitive science and the developmental systems approach in evolutionary biology, see below, as well as Wagman and Miller 2003a,b; Chemero and Turvey 2007a; Chemero and Silberstein 2008a,b; Silberstein and Chemero under review.

12. This may not be true if you are reading this many years after I wrote it, in a terrifying future in which there are no books. If this is you, you can imagine holding a glass of Dogfish Head Ninety Minute Imperial India Pale Ale. If the Dogfish Head Brewery is gone, you should stop reading and weep about missed gustatory affordances.

13. All ecological psychologists acknowledge Gibson's (1962) experiments on active touch as foundational. I start with Solomon and Turvey because I am specifically interested in the inertial tensor.

14. Notice that the moment of inertia is a function of mass and length, so it does not specify the rod's length. See chapter 6 on specificity and information.

15. If this is actually a mistake. Wagman, Zimmerman, and Sorric (2007) show that when they are put into containers of the same size, a pound of lead is consistently judged by subjects to be heavier than a pound of feathers. That is, a pound of lead *feels* heavier than a pound of feathers.

16. Thanks to Claudia Carello for a discussion that inspired this section.

8 Neurophilosophy Meets Radical Embodied Cognitive Science

1. This chapter is based on Chemero and Heyser 2005. For a more detailed discussion of the same material, see Chemero and Heyser 2009.

2. The Churchlands are even more famous for being eliminativists about folk psychology. Their guiding idea is that the cognitive science that is ultimately reduced to cognitive neuroscience will make folk psychology a predictive and explanatory embarrassment. They are *not* eliminativists about cognitive science.

3. To match the intake of our rats, a 150-pound human would need to drink a six-pack in one hour, and then one additional beer every hour for the next two weeks.

4. I have not included the citations for these papers. The list of full citations for the 116 articles reviewed is longer than the current chapter. Furthermore, notice that we restricted ourselves to the neuroscience literature. Animal behaviorists who are not neuroscientists also use object exploration, and use it very differently than neuroscientists do. For one thing, they do not tend to cite the Ennaceur/Delacour papers. It is not clear to what extent the animal behavior literature follows the patterns of the neuroscience literature that I will be complaining about. Maricia Bernstein (unpublished) suggests that the animal behavior literature is no better off than the neuroscience literature.

5. See Chemero and Heyser 2005 for a detailed description of a study reported in Morrow, Ellsworth, and Roth 2002 in which different objects (which were not described) clearly were explored differently. After presenting data showing that objects were explored differently, Morrow et al. averaged over them.

6. In this study, they are strain C57BL/6. In another study, we've shown that C57BL/6s explore objects differently than DBA/2Js do (Heyser, Vishnevetsky, and Chemero 2005). This strain difference does not affect the results discussed here.

9 The Metaphysics of Radical Embodiment

1. This is unsurprising considering that my 1998b argument is parallel to Putnam's. Putnam argued that because ideal scientific theories have many models that conflict with one another, there is no reason to trust that any one gets the theory-independent world just right. I have argued that because we actually do have many

equally good, conflicting sensory systems, there is no reason to trust that one maps the animal-independent world just right.

2. Churchland (1979) embraces both scientific realism and theory-laden perception. But Churchland's scientific realism is highly nonstandard.

3. In an extended critique of arguments by Varela, Thompson, and Rosch and by myself, Mandik and Clark (2002) point to perceptual extensibility, but not to the reorganization that might come with it. Clark (2003), however, is a big fan of cognitive reorganization.

4. See also Churchland 1979, which is a book-length paean to plasticity.

5. Incidentally, this is something Churchland and Fodor agree on. For Churchland, a mind is one big theory; for Fodor, the mind is a bunch of little theories. Taking minds to be (analogous to) theories is also a key feature of some theories of development (Gopnik 1996; Gopnik and Meltzoff 1997).

6. Note that there is no contradiction between claiming that perceptual or cognitive systems are plastic and claiming that they are not theories. For the (radical) embodied cognitive scientist, modifications of perceptual systems come from learning new skills, not alterations of theories.

7. Note that, despite what everyone seems to think about him, Feyerabend was a realist. See Tsou 2003.

8. These studies parallel the Shockley et al. study described in chapter 7. What Shockley et al. (2004) showed was that subjects make mistaken judgments about weight, while making accurate judgments about the affordance moveability. Similary, studies in the Proffitt lab show that subjects make inaccurate judgments about distance and slant because they are actually perceiving affordances (walkability, throwability). So the Proffitt studies are further evidence that there is information specifying affordances available to perceivers, supporting the case made there. At the same time, the Shockley et al. studies are another instance of manipulating an affordance (moveability) to study something else (the size-weight illusion), supporting the case made here.

9. The arguments in this section are all made in much more detail in Silberstein and Chemero, under review. In that paper, we also mount a detailed defense of neutral monism.

10. Others who are in no way in the radical embodied camp who have made claims like this are Dretske 1988; Tye 1995; Horgan and Tienson 2002. Dennett isn't really in the radical embodied camp either, though I would still claim him as inspiration on this point.

11. Of course, the question here is not whether you could perceive and act upon these affordances without purposefully attending to them. I take it as obvious that we do not attend to most of the things we experience.

References

Adams, F., and K. Aizawa (2008). *The Bounds of Cognition*. Malden, Mass.: Blackwell.

Agre, P. (1997). *Computation and Human Experience*. New York: Oxford.

Agre, P., and D. Chapman (1987). Pengi: An implementation of a theory of activity. *Proceedings of the Sixth National Conference on Artificial* Intelligence, 268–272. Menlo Park, Calif.: AAAI Press.

Aizawa, K. (2003). *The Systematicity Arguments*. Dordrecht: Kluwer.

Amazeen, E. L., D. Sternad, and M. T. Turvey (1996). Predicting the nonlinear shift of stable equilibria in interlimb rhythmic coordination. *Human Movement Science, 15*, 521–542.

Amazeen, E. L., and M. T. Turvey (1996). Weight perception and the haptic size-weight illusion are functions of the inertia tensor. *Journal of Experimental Psychology: Human Perception and Performance, 22*, 213–232.

Anderson, M. (2003). Embodied cognition: A field guide. *Artificial Intelligence, 149*, 91–130.

Anderson, M. (2006). Cognitive science and epistemic openness. *Phenomenology and the Cognitive Sciences, 5*, 125–154.

Anderson, M., and G. Rosenberg (2008). Content and action: The guidance theory of representation. *Journal of Mind and Behavior, 29*, 55–86.

Balasubramaniam, R., and A. Wing (2002). The dynamics of standing balance. *Trends in Cognitive Sciences, 6*, 531–536.

Barkow, K., L. Cosmides, and J. Tooby (eds.) (1992). *The Adapted Mind*. New York: Oxford University Press.

Barwise, J., and J. Perry (1981). Situations and attitudes. *Journal of Philosophy, 77*, 668–691.

Barwise, J., and J. Perry (1983). *Situations and Attitudes*. Cambridge, Mass.: MIT Press.

Barwise, J., and J. Seligman (1994). The rights and wrongs of natural regularity. *Philosophical Perspectives, 8,* 331–364.

Barwise, J., and J. Seligman (1997). *Information Flow.* Cambridge: Cambridge University Press.

Beaumont, B. (1954). Hegel and the seven planets. *Mind, 63,* 246–248.

Bechtel, W. (1988). *Philosophy of Science: An Overview of Cognitive Science.* Hillsdale, N.J.: Erlbaum.

Bechtel, W. (1998). Representations and cognitive explanations: Assessing the dynamicist challenge in cognitive science. *Cognitive Science, 22,* 295–318.

Bechtel, W., and J. Mundale (1999). Multiple realizability revisited: Linking cognitive and neural states. *Philosophy of Science, 66,* 175–207.

Beer, R. (1995a). Computational and dynamical languages for autonomous agents. In *Mind as Motion,* ed. R. Port and T. van Gelder. Cambridge, Mass.: MIT Press.

Beer, R. (1995b). A dynamical systems perspective on agent-environment interactions. *Artificial Intelligence, 72,* 173–215.

Beer, R. (1996). Toward the evolution of dynamical neural networks for minimally cognitive behavior. In *From Animals to Animats 4: Proceedings of the Fourth International Conference on Simulation of Adaptive Behavior,* ed. P. Maes, M. Mataric, J. Meyer, J. Pollack, and S. Wilson, 421–429. Cambridge, Mass: MIT Press.

Beer, R. (2000). Dynamical approaches to cognitive science. *Trends in Cognitive Sciences, 4,* 91–99.

Beer, R. (2003). The dynamics of active categorical perception in an evolved model agent. *Adaptive Behavior, 11,* 209–243.

Beer, R., and J. Gallagher (1992). Evolving dynamical neural networks for adaptive behavior. *Adaptive Behavior, 1,* 91–122.

Behe, M. (1996). *Darwin's Black Box.* New York: Free Press.

Bernstein, M. (unpublished). Comments on Chemero and Heyser.

Bhalla, M., and D. R. Proffitt (1999). Visual-Motor recalibration in geographical slant perception. *Journal of Experimental Psychology: Human Perception and Performance, 25,* 1076–1096.

Bickhard, M. H. (1993). Representational content in humans and machines. *Journal of Experimental and Theoretical Artificial Intelligence, 5,* 285–333.

Bickhard, M. H. (2003). Process and emergence: Normative function and representation. In *Process Theories: Crossdisciplinary Studies in Dynamic Categories,* ed. J. Seibt. Dordrecht: Kluwer Academic.

Bickle, J. (1998). *Psychoneural Reduction: The New Wave*. Cambridge, Mass.: MIT Press.

Bickle, J. (2003). *Philosophy and the Neurosciences: A Ruthlessly Reductionist Account*. Dordrecht: Kluwer Academic.

Boltzmann, L. (1900). The recent development of method in theoretical physics. *Monist, 11*, 226–257.

Boyer, P. (2001). Natural epistemology or evolved metaphysics? Developmental evidence for early-developed, intuitive, category-specific, incomplete, and stubborn metaphysical presumptions. *Philosophical Psychology, 13*, 277–297.

Breazeal, C. (2002). *Designing Sociable Robots*. Cambridge, Mass.: MIT Press.

Bressler, S. L. (2002). Understanding cognition through large-scale cortical networks. *Current Directions in Psychological Science, 11*, 58–61.

Bressler, S., and J. A. S. Kelso (2001). Cortical coordination dynamics and cognition. *Trends in Cognitive Sciences 5*, 26–36.

Brooks, R. (1991). Intelligence without representation. *Artificial Intelligence, 47*, 139–159.

Brooks, R. (1999). *Cambrian Intelligence*. Cambridge, Mass.: MIT Press.

Bruce, V., P. Green, and M. Georgeson (2003). *Visual Perception: Physiology, Psychology, and Ecology*. New York: Psychology Press.

Buller, D. (2005). *Adapting Minds: Evolutionary Psychology and the Persisting Quest for Human Nature*. Cambridge, Mass.: MIT Press.

Burton, G. (1992). Nonvisual judgement of the crossability of path gaps. *Journal of Experimental Psychology: Human Perception and Performance, 18*, 698–713.

Burton, G. (1993). Non-neural extensions of haptic sensitivity. *Ecological Psychology, 5*, 105–124.

Burton, G. (1994). Crossing without vision of path gaps. *Journal of Motor Behavior, 26*, 2, 147–161.

Burton, G., M. Turvey, and H. Solomon (1990). Can shape be perceived by dynamic touch? *Perception and Psychophysics, 5*, 477–487.

Busemeyer, J., and J. Townsend (1995). Decision field theory. In *Mind as Motion*, ed. R. Port and T. van Gelder. Cambridge, Mass.: MIT Press.

Busemeyer, J., J. T. Townsend, and J. Stout (2002). Motivational underpinnings of utility in decision making. In *Emotional Cognition*, ed. S. Moore and M. Oaksford. Philadelphia: John Benjamins.

Carello, C., and M. T. Turvey (2000). Rotational dynamics and dynamic touch. In *Touch, Representation, and Blindness*, ed. M. Heller. Oxford: Oxford University Press.

Carello, C., and M. T. Turvey (2004). Physics and psychology of the muscle sense. *Current Directions in Psychological Science, 13*, 25–28.

Carello, C., S. Thuot, K. L. Anderson, and M. T. Turvey (1999). Perceiving the sweet spot. *Perception, 28*, 307–320.

Cartwright, H. (1983). *How the Laws of Physics Lie*. New York: Oxford University Press.

Cartwright, H. (1999). *The Dappled World*. New York: Cambridge University Press.

Cash, M. (2008a). Thoughts and oughts. *Philosophical Explorations, 11*, 93–119.

Cash, M. (2008b). The normativity problem: Evolution and naturalized semantics. *Journal of Mind and Behavior, 29*, 99–137.

Casler, K., and D. Kelemen (2005). Young children's rapid learning about artifacts. *Developmental Science, 8*, 472–480.

Casler, K., and D. Kelemen (2007). Reasoning about artifacts at 24 months: The developing teleo-functional stance. *Cognition, 103*, 120–130.

Cesari, P., F. Formenti, and P. Olivato (2003). A common perceptual parameter for stair climbing for children, young and old adults. *Human Movement Science, 22*, 111–124.

Chalmers, D. (1990). Why Fodor and Pylyshyn were wrong: The simplest refutation. *Proceedings of the Twelfth Annual Conference of the Cognitive Science Society*, 340–347.

Chalmers, D. (1996). *The Conscious Mind*. New York: Oxford University Press.

Charpentier, A. (1891). Analyse experimentale de quelques elements de la sensation de poids. *Archives Physiologique Normals and Pathologiques, 18*, 79–87.

Chemero, A. (1998a). How to be an anti-representationalist. Unpublished Ph.D. Dissertation in Philosophy and Cognitive Science, Indiana University.

Chemero, A. (1998b). A Stroll through the worlds of animats and persons: A review of Andy Clark's *Being There*. *Psyche, 4*, 14.

Chemero, A. (2000a). Anti-representationalism and the dynamical stance. *Philosophy of Science, 67*, 625–647.

Chemero, A. (2000b). What events are. *Ecological Psychology, 12*, 1, 37–42.

Chemero, A. (2001a). Making space for embodiment. *Trends in Cognitive Science, 5*, 317–318.

Chemero, A. (2001b). Dynamical explanation and mental representation. *Trends in Cognitive Science, 5*, 140–141.

Chemero, A. (2001c). What we perceive when we perceive affordances. *Ecological Psychology, 13*, 111–116.

Chemero, A. (2003a). An outline of a theory of affordances. *Ecological Psychology, 15,* 181–195.

Chemero, A. (2003b). Information for perception and information processing. *Minds and Machines, 13,* 577–588.

Chemero, A. (2003c). Radical empiricism through the ages. *Contemporary Psychology, 48,* 18–20.

Chemero, A. (2008). Self-organization, writ large. *Ecological Psychology, 20,* 257–269.

Chemero, A., and D. Eck (1999). An exploration of representational complexity via coupled oscillator systems. In *Proceedings of the 1999 Midwest AI and Cognitive Science Conference,* ed. U. Priss. Cambridge: AAAI Press.

Chemero, A., and C. Heyser (2005). Object exploration and a problem with reductionism. *Synthese, 147,* 403–423.

Chemero, A., and C. Heyser (2009). Methodology and ontology in the behavioral neurosciences: Object exploration as a case study. In *Oxford Handbook of Philosophy and Neuroscience,* ed. J. Bickle. New York: Oxford University Press.

Chemero, A., C. Klein, and W. Cordeiro (2003). Events as changes in the layout of affordances. *Ecological Psychology, 15,* 19–28.

Chemero, A., and M. Silberstein (2008a). After the philosophy of mind. *Philosophy of Science, 75,* 1–27.

Chemero, A., and M. Silberstein (2008b). Defending extended cognition. In *Proceedings of the 30th Annual Meeting of the Cognitive Science Society,* ed. B. Love, K. McRae, and V. Sloutsky. Austin, Texas: Cognitive Science Society.

Chemero, A., and M. Turvey (2007a). Hypersets, complexity, and the ecological approach to perception-action. *Biological Theory, 2,* 23–36.

Chemero, A., and M. Turvey (2007b). Gibsonian affordances for roboticists. *Adaptive Behavior, 15,* 473–480.

Chen, G., K. S. Chen, J. Knox, J. Inglis, A. Bernard, S. J. Martin, A. Justice, L. McConlogue, D. Games, S. B. Freedman, and R. G. M. Morris (2000). A learning deficit related to age and B-amyloid plagues in a mouse model of Alzheimer's disease. *Nature, 408,* 975–979.

Chomsky, N. (1959). Review of B. F. Skinner's *Verbal Behavior. Language, 35,* 26–58. Reprinted in *The History of Psychology: Fundamental Questions,* ed. M. Munger. New York: Oxford University Press. Page references are to reprinted version.

Christiansen, M., and N. Chater (2008). Language as shaped by the brain. *Behavioral and Brain Sciences, 30,* 489–509.

Churchland, P. M. (1979). *Scientific Realism and the Plasticity of Mind.* Cambridge: Cambridge University Press.

Churchland, P. M. (1985). Reduction, qualia, and the direct introspection of brain states. *Journal of Philosophy, 82,* 8–28.

Churchland, P. M. (1988). Perceptual plasticity and theoretical neutrality: A reply to Jerry Fodor. *Philosophy of Science, 55,* 167–187.

Churchland, P. M. (1989). *A Neurocomputational Perspective.* Cambridge, Mass.: MIT Press.

Churchland, P. S. (1986). *Neursphilosophy.* Cambridge, Mass.: MIT Press.

Churchland, P. S. (2002). *Brain-Wise.* Cambridge, Mass.: MIT Press.

Clancey, W. (1997). *Situated Cognition: On Human Knowledge and Computer Representations.* Cambridge: Cambridge University Press.

Clark, A. (1997). *Being There.* Cambridge, Mass.: MIT Press.

Clark, A. (1999). An embodied cognitive science? *Trends in Cognitive Sciences, 3,* 345–351.

Clark, A. (2001). *Mindware.* New York: Oxford University Press.

Clark, A. (2003). *Natural Born Cyborgs.* New York: Oxford University Press.

Clark, A., and R. Grush (1999). Towards a cognitive robotics. *Adaptive Behavior, 7,* 5–16.

Clark, A., and J. Toribio (1994). Doing without representing? *Synthese, 101,* 401–431.

Clark, P. (1976). Atomism versus thermodynamics. In *Method and Appraisal in the Physical Sciences,* ed. C. Howson. Cambridge: Cambridge University Press.

Clarke, S. (2001). Defensible territory for entity realism. *British Journal for the Philosophy of Science, 52,* 701–722.

Cooper, M., C. Carello, and M. T. Turvey (1999). Further evidence of perceptual independence (specificity) in dynamic touch. *Ecological Psychology, 11,* 269–281.

Cornus, S., G. Montagne, and M. Laurent (1999). Perception of a stepping-across affordance. *Ecological Psychology, 11,* 249–267.

Cosmelli, D., J.-P. Lachaux, and E. Thompson (2007). Neurodynamics of consciousness. In *The Cambridge Handbook of Consciousness,* ed. P. Zelazo, M. Moscovitch, and E. Thompson. New York: Cambridge University Press.

Cussins, A. (1992). Content, embodiment, and objectivity: The theory of cognitive trails. *Mind, 101,* 651–688.

Dale, R. (2008). The possibility of a pluralist cognitive science. *Journal of Experimental and Theoretical Artificial Intelligence, 20*, 155–179.

Dale, R., and M. Spivey (2006). Unraveling the dyad: Using recurrence analysis to explore patterns of syntactic coordination between children and caregivers in conversation. *Language Learning, 56*, 391–430.

Deacon, T. (1997). *The Symbolic Species*. New York: W. W. Norton.

Dennett, D. (1969). *Content and Consciousness*. New York: Humanities Press.

Dennett, D. (1984). Cognitive wheels: The frame problem in AI. In *Minds, Machines, and Evolution*, ed. C. Hookway. Cambridge: Cambridge University Press.

Dennett, D. (1987). *The Intentional Stance*. Cambridge, Mass.: MIT Press.

Dennett, D. (1991). *Consciousness Explained*. Boston: Little, Brown.

Dennett, D. (1998). *Brainchildren*. Cambridge, Mass.: MIT Press.

Devlin, K. (1991). *Logic and Information*. Cambridge: Cambridge University Press.

Dewey, J. (1896). The reflex arc conecpt in psychology. *Psychological Review, 3*, 357–370.

Dietrich, E., and A. Markman (2003). Discrete thoughts: Why cognition must use discrete representations. *Mind and Language, 18*, 95–119.

Di Paolo, E. A. (2003). Organismically-inspired robotics: Homeostatic adaptation and natural teleology beyond the closed sensorimotor loop. In *Dynamical Systems Approach to Embodiment and Sociality*, ed. K. Murase and T. Asakura. Adelaide: Advanced Knowledge International.

Dotov, D., and A. Chemero (2006). Entropy detection in a 2-layer neural network. Paper presented at the International Conference on Comparative Cognition.

Dourish, P. (2001). *Where the Action Is*. Cambridge, Mass.: MIT Press.

Dretske, F. (1981). *Knowledge and the Flow of Information*. Cambridge, Mass.: MIT Press.

Dretske, F. (1988). *Naturalizing the Mind*. Cambridge, Mass.: MIT Press.

Dreyfus, H. (1964). Alchemy and artificial intelligence. RAND Paper P-3244.

Dreyfus, H. (1972). *What Computers Can't Do*. New York: Harper and Row.

Ebenholtz, S. (2001). *Oculomotor Systems and Perception*. Cambridge: Cambridge University Press.

Eck, D., M. Gasser, and R. Port (2000). Dynamics and embodiment in beat induction. In *Rhythm Perception and Production*, ed. P. Desain and L. Windsor. Lisse, the Netherlands: Swets and Zeitlinger.

Edelman, S. (2003). But will it scale up? Not without representations. *Adaptive Behavior, 11*, 273–275.

Ennaceur, A., and J. Delacour (1988). A new one-trial test for neurobiological studies of memory in rats. 1: Behavioral data. *Behavioral Brain Research, 31*, 47–59.

Fagot, J., E. Wasserman, and M. Young (2001). Discriminating the relation between relations: The role of entropy in abstract conceptualization by baboons (Papio papio) and humans (Homo sapiens). *Journal of Experimental Psychology: Animal Behaviour Processes, 27*, 316–328.

Fajen, B. (2005). Perceiving possibilities for action: On the necessity of calibration and perceptual learning for the visual guidance of action. *Perception, 6*, 717–740.

Feyerabend, P. (1963). How to be a good empiricist. In *Philosophy of Science: The Delaware Seminar*, vol. 2, ed. B. Baumrin. New York: Interscience Publishers.

Feyerabend, P. (1965). Problems of empiricism. In *Beyond the Edge of Certainty*, ed. R. Colodny. Englewood Cliffs, N.J.: Prentice Hall.

Feyerabend, P. (1975). *Against Method.* New York: New Left Press.

Feyerabend, P. (1995). *Killing Time.* Chicago: University of Chicago Press.

Fitzhugh, R. (1961). Impulses and physiological states in theoretical models of nerve membrane. *Biophysical Journal, 1*, 445.

Fodor, J. (1975). *The Language of Thought.* London: Thomas Crowell.

Fodor, J. (1981). *Representations.* Cambridge, Mass.: MIT Press.

Fodor, J. (1983). *The Modularity of Mind.* Cambridge, Mass.: MIT Press.

Fodor, J. (1984). Observation reconsidered. *Philosophy of Science, 51*, 23–43.

Fodor, J. (1988). A reply to Churchland's "Perceptual plasticity and theoretical neutrality." *Philosophy of Science, 55*, 188–198.

Fodor, J. (1990). *A Theory of Content and Other Essays.* Cambridge, Mass.: MIT Press.

Fodor, J. (2007). Why pigs don't have wings. *London Review of Books, 29*, 20, 19–22.

Fodor, J. (2008). *LOT 2.* New York: Oxford University Press.

Fodor, J., and Z. Pyslshyn (1981). How direct is visual perception? Some reflections on Gibson's "ecological approach." *Cognition, 9*, 139–196.

Fodor, J., and Z. Pylyshyn (1988). Connectionism and the cognitive architecture. *Cognition, 28*, 3–71.

Freeman, W. (1975). *Mass Action in the Nervous System.* New York: Academic Press.

Freeman, W. (1999). *How Brains Make Up Their Minds.* London: Orion Press.

Gallagher, S. (2005). *How the Body Shapes the Mind.* New York: Oxford University Press.

Gallagher, S., and D. Zahavi (2008). *The Phenomenological Mind.* New York: Routledge.

Gibbs, R. (2005). *Embodiment and Cognitive Science.* New York: Cambridge University Press.

Gibson, J. (1962). Observations on active touch. *Psychological Review, 69,* 477–490.

Gibson, J. (1966). *The Senses Considered as Perceptual Systems.* Boston: Houghton-Mifflin.

Gibson, J. (1979). *The Ecological Approach to Visual Perception.* Boston: Houghton-Mifflin.

Goldstein, M., M. West, and A. King (2003). Social interaction shapes babbling. *Proceedings of the National Academy of Sciences, 100,* 8030–8035.

Gopnik, A. (1996). The scientist as child. *Philosophy of Science, 63,* 485–514.

Gopnik, A., and A. Meltzoff (1997). *Words, Thoughts, and Theories.* Cambridge, Mass.: MIT Press.

Griffiths, P., and R. Gray (2001). Darwinism and developmental systems. In *Cycles of Contingency,* ed. S. Oyama, P. Griffiths, and R. Gray. Cambridge, Mass.: MIT Press.

Grush, R. (1997). The architecture of representation. *Philosophical Psychology, 10,* 5–24.

Grush, R. (2003). In defence of some "Cartesian" assumptions concerning the brain and its operation. *Biology and Philosophy, 18,* 53–93.

Grush, R. (2004). The emulation theory of representation: Motor control, imagery, and perception. *Behavioral and Brain Sciences, 27,* 377–442.

Hacking, I. (1982). Experimentation and scientific realism. *Philosophical Topics, 13,* 71–87.

Hacking, I. (1983). *Representing and Intervening.* Cambridge: Cambridge University Press.

Haken, H., J. A. S. Kelso, and H. Bunz (1985). A theoretical model of phase transitions in human hand movements. *Biological Cybernetics, 51,* 347–356.

Hanson, N. (1958). *Patterns of Discovery.* Cambridge: Cambridge University Press.

Hartmann, S. (1999). Models and stories in Hadron physics. In *Models as Mediators,* ed. M. Morgan and M. Morrison. New York: Cambridge University Press.

Harvey, I., P. Husbands, and D. Cliff (1994). Seeing the light: Artificial evolution, real vision. In *From Animals to Animats 3,* ed. D. Cliff, P. Husbands, J.-A. Meyer, and S. W. Wilson. Cambridge, Mass.: MIT Press.

Harvey, I., P. Husbands, D. Cliff, A. Thompson, and N. Jakobi (1997). Evolutionary robotics: The Sussex approach. *Robotics and Autonomous Systems, 20,* 205–224.

Haselager, W. (1997). *Cognitive Science and Folk Psychology: The Right Frame of Mind.* London: Sage.

Haselager, W., A. de Groot, and J. van Rappard (2003). Representationalism versus anti-representationalism: A debate for the sake of appearance. *Philosophical Psychology, 16,* 5–23.

Haselager, W. F. G., and J. van Rappard (1998). Connectionism, systematicity, and the frame problem. *Minds and Machines, 8,* 161–179.

Haugeland, J. (1985). *Artificial Intelligence: The Very Idea.* Cambridge, Mass.: MIT Press.

Haugeland, J. (1991). Representational genera. In *Philosophy and Connectionist Theory,* ed. W. Ramsey, S. Stich, and D. Rumelhart. Hillsdale, N.J.: Erlbaum.

Heft, H. (1989). Affordances and the body: An intentional analysis of Gibson's ecological approach to visual perception. *Journal for the Theory of Social Behavior, 19,* 1–30.

Heft, H. (2001). *Ecological Psychology in Context: James Gibson, Roger Barker, and the Legacy of William James's Radical Empiricism.* Mahwah, N.J.: Erlbaum.

Heidegger, M. (1927). *Sein und Zeit.* Trans. as *Being and Time,* J. Macquarrie and E. Robinson, 1962. New York: Harper and Row.

Hempel, C. (1966). *The Philosophy of Natural Science.* Englewood: Prentice Hall.

Heyser, C., M. Rosen, and A. Chemero (2003). Novel object exploration in rodents: Not all objects are created equally. Poster presented at the meeting of the Society for Neuroscience.

Heyser, C., D. Vishnevetsky, and A. Chemero (2005). Novel object exploration in rodents: What does it mean to be novel? Poster presented at the meeting of the Society for Neuroscience.

Hobbes, T. (1651). *Leviathan.* Downloaded from http://www.mdx.ac.uk/WWW/STUDY/xhob01.htm, January 3, 2008.

Hodgkin, A. and A. Huxley. (1952). A quantitative description of membrane current and its application to conduction and excitation in nerve. *Journal of Physiology, 117,* 500–544.

Hooker, C. A. (1981a). Towards a general theory of reduction. Part I: Historical and scientific setting. *Dialogue* 20: 38–59.

Hooker, C. A. (1981b). Towards a general theory of reduction. Part II: Identity in reduction. *Dialogue* 20: 201–236.

Hooker,C. A. (1981c). Towards a general theory of reduction. Part III: Cross-categorial reduction. *Dialogue* 20: 496–529.

Horgan, T. and J, Tienson (2002). The intentionality of phenomenology and the phenomenology of intentionality. In *Philosophy of Mind: Classical and Contemporary Readings*, ed. D. Chalmers. New York: Oxford University Press.

Hughes, R. N. (1997). Intrinsic exploration in animals: Motives and measurement. *Behavioural Processes, 41*, 213–226.

Hurley, S. (1998). *Consciousness in Action*. Cambridge, Mass.: Harvard University Press.

Husbands, P., I. Harvey, and D. Cliff (1995). Circle in the round: State space attractor for evolved sight robots. *Journal of Robotics and Autonomous Systems, 15*, 83–106.

Hutchins, E. (1995). *Cognition in the Wild*. Cambridge, Mass.: MIT Press.

Hutto, D. (2005). Knowing what? Radical versus conservative enactivism. *Phenomenology and the Cognitive Sciences, 4*, 389–405.

Hutto, D. (2007). *Folk Psychological Narratives*. Cambridge, Mass.: MIT Press.

Israel, D., and J. Perry (1990). What is information? In *Information, Language, and Cognition*, ed. P. Hanson. Vancouver: University of British Columbia Press.

Jackendoff, R. (1987). *Consciousness and the Computational Mind*. Cambridge, Mass.: MIT Press.

Jacobs, D., and C. Michaels (2007). Direct learning. *Ecological Psychology, 19*, 321–349.

Jacobs, D., C. Michaels, and S. Runeson (2000). Learning to perceive the relative mass of colliding balls: The effects of ratio-scaling and feedback. *Perception and Psychophysics, 62*, 1332–1340.

Jacobs, D., S. Runeson, and C. Michaels (2001). Learning to perceive the relative mass of colliding balls in globally and locally constrained task ecologies. *Journal of Experimental Psychology: Human Perception and Performance, 27*, 1019–1038.

Jacobson, A. (2003). Mental representations: What philosophy leaves out and neuroscience puts in. *Philosophical Psychology, 16*, 189–203.

Jacobson, A. (2008). What should a theory of vision look like? *Philosophical Psychology, 21*, 585–599.

James, W. (1912/1976). *Essays in Radical Empiricism*. Cambridge, Mass.: Harvard University Press.

Jiang, Y., and L. Mark (1994). The effect of gap depth on the perception of whether a gap is crossable. *Perception and Psychophysics, 56*, 691–700.

Jones, M., and M. Boltz (1989). Dynamic attending and responses to time. *Psychological Review, 96*, 459–491.

Kay, B., E. Saltzman, and J. Kelso (1991). Steady state and perturbed rhythmical movements: A dynamical analysis. *Journal of Experimental Psychology: Human Perception and Performance, 17*, 183–197.

Keijzer, F. (1998). Doing without representation which specify what to do. *Philosophical Psychology, 11*, 269–302.

Keijzer, F. (2001). *Representation and Behavior*. Cambridge, Mass.: MIT Press.

Keller, E. F. (2002). *Making Sense of Life*. Cambridge, Mass.: Harvard University Press.

Kelso, J. A. S. (1984). Phase transitions and critical behavior in human bimanual coordination. *American Journal of Physiology: Regulatory, Integrative and Comparative, 15*, R1000–R1004.

Kelso, J. A. S. (1995). *Dynamic Patterns*. Cambridge, Mass.: MIT Press.

Kelso, J. A. S., J. DelColle, and G. Schöner (1990). Action-perception as a pattern formation process. In *Attention and Performance XIII*, ed. M. Jeannerod, 139–169. Hillsdale, N.J.: Erlbaum.

Kelso, J. A. S., and D. Engstrøm (2006). *The Complementary Nature*. Cambridge, Mass.: MIT Press.

Kirsh, D. (1991). Today the earwig, tomorrow man? *Artificial Intelligence, 47*, 161–184.

Kirsh, D. (1995). The intelligent use of space. *Artificial Intelligence, 72*, 31–68.

Kirsh, D., and P. Maglio (1994). On distinguishing epistemic from pragmatic action. *Cognitive Science, 18*, 513–549.

Kugler, P. N., J. A. S. Kelso, and M. T. Turvey (1980). Coordinative structures as dissipative structures I. Theoretical lines of convergence. In *Tutorials in Motor Behavior*, ed. G. E. Stelmach and J. Requin. Amsterdam: North Holland.

Kugler, P. N., and M. Turvey (1987). *Information, Natural Law, and the Self-Assembly of Rhythmic Movement*. Hillsdale, N.J.: Erlbaum.

Kuhn, T. (1962). *The Structure of Scientific Revolutions*. Chicago: University of Chicago Press.

Lakatos, I. (1970). Falsification and the methodology of scientific research programmes. In *Criticism and the Growth of Knowledge*, ed. I. Lakatos and A. Musgrave. Cambridge: Cambridge University Press.

Lakatos, I., and A. Musgrave (eds.) (1970). *Criticism and the Growth of Knowledge*. Cambridge: Cambridge University Press.

Lakoff, G., and M. Johnson (1999). *Philosophy in the Flesh.* New York: Basic Books.

Large, E., and J. Kolen (1994). Resonance and the perception of musical meter. *Connection Science, 6,* 177–120.

Large, E. W., and M. R. Jones (1999). The dynamics of attending: How we track time-varying events. *Psychological Review, 106,* 119–159.

Laudan, L. (1977). *Progress and Its Problems.* Berkeley, Calif.: University of California Press.

Leahey, T. (2001). *History of Psychology.* 3rd edition. Englewood Cliffs, N.J.: Prentice Hall.

Lee, D. N. (1980). The optic flow-field: The foundation of vision. *Philosophical Transactions of the Royal Society London B, 290,* 169–179.

Lee, D. N. (2006). How movement is guided. Retrieved March 2008 from http://www.perception-in-action.ed.ac.uk/PDF_s/Howmovementisguided.pdf.

Lee, D. N., and P. E. Reddish (1981). Plummeting gannets: A paradigm of ecological optics. *Nature, 293,* 293–294.

Lewontin, R. (1994). *Inside and Outside.* Worcester, Mass.: Clark University Press.

Lloyd, D. (2000). Popping the thought balloon. In *Dennett's Philosophy: A Comprehensive Assessment,* ed. D. Ross, A. Brook, and D. Thompson. Cambridge, Mass.: MIT Press.

Lopresti-Goodman, S. M., M. Richardson, P. Silva, and R. Schmidt (2008). Period basin of entrainment for unintentional visual coordination. *Journal of Motor Behavior, 40,* 3–10.

Mace, W. (1977). James Gibson's strategy for perceiving: Ask not what's inside your head, but what your head's inside of. In *Perceiving, Acting, and Knowing,* ed. R. Shaw and J. Bransford. Hillsdale, N.J.: Erlbaum.

Mach, E. (1886). *The Analysis of Sensations.* Trans. C. Williams. New York: Dover.

Mandik, P. (2005). Action-oriented representation. In *Cognition and the Brain: The Philosophy and Neuroscience Movement,* ed. Kathleen Akins and Adrew Brook. Cambridge: Cambridge University Press.

Mandik, P., and A. Clark (2002). Selective representing and world making. *Minds and Machines, 12,* 383–395.

Mark, L. (1987). Eye height-scale information about affordances: A study of sitting and stair climbing. *Journal of Experimental Psychology: Human Perception and Performance, 13,* 360–370.

Mark, L., Y. Jiang, S. S. King, and J. Paasche (1999). The impact of visual exploration on judgements of whether a gap is crossable. *Journal of Experimental Psychology: Human Perception and Performance, 25,* 287–295.

Markman, A. B., and E. Dietrich (2000a). In defense of representation. *Cognitive Psychology, 40,* 138–171.

Markman, A. B., and E. Dietrich (2000b). Extending the classical view of representation. *Trends in Cognitive Sciences, 4,* 70–75.

Marsh, K. L., M. J. Richardson, R. M. Baron, and R. C. Schmidt (2006). Contrasting approaches to perceiving and acting with others. *Ecological Psychology, 18,* 1–37.

Massimi, M. (2004). Non-defensible middle ground for experimental realism: Why we are justified to believe in colored quarks. *Philosophy of Science, 71,* 36–60.

Maturana, H., and F. Varela (1980). Autopoiesis and cognition: The realization of the living. In *Boston Studies in the Philosophy of Science 42,* ed. R. Cohen and W. Wartofsky. Dordecht: D. Reidel.

McAuley, J. D. (1996). On the nature of timing mechanisms in cognition. *Proceedings of the Eighteenth Annual Conference of the Cognitive Science Society.* Hillsdale, N.J.: Erlbaum.

McKinstry, C., R. Dale, and M. Spivey (2008). Action dynamics reveal parallel competition in decision making. *Psychological Science, 19,* 22–24.

Menary, R. (2007). *Cognitive Integration.* New York: Palgrave.

Merleau-Ponty, M. (1962). *The Phenomenology of Perception.* Trans. Colin Smith. New York: Routledge.

Michaels, C. F. (2000). Information, perception, and action: What should ecological psychologists learn from Milner and Goodale (1995)? *Ecological Psychology, 12* (3), 241–258.

Michaels, C. F., and C. Carello (1981). *Direct Perception.* Englewood Cliffs, N.J.: Prentice Hall.

Michaels, C. F., E. Zeinstra, and R. R. D. Oudejans (2001). Information and action in timing the punch of a falling ball. *Quarterly Journal of Experimental Psychology, 54A,* 69–93.

Miller, G., E. Galanter, and K. Pribam (1960). *Plans and Structure of Behaviour.* New York: Holt, Rinehart, and Winston.

Millikan, R. (1984). *Language, Thought, and Other Biological Categories.* Cambridge, Mass.: MIT Press.

Millikan, R. (1993). *White Queen Psychology and Other Essays for Alice.* Cambridge, Mass.: MIT Press.

Millikan, R. (1995). Pushmi-pullyu Representations. In *Philosophical Perspectives, 9*, ed. J. Tomberlin, 185–200. Atascadero, Calif.: Ridgeview.

Millikan, R. (2000). *On Clear and Confused Ideas*. Cambridge: Cambridge University Press.

Milner, D., and M. Goodale (1995). *The Visual Brain in Action*. New York: Oxford University Press.

Morris, C., and H. LeCar (1981). Voltage oscillations in the barnacle giant muscle fiber. *Biophysical Journal, 35*, 193–213.

Morrison, M. (1998). Modelling nature: Between physics and the physical world. *Philosophia Naturalis, 35*, 65–85.

Morrison, M. (2007). Where have all the theories gone? *Philosophy of Science, 74*, 195–228.

Morrow, B., M. Elsworth, and R. Roth (2002). Prenatal cocaine exposure disrupts non-spatial, short-term memory in adolescent and adult male rat. *Behavioral Brain Research, 129*, 217–223.

Murray, D. J., R. R. Ellis, C. A. Bandomir, and H. E. Ross (1999). Charpentier (1891) on the size-weight illusion. *Perception and Psychophysics, 61*, 1681–1685.

Nagel, E. (1961). *The Structure of Science: Problems in the Logic of Scientific Explanation*. New York: Harcourt, Brace, and World.

Nagumo, J., S. Arimoto, and S. Yoshizawa (1962). An active pulse transmission line simulating nerve axon. In *Proceedings of the Institute for Radio Engineers, 50*, 2061–2070.

Noë, A. (2005). *Action in Perception*. Cambridge, Mass.: MIT Press.

Noë, A., and E. Thompson (2004). Are there neural correlates of consciousness? *Journal of Consciousness Studies, 11*, 3–28.

Nolfi, S., and D. Floreano (2000). *Evolutionary Robotics*. Cambridge, Mass.: MIT Press.

Norman, D. (1988). *The Psychology of Everyday Things*. New York: Basic Books.

Norman, J. (2002). Two visual systems and two theories of perception: An attempt to reconcile the constructivist and ecological approaches. *Behavioral and Brain Sciences, 25*, 73–144.

Oden, D., R. Thompson, and D. Premack (1990). Infant chimpanzees spontaneously perceive both concrete and relational same/different relations. *Child Development, 61*, 621–631.

Odling-Smee, F., K. Laland, and M. Feldman (2003). *Niche Construction: The Neglected Process in Evolution*. Princeton, N.J.: Princeton University Press.

Oullier, O., G. C. de Guzman, K. J. Jantzen, J. F. Lagarde, and J. A. S. Kelso (2005). Spontaneous interpersonal synchronization. In *European Workshop on Movement Sciences: Mechanics-Physiology-Psychology*, ed. C. Peham, W. Schöllhorn, and W. Verwey. Cologne: Sportverlag.

Owens, D. A., L. Chiang, and C. Muller (1996). Visual control of vehicle stopping distance: Do we see speed or kinetic energy? *Investigative Ophthalmology and Visual Science (Suppl.), 37*, S525.

Pagano, C., and M. Turvey (1998). Eigenvectors of the inertia tensor and perceiving the orientations of limbs and objects. *Journal of Applied Biomechanics, 14*, 331–359.

Pfeiffer, R., and C. Scheier (1999). *Understanding Intelligence*. Cambridge, Mass.: MIT Press.

Pinker, S. (1984). *Language Learnability and Language Development*. Cambridge, Mass.: Harvard University Press.

Plotkin, H. (1993). *Darwin Machines and the Nature of Knowledge*. Cambridge, Mass.: Harvard University Press.

Popper, K. (1945). *The Open Society and Its Enemies*, volume 2: *The High Tide of Prophesy: Hegel, Marx, and the Aftermath*. London: Routledge and Kegan Paul.

Port, R. (2003). Meter and speech. *Journal of Phonetics, 31*, 599–611.

Port, R., and T. van Gelder (1995). *Mind as Motion*. Cambridge, Mass.: MIT Press.

Proffitt, D. R., J. Stefanucci, T. Banton, and W. Epstein (2003). The role of effort in perceiving distance. *Psychological Science, 14*, 106–112.

Putnam, H. (1975). *Philosophical Papers*, volume 2: *Mind, Language, and Reality*. Cambridge: Cambridge University Press.

Putnam, H. (1985). *Philosophical Papers*, volume 3: *Realism and Reason*. Cambridge: Cambridge University Press.

Pynchon, T. (1997). *Mason and Dixon*. New York: Henry Holt.

Pynchon, T. (2006). *Against the Day*. New York: Viking.

Ramsey, W. (1997). Do connectionist representations earn their explanatory keep? *Mind and Language, 12*, 34–66.

Ramsey, W. (2007). *Representation Reconsidered*. Cambridge: Cambridge University Press.

Reali, F., and M. H. Christiansen (2005). Uncovering the richness of the stimulus: Structure dependence and indirect statistical evidence. *Cognitive Science, 29*, 1007–1028.

Reed, E. (1996). *Encountering the World*. New York: Oxford University Press.

Reiner, R., and R. Pierson (1995). Hacking's experimental realism: An untenable middle ground. *Philosophy of Science, 62,* 60–69.

Renner, M. (1990). Neglected aspects of exploratory and investigatory behavior. *Psychobiology, 18,* 16–22.

Renner, M., and M. Rosenzweig (1986). Object interactions in juvenile rats (*Rattus norvegicus*): Effects of differential experiential histories. *Journal of Comparative Psychology, 100,* 229–236.

Resnik, D. (1994). Hacking's experimental realism. *Canadian Journal of Philosophy, 24,* 395–412.

Reynolds, P. (2001). Growth, decay, digestion, and resurrection. *History Today, 51,* 42–47.

Richardson, D., R. Dale, and N. Kirkham (2007). The art of conversation is coordination: Common ground and the coupling of eye movements during dialogue. *Psychological Science, 18,* 407–413.

Richardson, M., K. Marsh, R. Isenhower, J. Goodman, and R. Schmidt (2007). Rocking together: Dynamics of intentional and unintentional interpersonal coordination. *Human Movement Science, 26,* 867–891.

Richardson, M. J., K. L. Marsh, and R. C. Schmidt (2005). Effects of visual and verbal couplings on unintentional interpersonal coordination. *Journal of Experimental Psychology: Human Performance and Perception, 31,* 62–79.

Richardson, R. (2007). *Evolutionary Psychology as Maladapted Psychology.* Cambridge, Mass.: MIT Press.

Riley, M. A., E. L. Amazeen, P. G. Amazeen, P. J. Treffner, and M. T. Turvey (1997). Effects of temporal scaling and attention on the asymmetric dynamics of bimanual coordination. *Motor Control, 1,* 263–283.

Rockwell, T. (2005). *Neither Brain nor Ghost.* Cambridge, Mass.: MIT Press.

Roe, R. M., J. Busemeyer, and J. T. Townsend (2001). Multialternative decision field theory: A dynamic artificial neural network model of decision making. *Psychological Review, 108,* 370–392.

Rohde, M., and J. Stewart (2008). Genuine and ascriptional autonomy. *BioSystems, 91,* 424–433.

Rorty, R. (1979). *Philosophy and the Mirror of Nature.* Princeton, N.J.: Princeton University Press.

Rosa, J., and A. Malter (2003). E-(embodied) knowledge and e-commerce: How physiological factors affect online sales of experiential products. *Journal of Consumer Psychology,* 13, 63–73.

Rosenberg, G., and M. Anderson (2004). A brief introduction to the guidance theory of representation. In *Proceedings of the 26th Annual Conference of the Cognitive Science Society*, ed. K. Forbus, D. Gentner, and T. Regier. Hillsdale, N.J.: Erlbaum.

Roullet, P., A. Mele, and M. Ammassari-Teule (1997). Ibotenic lesions of the nucleus accumbens promote reactivity to spatial novelty in nonreactive DBA mice: Implications for neural mechanisms subserving spatial information encoding. *Behavioral Neuroscience, 111*, 976–984.

Rovee-Collier, C., and M. Sullivan (1980). Organization of infant memory. *Journal of Experimental Psychology: Human Perception and Performance, 6*, 798–807.

Rowlands, M. (2006). *Body Language*. Cambridge, Mass.: MIT Press.

Rumelhart, D., J. McClelland, and the PDP Research Group (1986). *Parallel Distributed Processing*, volumes 1 and 2. Cambridge, Mass.: MIT Press.

Rupert, R. (2004). Challenges to the hypothesis of extended cognition. *Journal of Philosophy, 101*, 389–428.

Sahin, E., M. Cakmak, M. Dogar, E. Ugur, and G. Ucoluk (2007). To afford or not to afford: A new formulation of affordances toward affordance-based robotic control. *Adaptive Behavior, 15*, 447–472.

Save, E., B. Poucet, N. Foreman, and M. C. Buhot (1992). Object exploration and reactions to spatial and nonspatial changes in hooded rats following damage to parietal cortex or hippocampal formation. *Behavioral Neuroscience, 106*, 447–456.

Scarantino, A. (2003). Affordances explained. *Philosophy of Science, 70*, 949–961.

Schöner, G., H. Haken, and J. A. S. Kelso (1986). A stochastic theory of phase transitions in human hand movement. *Biological Cybernetics, 53*, 247–257.

Schöner, G., and J. A. S. Kelso (1988a). Dynamic pattern generation in behavioral and neural systems. *Science, 239*, 1513–1520.

Schöner, G., and J. A. S. Kelso (1988b). A synergetic theory of environmentally-specified and learned patterns of movement coordination. II. Component oscillator dynamics. *Biological Cybernetics, 58*, 81–89.

Schmidt, R., C. Carello, and M. Turvey (1990). Phase transitions and critical fluctuations in the visual coordination of rhythmic movements between people. *Journal of Experimental Psychology: Human Perception and Performance, 16*, 227–247.

Searle, J. (1980). Minds, brains, and programs. *Behavioral and Brain Sciences, 3*, 417–457.

Sedgewick, H. (1973). The visible horizon. Unpublished Doctoral Dissertation, Cornell University.

Sellars, W. (1956). Empiricism and the philosophy of mind. In *Minnesota Studies in the Philosophy of Science*, volume I: *The Foundations of Science and the Concepts of Psychology and Psychoanalysis*, ed. H. Feigl and M. Scriven. Minneapolis: University of Minnesota Press.

Semjen, A., and R. B. Ivry (2001). The coupled oscillator model of between-hand coordination in alternate hand tapping: A re-appraisal. *Journal of Experimental Psychology: Human Perception and Performance, 27*, 251–265.

Shapere, D. (1993). Astronomy and anti-realism. *Philosophy of Science, 60*, 134–150.

Shaw, R., and M. McIntyre (1974). Algoristic foundations to cognitive psychology. In *Cognition and Symbolic Processes*, ed. W. Weimer and D. Palermo. Hillsdale, N.J.: Erlbaum.

Shaw, R., M. Turvey, and W. Mace (1982). Ecology psychology: The consequence of a commitment to realism. In *Cognition and the Symbolic Processes II*, ed. W. Weimer and D. Palermo. Hillsdale, N.J.: Erlbaum.

Shepard, R., and L. Cooper (1982). *Mental Images and Their Transformations*. Cambridge, Mass.: MIT Press.

Shockley, K., C. Carello, and M. T. Turvey (2004). Metamers in the haptic perception of heaviness and moveableness. *Perception and Psychophysics, 66*, 731–742.

Silansky, C., and A. Chemero (2002). A neural network model of same/different perception. Paper presented at the Internation Conference on Comparative Cognition.

Silberstein, M. (2002). Reduction, emergence, and explanation. In *The Blackwell Guide to the Philosophy of Science*, ed. P. Machamer and M. Silberstein. New York: Blackwell.

Silberstein, M. and A. Chemero (under review). Extended phenomenology-cognition.

Singer, W., and C. Gray (1995). Visual feature integration and the temporal correlation hypothesis. *Annual Review of Neuroscience, 18*, 555–586.

Skarda, C., and W. Freeman (1987). How the brain makes chaos in order to make sense of the world. *Behavioral and Brain Sciences, 10*, 161–195.

Smith, B. C. (1991). The owl and the electric encyclopedia. *Artificial Intelligence, 47*, 251–288.

Smith, B. C. (1996). *On the Origin of Objects*. Cambridge, Mass.: MIT Press.

Smolensky, P. (1990). Tensor product variable binding and the representation of symbolic structures in connectionist networks. *Artificial Intelligence, 46*, 159–216.

Solomon, H., and M. Turvey (1988). Haptically perceiving the distances reachable with hand-held objects. *Journal of Experimental Psychology: Human Perception and Performance, 14*, 404–427.

Spade, P. V. (unpublished). *A Survey of Medieval Philosophy.*

Spivey, M., and R. Dale (2006). Continuous temporal dynamics in real-time cognition. *Current Directions in Psychological Science, 15,* 207–211.

Stefanucci, J., D. Proffitt, T. Banton, and W. Epstein (2005). Distances appear different on hills. *Perception and Psychophysics,* 67, 1052–1060.

Stephen, D., and J. Dixon (in press). The self-organization of insight: Entropy and power laws in problem solving. *Journal of Problem Solving.*

Stephen, D., J. Dixon, and R. Isenhower (2007). Dynamics in development: New structure through self-organization. Paper presented at the 14th International Conference on Perception and Action.

Stephen, D., J. Dixon, and R. Isenhower (in press). Dynamics of representational change: Entropy, action, cognition. *Journal of Experimental Psychology: Human Perception and Performance.*

Stevens, C. E., and I. D. Hume (1995). *Comparative Physiology of the Vertebrate Digestive System.* New York: Cambridge University Press.

Stich, S. (1983). *From Folk Psychology to Cognitive Science: The Case against Belief.* Cambridge, Mass.: MIT Press.

Stich, S. (1996). *Deconstructing the Mind.* New York: Oxford University Press.

Stoffregen, T. (2000). Affordances and events. *Ecological Psychology, 12,* 1–28.

Stoffregen, T. (2003). Affordances as properties of the animal–environment system. *Ecological Psychology, 15,* 149–180.

Strawson, P. F. (1959). *Individuals.* London: Methuen.

Suppes, P. (1969). *Studies in the Methodology and Foundations of Science: Selected Papers from 1951–1969.* Dordrecht: Reidel.

Thelen, E. (1994). Three-month-old infants can learn task-specific patterns of interlimb coordination. *Psychological Science, 5,* 280–285.

Thelen, E. (1995). Time-scale dynamics and the embodiment of embodied cognition. In *Mind as Motion,* ed. R. Port and T. van Gelder. Cambridge, Mass.: MIT Press.

Thelen, E., and L. B. Smith (1994). *A Dynamic Systems Approach to the Development of Cognition and Action.* Cambridge, Mass.: MIT Press.

Thompson, E. (2007). *Mind in Life.* Cambridge, Mass.: Harvard University Press.

Thompson, E., and F. Varela (2001). Radical embodiment: Neural dynamics and consciousness. *Trends in Cognitive Sciences, 5,* 418–425.

Thompson, R., and D. Oden (2000). Categorical perception and conceptual judgments by nonhuman primates: The paleological monkey and the analogical ape. *Cognitive Science, 24,* 363–396.

Thompson, R., D. Oden, and S. Boysen (1997). Language-naive chimpanzees (Pan troglodytes) judge relations between relations in a conceptual matching-to-sample task. *Journal of Experimental Psychology: Animal Behavior Processes, 23,* 31–43.

Titchener, E. (1895). Simple reactions. *Mind, 4,* 74–81.

Torretti, R. (1986). Observation. *British Journal for the Philosophy of Science, 37,* 1–23.

Treffner, P., and M. Turvey (1995). Symmetry, broken symmetry, and handedness in bimanual coordination dynamics. *Experimental Brain Research, 107,* 163–178.

Tsou, J. (2003). Reconsidering Feyerabend's "anarchism." *Perspectives on Science, 11,* 208–235.

Tuller, B., P. Case, M. Ding, and J. A. S. Kelso (1994). The nonlinear dynamics of speech categorization. *Journal of Experimental Psychology: Human Perception and Performance, 20,* 1–16.

Turvey, M. (1977). Preliminaries to a theory of action with reference to vision. In *Perceiving, Acting, and Knowing,* ed. R. Shaw and J. Bransford. Hillsdale, N.J.: Erlbaum.

Turvey, M. (1990a). Coordination. *American Psychologist, 45,* 938–953.

Turvey, M. (1990b). The challenge of a physical account of action: A personal view. In *The Natural Physical Approach to Movement Control,* ed. H. T. A. Whiting, O. G. Meijer, and P. C. W. van Wieringen. Amsterdam: Free University Press.

Turvey, M. (1992). Affordances and prospective control: An outline of the ontology. *Ecological Psychology, 4,* 173–187.

Turvey, M. (1996). Dynamic touch. *American Psychologist, 51,* 1134–1152.

Turvey, M., and C. Carello (1995). Some dynamical themes in perception and action. In *Mind as Motion,* ed. R. F. Port and T. van Gelder. Cambridge, Mass.: MIT Press.

Turvey, M. T., and M. Moreno (2006). Physical metaphors for the mental lexicon. *Mental Lexicon, 1,* 7–33.

Turvey, M., and R. Shaw (1979). The primacy of perceiving: An ecological reformulation of perception for understanding memory. In *Perspectives on Memory Research,* ed. L. G. Nillson. Hillsdale, N.J.: Erlbaum.

Turvey, M. T., R. Shaw, E. Reed, and W. Mace (1981). Ecological laws of perceiving and acting: In reply to Fodor and Pylyshyn (1981). *Cognition, 9,* 237–304.

Tye, M. (1995). *Ten Problems of Consciousness.* Cambridge, Mass: MIT Press.

Ullman, S. (1980). Against direct perception. *Behavioral and Brain Sciences, 3,* 373–415.

van Fraassen, B. (1980). *The Scientific Image.* New York: Oxford University Press.

van Fraassen, B. (2002). *The Empirical Stance.* New Haven: Yale University Press.

van Gelder, T. (1990). Compositionality: A connectionist variation on a classical theme. *Cognitive Science, 14,* 355–384.

van Gelder, T. (1995). What might cognition be if not computation? *Journal of Philosophy, 91,* 345–381.

van Gelder, T. (1998). The dynamical hypothesis in cognitive science. *Behavioral and Brain Sciences, 21,* 615–628.

van Gelder, T., and R. Port (1995). It's about time. In *Mind as Motion,* ed. R. Port and T. van Gelder. Cambridge, Mass.: MIT Press.

van Orden, G., J. Holden, and M. Turvey (2005). Human cognition and 1/f scaling. *Journal of Experimental Psychology: General, 134,* 117–123.

van Rooij, I., R. Bongers, and W. Haselager (2002). A non-representational approach to imagined action. *Cognitive Science, 26,* 345–375.

Varela, F., J. P. Lachaux, E. Rodriguez, and J. Martiniere (2001). The brainweb: Phase synchronization and large-scale integration. *Nature Reviews Neuroscience, 4,* 229–239.

Varela, F., E. Thompson, and E. Rosch (1991). *The Embodied Mind.* Cambridge, Mass.: MIT Press.

Vera, A. H., and H. A. Simon (1993). Situated action: A symbolic interpretation. *Cognitive Science, 17,* 7–48.

Wagman, J. B., and C. Carello (2001). Affordances and inertial constraints on tool use. *Ecological Psychology, 13,* 173–195.

Wagman, J. B., and C. Carello (2003). Haptically creating affordances: The user-tool interface. *Journal of Experimental Psychology: Applied, 9,* 175–186.

Wagman, J. B., and D. B. Miller (2003a). Nested reciprocities: The organism-environment system in perception-action and development. *Developmental Psychobiology, 42,* 317–334.

Wagman, J. B., and D. B. Miller (2003b). The womb and the skin as false boundaries in perception-action and development: A response. *Developmental Psychobiology, 42,* 362–367.

Wagman, J. B., and K. Taylor (2004). Chosen striking location and the user-tool-environment system. *Journal of Experimental Psychology: Applied, 10,* 267–280.

Wagman, J. B., C. Zimmerman, and C. Sorric (2007). Which feels heavier—a pound of lead or a pound of feathers? A potential perceptual basis of a cognitive riddle. *Perception, 36,* 1709–1711.

Warren, W. H. (1984). Perceiving affordances: Visual guidance of stair climbing. *Journal of Experimental Psychology: Human Perception and Performance, 10,* 683–703.

Warren, W. H. (2004). Optic flow. In *The Visual Neurosciences,* ed. L. Chalupa and J. Werner, 1247–1259. Cambridge, Mass.: MIT Press.

Warren, W. H. (2005). Direct perception: The view from here. *Philosophical Topics, 33,* 335–361.

Warren, W. H. (2006). The dynamics of perception and action. *Psychological Review, 113,* 358–389.

Warren, W. H., and D. Hannon (1988). Direction of self-motion is perceived from optical flow. *Nature, 336,* 162–163.

Wasserman, E., M. Young, and R. Cook (2004). Variability discrimination in humans and animals: Implications for adaptive action. *American Psychologist, 59,* 879–890.

Webb, B. (2004). Neural mechanisms for prediction: Do insects have forward models? *Trends in Neurosciences, 27,* 278–282.

Wheeler, M. (1996). From robots to Rothko. In *The Philosophy of Artificial Life,* ed. M. Boden. New York: Oxford University Press.

Wheeler, M. (2005). *Reconstructing the Cognitive World.* Cambridge, Mass.: MIT Press.

Wheeler, M., and A. Clark (1999). Genic representation: Reconciling content and causal complexity. *British Journal for the Philosophy of Science, 50,* 103–135.

Wilson, R. (2004). *Boundaries of the Mind.* Cambridge: Cambridge University Press.

Winsberg, E. (2001). Simulations, models, and theories: Complex physical systems and their representations. *Philosophy of Science, 68,* S442–S454.

Winsberg, E. (2006). Models of success vs. the success of the models: Reliability without truth. *Synthese, 152,* 1–19.

Withagen, R. (2004). The pickup of nonspecifying variables does not entail indirect perception. *Ecological Psychology, 16,* 237–253.

Withagen, R., and A. Chemero (2009). Naturalizing perception: Developing the Gibsonian approach to perception along evolutionary lines. *Theory and Psychology.*

Withagen, R., and C. F. Michaels (2005). Information for calibration and information for attunement in length perception by dynamic touch. *Journal of Experimental Psychology: Human Perception and Performance, 31,* 1379–1390.

Witt, J. K., D. R. Proffitt, and W. Epstein (2004). Perceiving distance: A role of effort and intent. *Perception, 33,* 570–590.

Young, M., and E. Wasserman (1997). Entropy detection by pigeons: Response to mixed visual displays after same-different discrimination training. *Journal of Experimental Psychology: Animal Behavior Processes, 23,* 157–170.

Young, M., and E. Wasserman (2001). Entropy and variability discrimination. *Journal of Experimental Psychology: Learning, Memory, and Cognition, 27,* 278–293.

Index